ID0757953

George Scarborough

George Adolphus Scarborough. *Courtesy Western History Collections, University of Oklahoma Library.*

George Scarborough

The Life and Death of a Lawman on the Closing Frontier

By Robert K. DeArment

Foreword by Leon C. Metz

University of Oklahoma Press : Norman and London

By Robert K. DeArment

Bat Masterson: The Man and the Legend (Norman, 1979)
Knights of the Green Cloth: The Saga of the Frontier Gamblers (Norman, 1982)
George Scarborough: The Life and Death of a Lawman on the Closing Frontier (Norman, 1992)

For
Rosemary, Paul, Joan, and Diana
of whom I am very proud

Library of Congress Cataloging-in-Publication Data

DeArment, Robert K., 1925–
  George Scarborough : the life and death of a lawman on the closing
frontier / by Robert K. DeArment ; foreword by Leon C. Metz.—1st
ed.
    p. cm.
  Includes bibliographical references and index.
  ISBN 0-8061-2406-7 (alk. paper)
  1. Scarborough, George Adolphus, 1859–1900. 2. Peace officers—
Southwest, New—Biography. 3. Frontier and pioneer life—
Southwest, New. 4. Southwest, New—Biography. 5. Law
enforcement—Southwest, New—History—19th century. I. Title.
F786.S3D43 1992
363.2′092—dc20
[B]   91-30145

The paper in this book meets the guidelines for permanence and durability of the Committee on Production Guidelines for Book Longevity of the Council on Library Resources, Inc.♾

Contents

Illustrations

Maps

Foreword
by Leon C. Metz

The name George A. Scarborough is not a household word among western historians. The men he killed were, for the most part, footnotes to an era. The men he rode with, and sometimes entrusted his life to, were, for the most part, obscure individuals.

Yet to read *George Scarborough* is to understand how law and order prevailed in the American West. Such methods were not easy, were not pretty, and only rarely were professional, but they worked. In its way, the name George A. Scarborough epitomizes legitimate law enforcement far more than the handful of Wyatt Earps and Wild Bill Hickoks.

In this respect, Robert K. DeArment has done something rare. He has taken a vague figure, raised him from the dust of ancient ledgers and journals, and given him form, flesh, blood, spirit, and, above all, significance. Anybody can write a biography about an individual who already has a dozen biographies. It takes a heroic and determined writer to see strengths where others see smoke, to lift a character out of nothing and place upon his shoulders the mantle of relevance, interest, and importance.

Until now, Scarborough has been best remembered as the man who killed the man who killed the man who killed the men. George killed John Selman, who had recently killed John Wesley Hardin, who had, over a lifetime and according to his own memoirs, killed perhaps forty men.

However, what separated Scarborough from Selman and Hardin is that George was not just a manslayer; he was a legal, deputized manhunter, a relentless pursuer of desperadoes. No trails were too

ix

dim, no odds too great, no obstacles too difficult. Scarborough
relished the pursuit.

Scarborough's tenacity forced outlaws into two choices: surrender
or die. A final option for the desperado was to kill the lawman, and
eventually that happened too.

In relating the Scarborough story, DeArment has uncovered new
detail regarding the last days of John Wesley Hardin, easily the
greatest gunfighter of his time. Furthermore, DeArment has rounded
out the shadowy figure of John Selman, a notorious gunman in his
own right.

The author provides a fresh assessment of Jeff Milton, described
by historian J. Evetts Haley in *A Good Man with a Gun*. DeArment
also untangles a complex West Texas–New Mexico–Arizona envi-
ronment that allowed notorious outlaw gangs to flourish.

This biography abounds with U.S. marshals, deputy marshals,
city marshals, sheriffs, rangers, constables, customs officers, border
patrolmen, Pinkerton agents, railroad police, and occasional oddballs
looking for something to do. Law work was like that. The pay
was not much, the benefits nonexistent, the future unpromising. A
lawman worth his salt never asked for more and never expected less.

Almost nothing in the Southwest occurred without controversy.
DeArment displays a fascinating ability to sort out events, to place
the figures, dates, times, and details in perspective. A variety of
possibilities are evaluated regarding the deaths of Selman, Hardin,
and Scarborough.

Scarborough's life spanned an era that saw not only the last of the
badmen but the demise of the lawmen who crossed jurisdictional
lines and depended upon instinct and courage to make arrests. Their
warrant was a six-gun. Their alternative was the grave. Lawmen and
lawbreakers alike would never have understood or even counte-
nanced modern-day rules that shackle everything but crime.

In the end, Scarborough's only monument has been a granite
stone in the cemetery at Deming, New Mexico. This biography by
DeArment, however, has resurrected a man whose memory and
career is worthy of better. The name George Scarborough deserves
to be spoken in the same breath with those of other great western
lawmen. He was one of the best.

Preface

George Scarborough was tried for murder on three occasions. Although he had spent most of his adult life as an officer of the law and was wearing a badge when each of the killings took place, sufficient questions surrounded the cases to prompt authorities to indict him and bring him to trial. Scarborough's activities as a lawman on the closing American western frontier during the final years of the nineteenth century were marked by controversy in his lifetime and are disputed to this day by students of the period. Unresolved mystery also surrounds the circumstances of his death.

Scarborough lived by the law of the gun in the waning days of the gunfighter era and was the peer of the elite of that uniquely western American fraternity. His story has never before been told, largely because he shunned publicity during his lifetime and his family refused to talk to writers after his death. He did not immortalize himself in published memoirs as did contemporary gunmen like John Wesley Hardin, Tom Horn, and Frank Canton, nor were his experiences popularized by literary admirers as were those of Wyatt Earp, Bat Masterson, and Ben Thompson. The reluctance of family members to cooperate with writers was in part an effort to protect Scarborough's eldest son, who tried to follow in his father's footsteps and succeeded only in slipping down a precipitous slope to become one of those fugitives from the law his father had pursued so assiduously.

Because he was born just before the outbreak of the War Between the States, George Scarborough's earliest recollections would be of civil war. In childhood he would be exposed to the violence spawned by the clash of cultures between red man and white and white man and black. At the age of puberty he would witness one of the most brutal racial upheavals of the turbulent Reconstruction period. The potential for sudden violence would be constant throughout his life as he matched nerve and skill with some of the deadliest killers and wiliest outlaws of the American West. He would himself meet a violent death.

Scarborough was both a typical specimen of the dedicated frontier lawman and a singular individual in a unique historical period and locale.

This is his story.

Robert K. DeArment

Sylvania, Ohio

Acknowledgments

Many people contributed to the creation of this book and I want to acknowledge their help and express my appreciation. The following members of the Scarborough family were most generous with their time and assisted me immeasurably in reconstructing and interpreting the history of George Scarborough: Dan Scarborough Abbott, Abilene, Texas, grandson of Ethel Abbott, fourth child of George and Mollie Scarborough; Mrs. Sarita Abbott, Abilene, Texas, daughter-in-law of Ethel Abbott; Mrs. Evelyn Linebery, Midland, Texas, daughter of W. F. Scarborough, George's brother; Mrs. Ada Phillips, Midland, Texas, daughter of Ada McCargo, George's sister; The late Moliere Scarborough, San Antonio, Texas, son of Cicero Battle Scarborough, George's brother; Moliere Scarborough, Jr., Tyler, Texas, grandson of C. B. Scarborough; Stuart M. Scarborough, Houston, Texas, great-grandson of C. B. Scarborough.

The librarians, court employees, genealogists, historians, collectors, newspaper personnel, former law officers, and western history enthusiasts listed below all contributed to the book in the form of information or illustrations and to them I am very grateful: Susan K. Anderson, Silver City, New Mexico; T. Lindsay Baker, Canyon, Texas; Larry Ball, Arkansas State University, State University, Arkansas; Jan M. Barnhart, University of New Mexico, Albuquerque; Ed Bartholomew, Fort Davis, Texas; Jim Baum, Colorado City, Texas; Jemison Beshears, San Francisco, California; Cleola Blackwell, Yuma Territorial Prison State Historic Park, Yuma, Arizona; John Boessenecker, Foster City, California; Susan C. Calloway, Cochise County Courthouse, Bisbee, Arizona; Robert H. Carlock of the Aztec Land and Cattle Company, Ltd., Mesa, Arizona; Don Cline, Albuquerque, New Mexico; Gay G. Craft, Tulane University Library, New Orleans, Louisiana; Lori Davisson, Arizona Historical Society, Tucson, Arizona; Diane Dubose, *Western Observer*, Anson, Texas; Jim Earle, College Station, Texas; Harold L. Edwards, Bakersfield, California; Gary Fitterer, Kirkland, Washington; Geraldine I. Goodwin, Sacramento, California; J. Evetts Haley, Midland, Texas; H. R. ("Skip") Hall, Tyler, Texas; Mary R. Harper, Cochise County Courthouse, Bisbee, Arizona; Chuck Hornung, Lubbock, Texas; Kay Hull, Luna County Courthouse, Deming, New Mexico; Homer Hutto, Tuscola, Texas; Elaine Johnston, Louisiana State Library, Baton Rouge, Louisiana; Sue Kethley, Waco–McLennan County Library, Waco, Texas; Billie D. Lipham, Abilene, Texas; Bob McCubbin, El Paso, Texas; Robin McWilliams, Nita Stewart Haley Memorial Library, Midland, Texas; Elizabeth Shown Mills, Tuscaloosa, Alabama; Sylvia Moreland, Jones County Historical Society, Anson, Texas; Pat Morris, El Paso Public Library, El Paso, Texas; Irvin Munn, Chickasha, Oklahoma; Lt. Col. Phillip G. Nickell, Mesilla, New Mexico; Bill O'Neal, Carthage, Texas; Chuck Parsons, South Wayne, Wisconsin; Bob Petrucco, Burbank Public Library, Burbank, California; Bill Reynolds, Bakersfield, California; Bill Robinson, Corning, Arkansas; Mrs. Buryl Rye, Jones County Courthouse, Anson, Texas; J. Richard Salazar, State Records Center and Archives, Santa Fe, New Mexico; Beth Schneider, Nita Stewart Haley Memorial Library, Midland, Texas; Mary Kay Shannon, Fort Stockton, New Mexico; Woodrow Simmons, former sheriff, Jones County, Texas; Arthur Soule, APO San Francisco, California; Bob Stephens, Dallas, Texas; Steven D. Tilley, National Archives, Washington, D.C.; John D. Voliva, Albuquerque, New Mexico; William Reese Walker, Hot Springs Village, Arkansas; and Leon C. Metz, who provided the introduction.

R.K.D.

George Scarborough

His old gun went off, and he killed five of them with two shots.
Then it was like popcorn in a skillet. They killed those
forty-eight.

—W. Lod Tanner, December 28, 1928

-1-

Introduction to Violence
Popcorn in a Skillet

George Adolphus Scarborough was a member of a proud and vigorous family of rock-solid southern American stock. His lineage could be traced back to Capt. Edmond Scarborough, who came to the New World from North Walsham, County Norfolk, England, about 1620 and settled in Virginia Colony only thirteen years after the establishment of Jamestown.[1] Sixteen twenty was also the year of the sailing of the *Mayflower*, and family members today say that although there were no Scarboroughs on the famous Pilgrim ship, Scarboroughs probably built it because they were shipbuilders in England.[2]

Devout Baptists, the family produced many ministers and religious teachers, but also a number of adventurous fighting men. In 1676 a grandson of Edmond, William Scarborough, was a leader of Bacon's Rebellion, a popular uprising against the corruption and despotic policies of the colonial governor, Sir William Berkeley. The rebellion was crushed and on March 16, 1677, by order of Governor Berkeley, William Scarborough was executed and his property confiscated.[3]

Three generations later, in 1758, David Scarborough, a direct descendant of Captain Edmond and William of Bacon's Rebellion, moved his family from Virginia to North Carolina, the first of many relocations this branch of the Scarboroughs would make as they pushed the southern frontier westward until, after another four generations, George Scarborough's widow and several of her children would fetch up at the Pacific Ocean and end the long migration.

The Scarboroughs and the Baptists of the Carolina colonies were leaders in the formation and activities of an organization called The

3

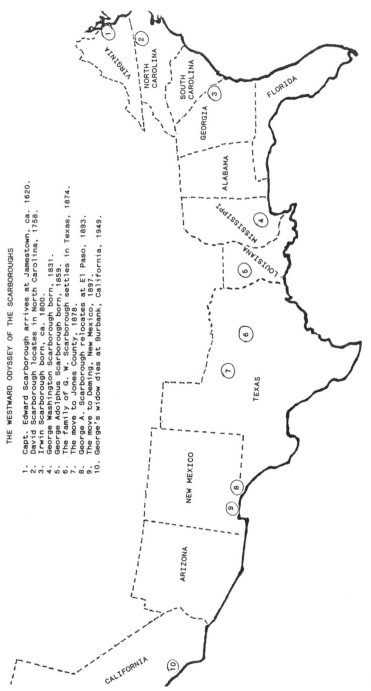

THE WESTWARD ODYSSEY OF THE SCARBOROUGHS

1. Capt. Edward Scarborough arrives at Jamestown, ca. 1620.
2. David Scarborough locates in North Carolina, 1758.
3. Irwin Scarborough born, ca. 1800.
4. George Washington Scarborough born, 1831.
5. George Adolphus Scarborough born, 1859.
6. The family of G. W. Scarborough settles in Texas, 1874.
7. The move to Jones County, 1878.
8. George A. Scarborough relocates at El Paso, 1893.
9. The move to Deming, New Mexico, 1897.
10. George's widow dies at Burbank, California, 1949.

The Westward Odyssey of the Scarboroughs.

Regulators which presaged the vigilance committees of California and Nevada a century later. Scarboroughs were active in the organization, which was organized in South Carolina to control lawlessness and enforce respect for life and property but was later reactivated in North Carolina in a revolt against the venality and oppression of the colonial government. When The Regulators drove out the local authorities, a military force dispatched by Gov. William Tryon confronted the rebellious colonists and defeated them in a bloody battle on May 16, 1771, an engagement considered by some historians as one of the opening battles of the American Revolution. With the outbreak of the War for Independence in 1776, David Scarborough's son James enlisted as a sergeant in Col. Henry Irwin's Edgecombe County Militia. He rose in the ranks and at war's end held a temporary commission as major in the Continental Army. After the war he commanded the Edgecombe County Regiment of Militia with the rank of major bestowed by the North Carolina General Assembly.[4] Perhaps because of lingering bitterness stemming from the prewar activities of The Regulators in the area, Allen Scarborough, son of Major James, moved soon after the war from North Carolina to Burke County, Georgia. Here was born a son, Irwin, named for Major James's commander. In 1818, Irwin moved west to Lawrence County, Mississippi, where his son, George Washington Scarborough, was born April 13, 1831.[5]

George W. Scarborough, who was to become the father of George Adolphus, was a boy of nine when his father joined other westering Scarboroughs and relocated his family in the uplands of western Louisiana. There, on June 20, 1850, in Bienville Parish, nineteen-year-old George W. Scarborough married Martha Elizabeth Rutland, a Graves County, Kentucky, girl. The first of the nine children Martha would bring into the world was a girl, Isadora Eugenia, born March 8, 1852, in neighboring Jackson Parish. Like three other of George and Martha Scarborough's offspring, Isadora died in infancy. On August 12, 1854, a son, christened Cicero Battle but always to be called C. B., was born in Bienville Parish.[6] About this time the family joined a procession of other cotton-planting Scarboroughs who quit the uplands for Natchitoches Parish and the rich bottomlands of the Red River Valley. George W. obtained farmland west of the town of Natchitoches near El Camino Real, the old

Spanish trail leading to Texas. Perhaps the very proximity of the road beckoning adventurers into the wild open country of Texas influenced Scarborough's future.[7]

Here in Natchitoches Parish on January 26, 1857, another son, James Monroe, was born, but, like Isadora, he did not survive infancy. On October 2, 1859, George Adolphus Scarborough entered this world and became the newest member of a large clan of Scarboroughs in Natchitoches Parish.[8] The census taken the following year enumerated thirty-six family members in the parish, with families headed by fifty-nine-year-old Irwin, the patriarch of the clan; his brother Joseph; a nephew, Thomas; and four of Irwin's sons, Matthias, Josiah, James Warren, and George W.[9]

The year 1861 brought the War Between the States and destruction of the cotton planters' way of life in the Red River Valley. George Washington Scarborough went off to fight for the Confederacy and became a second lieutenant in Capt. William W. Ferrill's Company, First Regiment of the Arizona Brigade, Mounted Partisan Rangers.[10] He spent most of the war in the commissary department and saw service throughout Louisiana, Mississippi, and Texas. Martha and her two young sons, C. B. and George, followed him to Mississippi in 1862 and there on May 9 a daughter was born in Claiborne County.[11] The infant girl, christened Sarah Idah, fell victim to the diseases that ravaged children of the time and died early.

G. W. Scarborough was impressed by the opportunities he saw in Texas and soon after war's end moved his family to the frontier county of Lampasas, where on August 20, 1865, daughter Ada Ann was born. She was the only one of his four daughters to attain adulthood. Probably because of the threat to his family posed by marauding Indian bands still roaming central Texas, George W. began a slow retreat to the east. In Burleson County, some 150 miles eastward, another son was born on February 3, 1868, and named William F.[12]

By 1870, George and Martha Scarborough were once again back in Louisiana, living in the Red River town of Colfax, seat of Grant Parish. Here they operated a hotel and here their last two children were born, Lee Rutland on July 4, 1870, and Nancy Frances on September 9, 1872. Nancy also died in childhood, leaving four sons and a daughter as the only survivors of the nine children born to Martha.[13]

If the terrors of Indian attack drove the Scarboroughs out of Texas, George W. may have wondered in the days to come whether the situation in Louisiana provided more security for his family. These were the days of Reconstruction, and chaotic political and economic conditions prevailed in the state. Within a few years the Scarboroughs would become enmeshed in one of the bloodiest episodes of a violent and tumultuous period.

Grant Parish had been created during the postwar administration of carpetbagger Gov. Henry Clay Warmoth, when a new Louisiana Constitution was framed, the Fourteenth Amendment to the U.S. Constitution ratified by the legislature, and the state readmitted to the Union. The very name of the new parish, chosen to immortalize the Union army hero and recently elected Republican president, Ulysses S. Grant, must have infuriated Confederate veterans like G. W. Scarborough. The name of the parish seat, a village on the north side of the Red River 30 miles from Alexandria and 350 miles northwest of New Orleans, also was a constant reminder of the war's victors, having been chosen to honor Grant's vice president, Schuyler Colfax.

Grant Parish was composed of two areas, distinct in topography and population composition. The narrow alluvial plain along the river was the site of large cotton and sugar-cane plantations and an overwhelming population of newly freed blacks; enumerated in the 1870 census of Ward 1, which included the village of Colfax, were 3 Indians, 196 whites, and 1,320 blacks. The hill country to the north and east was inhabited largely by white yeoman farmers.

Colfax itself contained only about five homes, two or three stores, G. W. Scarborough's modest hotel, and the most imposing edifice, a brick building which formerly had been a plantation stable and now served as the parish courthouse. The few whites in Colfax were largely represented by the families of G. W. Scarborough and William R. Rutland, brother of Martha and parish judge. Living with G. W. and Martha Scarborough and their four children at this time was Nancy Rutland Jackson, mother of Martha and William Rutland.

Nancy Rutland had been widowed in Graves County, Kentucky,

in 1840 and three years later had married Col. Hardy Jackson, who raised her children. In 1846, Hardy Jackson moved to Claiborne (later Bienville) Parish, Louisiana, where, in 1850, Martha Rutland married George W. Scarborough. Ties between the Rutlands and Scarboroughs were further strengthened two years later when Martha's sister, Nancy Sarah, married G. W. Scarborough's brother, James. William Rutland went on to college at Mount Vernon University, taught school in Natchitoches Parish, and studied law in the offices of a parish judge. He and G. W. Scarborough served in the Confederate army together and the two brothers-in-law became business partners and fast friends.[14]

The chaotic postwar political situation in Louisiana became even more confused after the elections of 1872, which were marked by massive fraud and corruption and resulted in two governments within the state, each claiming legitimacy. John McEnery was the gubernatorial candidate of the Fusion party, made up of elements of the Republican party loyal to Warmoth, who had broken with President Grant for attempting to limit his power, and the moribund Democratic organization. The Republicans were led by William Pitt Kellogg, who claimed victory and began taking executive action even as a delegation of McEnery adherents called on President Grant with an appeal to withhold recognition of either faction until an investigation of election irregularities had been completed.

In December 1872, McEnery sanctioned the election of Alphonse Cazabat and Christopher Columbus Nash as judge and sheriff of Grant Parish, but because of questions concerning the legitimacy of McEnery's governorship, in early March 1873, William Rutland and W. A. Richardson journeyed to New Orleans to request that Kellogg issue commissions to the two parish officers. Kellogg reportedly agreed to the request but later, exhibiting what a contemporary critic called "that duplicity and hypocrisy which is part of his nature," instead issued Grant Parish commissions to R. C. Register as judge and Daniel Shaw as sheriff.[15]

On March 23, Register and Shaw and a group of Kellogg supporters led by William Ward, a black representative in the Kellogg legislature, took possession of the parish courthouse in Colfax. Anticipating white resistance to their action, they issued a call to blacks in the area and began distributing arms and ammunition to the freedmen. Around-the-clock armed guards were posted at the courthouse, and trenches were dug. Old steam pipes were fitted to act as "artillery." Conflicting contemporary estimates placed the number of blacks assembled at the courthouse at fewer than two hundred and more than four hundred. But the entire group, brandishing weapons, was drilled daily in the street by Ward and two other black Union army veterans, Allen and Flowers.

Several attempts to have the contending black and white factions meet in an effort to reconcile their differences failed. Tension mounted as the blacks posted rifle-carrying pickets at the approaches to town and denied passage to white citizens. By April 1, Judge Rutland had returned from New Orleans to Colfax, bringing with him for reburial the remains of one of his children, who had died six years earlier in Calcasieu Parish. Threatened by a party of blacks reportedly led by Flowers, Rutland and his family were forced to abandon their home and flee the town, barely escaping by ferryboat across the river ahead of a black mob. Rutland's departure had been so sudden that he had to leave behind the casket containing the body of his child. The Rutland house was ransacked and the casket thrown into the street and smashed. This act of desecration probably incensed and galvanized the whites of Grant Parish to retaliatory action more than any other single outrage during those terrible days.

Anarchy reigned in Colfax. The other white residents, including the family of G. W. Scarborough, also were forced to depart, as was a black Colfax merchant named Butler. Postmaster Samuel Cluny, a black, closed the post office and fled. The house of W. A. Richardson was fired upon before he and his family hurriedly left town. Whites were fleeing thirty or forty miles into the hills to escape. There were blood-chilling reports that some blacks were threatening to "go to the country and kill from the cradle to old age."[16] Soon, passengers on riverboats arriving in New Orleans were reported seeing bands of armed blacks patrolling the bank of the river for several miles above and below the town of Colfax.

During the early days of April the Colfax tragedy crept toward its bloody climax. Register, Flowers, and Ward went to New Orleans, leaving Levi Allen in charge of the courthouse. Shaw, the Kellogg sheriff, was taken in charge by supporters of C. C. Nash, the other claimant to the office, and held prisoner. On April 4 shots were exchanged within a mile of Colfax by a small party of whites and a black patrol led by Allen.

After his narrow escape Judge Rutland had gone to Montgomery, a white settlement some ten miles upriver from Colfax, where he boarded a steamboat for New Orleans. The boat was scheduled to stop at Colfax, but a mob of blacks, having learned that Rutland was aboard, crowded the banks, howling for his skin. "Three times the steamboat circled and feigned a landing, and when the negroes perceived the pilot's intentions, they ran along the shore threatening to shoot him out of the pilot house unless he delivered Rutland into their hands."[17] Not surprisingly, the riverboat captain elected to pass up Colfax and went on downriver. At Alexandria, "Col. R. A. Hunter, an old and distinguished citizen of Louisiana, came on the boat and wrote a letter to Kellogg, advising him of the fearful state of affairs in Grant Parish, and warning him that unless he intervened there would be bloodshed. This letter he gave to Rutland to bear to Kellogg."[18]

At New Orleans on April 9, Rutland had a meeting with Kellogg to the Saint Louis Hotel during which he presented the letter from Hunter, a petition requesting state intervention signed by Grant Parish citizens, and a warrant for the arrest of those who had ransacked his home, which he said could not be executed because of the appalling conditions prevailing in the parish. Kellogg referred Rutland to James Longstreet, the state adjutant general, and offered the use of his personal carriage for Rutland to make the call.

Longstreet was sympathetic to Rutland's plea and promised to start for Colfax that evening with twenty Metropolitan Police, but Kellogg evidently overruled his adjutant general and no peacekeeping force was dispatched. Rutland also called on the United States district attorney in New Orleans and Major General William H. Emory, commander of the military district, seeking help, but both federal officers denied having proper authority to act in the situation.

The potentially explosive state of affairs in Grant Parish was common knowledge in New Orleans during those fateful days in early April, as attested by newspaper reports in the city's papers. The *Republican,* sympathetic to Kellogg and the black cause, published on Saturday, April 12, an inflammatory article which said in part:

> The local majority of Grant Parish is prepared to clean out the local minority of Grant in twenty-four hours or less. . . . There is a local majority of colored men, not only accustomed to the trade of war, but equipped with arms of the most perfect character. . . . The negroes . . . are no longer the weak and simple creatures they were before the war. The years of freedom which they have enjoyed have had their effect on them, as well as the military education which many of them received in the United States Army. The time is past, if ever it existed, when a handful of whites could frighten a regiment of colored men.[19]

The contrary view was expressed in the *Daily Picayune*, New Orleans's opposition paper: "We have been waiting to hear that the white men of Grant and the adjoining parishes had taken care of the lawlessness in their neighborhood."[20]

In the absence of state or federal intervention in the tinderbox Colfax situation, the tragedy was played out by the opposing parties in what had become an emotionally overheated atmosphere of fear, hatred, and vengeance. As the blacks drove all their perceived enemies from the town and paraded up and down the street with their weapons, the whites were assembling at the hamlet of Summerfield Springs, four miles to the north, under the leadership of C. C. Nash, the McEnery-commissioned sheriff. They came from the hill country of Grant and from the neighboring parishes of Winn, Rapides, Catahoula, and Natchitoches. By the second week of April, they numbered about 150 armed and determined men and were organized as a posse comitatus by Nash under his claimed authority as elected sheriff.

Nash chose Easter Sunday, April 13, to confront the entrenched black army at the courthouse. Early in the morning he deployed his forces in a line of battle around the town and under a flag of truce called for a conference with Levi Allen. He told the black leader that he had warrants for the arrest of those responsible for depredations in the town and demanded their surrender. He also ordered the dispersal of those holding the courthouse. When Allen refused to recognize Nash's authority and rejected his demands, Nash said he was prepared to take the courthouse and make his arrests by force;

he gave Allen half an hour to remove from the town all women, children, and men who did not want to fight.

After the noncombatants had been evacuated, rifle fire broke out and continued for several hours. Black casualties during this long-range phase of the fighting are not known, but one white was killed and eight or nine wounded. The blacks finally deserted their trenches and sought cover in the brick courthouse. Some of them continued to fire from the doorway, but Nash's men closed in on the building from the blind side. There they were able to ignite the wooden shingles on the roof and soon the place was ablaze.

A white flag of truce was waved from the doorway and some of the blacks began running from the courthouse with their hands in the air. A party of whites approached the doorway to accept the surrender, but suddenly shots were fired from within and James Hadnot and Sidney Harris, two of the negotiating party, crumpled. Hadnot, Colfax resident and popular figure, died later of his wounds.

Enraged by what they considered an act of cowardice and treachery, the besieging whites turned savage. Blacks fleeing the burning building were slaughtered and many "were ridden down in the open fields and shot without mercy."[21] The wounded were pinned to the ground with bayonets. Seeing the carnage outside, some blacks chose death in the burning building. About forty were taken prisoner. Few escaped. One witness described the awful scene: "By the time the job was finished it looked to me like any one could have walked on dead negroes almost an acre big."[22]

Among the reported dead were Daniel Shaw, the Kellogg sheriff and only white man supporting the blacks, and Alexander Fellman, who had served as a delegate to the constitutional convention of 1868. It is not known whether Levi Allen escaped or was killed, but he probably perished.[23]

By four o'clock in the afternoon all firing had ceased and by nightfall most of Nash's army was headed for home. The prisoners were being held in a fenced garden under guard, ostensibly to await removal to Alexandria for trial. Said a Grant Parish old-timer almost half a century later:

> About dark the steamboat *Southwestern* came down the river, taking Mr. Hadnot, who was then in a dying state, and other seriously wounded on board. While this boat was at the landing a number of

whites drank pretty freely and became intoxicated. . . . After the boat was gone, and nearly all the sober and influential men had lain down to sleep, these parties, all of whom were young, reckless and irresponsible men, determined to go to the yard where the negroes were. . . . About ten o'clock before anyone was aware of their intentions, they opened fire on the defenseless negroes, who broke and ran in all directions. Of the forty negroes in the yard, about twenty were killed.[24]

W. Lod Tanner also claimed to have been present that bloody night and told the story a little differently. He and others had gone to the garden to take some of the prisoners to Alexandria. Luke Hadnot, a relative of the dying man who had been shot down under a flag of truce, said, " 'I can take five,' and five men stepped out. Luke lined them up and his old gun went off, and he killed all five of them with two shots. Then it was like popcorn in a skillet. They killed those forty-eight."[25]

The number of defenseless blacks massacred in the garden is not known; some feigned death and later escaped to testify in court against members of the posse. Nor is it known how many blacks were killed in Colfax on that fateful Easter. Some of the bodies had been removed by relatives before a deputy U.S. marshal and Metropolitan Police arrived a day or two later and supervised the mass burial of sixty-nine bodies in a common grave.[26] "The number of negroes killed in the battle was variously estimated at from sixty-four to four hundred, from sixty to seventy being the most likely estimate. Privilege was given to the negroes to bury their dead but as only a few came to do this, most of the bodies were thrown into trenches, 'buried as it were in the graves dug with their own hands.' "[27]

Later in the week a contingent of United States troops arrived and assisted the Metropolitans in a search for participants in what came to be called the Colfax Riot. C. C. Nash and Jim Bird had been identified by surviving blacks as the leaders and headed the wanted lists, but Nash escaped by swimming his horse across the river with bullets slapping the water around him and Bird vanished into the woodlands. Finally, nine men were placed under arrest and taken to New Orleans to stand trial.[28]

The extent of the Scarboroughs' involvement in the calamitous events in Colfax is not known. The names of George W. and his sons are not mentioned in the various histories of the infamous event, and the family may have fled far from the town after being driven from their home and may have taken no part in the battle and subsequent bloodbath. But because of their close family ties to Judge Rutland, a central figure in the early development of the tragedy, and because they were among the very few white residents of the town, it is reasonable to believe that G. W. Scarborough, his eighteen-year-old son C. B., and possibly even thirteen-year-old George were members of the Nash posse. In any event, the extreme violence of the episode must have had a powerful effect on the adolescent George, whose life would be spent in an atmosphere of imminent danger and, for himself and those with whom he associated, the very real possibility of sudden and violent death.[29]

It was to me a glorious trip.

—LEE SCARBOROUGH, 1942

-2-

A Glorious Trip

Revolted by conditions in Louisiana with its bitter racial strife, soon after the Colfax Riot George W. Scarborough led his family once again into Texas, locating this time near Waco, McLennan County, in an area strongly dominated by Southern Baptists. There, on October 3, 1874, at White Hall Baptist Church, George Washington Scarborough was ordained to the gospel ministry. The following year there was another move: to a farm some sixteen miles west of Waco.[1]

C. B. was a grown man by 1875. Large and powerfully built like his father, he worked with Parson Scarborough, as George W. was now being called, raising cotton on the farm. The other children—George, fifteen; Ada, ten; Will, seven; and Lee, five—attended classes in a tiny schoolhouse at Hog Creek. Lee, who in later years received academic degrees and honors from several prestigious universities, said he remembered only one thing from those early school days, a Friday afternoon speech:

> My head is large,
> My breast is small;
> God bless the girls,
> I love them all.[2]

At fifteen George Scarborough had just about finished all the formal education he would ever receive. The balance of his learning would come from hard experience on the trail and in the saddle. And into the saddle he went at age sixteen. Rejecting a future as a cotton planter, he went west to McCulloch County in cattle country. This

15

George Washington Scarborough, farmer,
rancher, preacher, Confederate veteran, Texas
pioneer, and father of G. A. Scarborough.
Courtesy Mrs. Evelyn Linebery.

was the era of the great trail drives when half-wild longhorns that
had roamed freely and proliferated on the Texas plains during the
war years were rounded up and driven north to the new railheads in
western Kansas, ultimately to be shipped to beef-hungry markets in
the East.

James B. Gillett, who would later become a Texas Ranger, city
marshal at El Paso, sheriff of Brewster County and a successful
stockgrower in the Davis Mountains of West Texas, was himself
only fifteen years old when he participated in a roundup in McCulloch
County a few years before Scarborough began cowboying in the
area. He has left a vivid description of how it was to work cattle
there at the time:

> In the spring of 1871 I was working with Robert Trogden's cow
> outfit. Mr. Trogden . . . contracted to gather and deliver 2,000 big

steers to be driven up the trail. At that time all of western Texas was an open frontier—there was not a pasture of any size in that part of the state.

The woods and prairies were full of wild cattle. Mr. Trogden decided to go south of the Colorado River and into what is now McCulloch County. We began work at the Hall pens on Big Brady Creek. . . .

We had no mess wagon but carried our provisions and bedding on pack horses. Our supplies were flour, coffee and salt. We were not burdened with can goods, potatoes and "lick" like the big outfits had in later years. We had no special cook—everybody cooked and it was wonderful to see how quick twelve or fifteen hungry men could cook a meal, especially when they had only bread to bake, meat to cook and coffee to boil.

We killed a beef almost every day—anybody's beef, just so it was fat. It was not considered stealing. Other cow outfits did the same thing so this evened up matters. I ate my neighbor's beef and he ate mine. Besides, a calf or yearling was not worth much then.

Every cowboy of that day and time carried either a sixshooter or a Winchester. . . . They had to be carried for self-protection as Indians hung on the flanks of all cow outfits in that western country just watching for a chance to steal horses or kill a cowboy.

We found cattle had drifted in on the Bradys from everywhere, especially from the northern part of the state. . . . When the cold northers blew they just drifted south. There was no one to turn them back on their range. . . .

We gathered 100 to 150 steers each day. None but the most choice beeves were selected, regardless of whose brands they were—that was the custom then. We soon had more cattle than the pens would hold and had to herd out. . . .

When we reached home with our steers Mr. Trogden sent to Brownwood, the county seat, for the inspector, [who] would set down the brand and mark of each steer. . . . The inspector never asked any questions as to whom the steers belonged. When the herd was shaped up the inspector went back to town, [and] put these brands in a record book.[3]

Said D. H. Henderson, who came to McCulloch County from Louisiana with his father in 1874: "There were only a few settlers here, and no farming—only a few small patches in cultivation, with fences made of brush mostly. The whole country was a wide open and free-for-all. Land had no value; there was lots of public land and a man could pre-empt 160 acres."[4]

Although bands of Indians still roamed in McCulloch County and men went armed for protection against them, the last fatal raid occurred in the spring of 1875 when two East Texas greenhorns, out to look over this new country, camped for the night on the San Saba River. In the morning their horses were gone, stolen by Indians, and the men, afoot and unarmed, were soon captured also. Attaching the hobbles they had removed from the horses to the men's legs, the Indians drove them some distance before they tired of this sport and impaled them with spears.[5]

"When we moved to McCulloch County that was a wild region," said Wyatt Anderson, who came in 1876. "The Indians would come in and take all the horses they could find, leaving their poor, old, ridden-down horses with us."[6]

Many of the cowboys, after gathering the cattle, went up the trail with their herds to the Kansas railheads. It is not known whether George Scarborough joined any of these long trail drives, but if he did not stray far, he had a very good reason. He was courting Mary Frances McMahan, pretty daughter of McCulloch County pioneer Frank M. McMahan. Mollie, as she was called by everyone, turned seventeen in June 1877. George, also seventeen that summer, asked for her hand and in August took her to his father's place in McLennan County. There, on August 30, Parson Scarborough joined George and Mollie in marriage.[7]

In December of that same year Parson Scarborough purchased a tract of land in Jones County. For the sum of one dollar he was awarded title to more than five hundred acres of land on the Clear Fork of the Brazos River near old Phantom Hill, a deserted army post.[8] The Scarboroughs did not move until fall of the following year, 1878. Then they loaded their wagons and began the more than two-hundred-mile trek to the new homestead. In the Scarborough party were George W. and Martha, their three youngest children, and C. B., now married, his wife, Mattie, and their infant daughter, Cora. George came along to help in the move and settlement but left Mollie, pregnant with their first child, with her family in McCulloch County.

As might be expected, the difficult move was a wonderful adventure for eight-year-old Lee.

I remember very distinctly the trip. We went by wagons and carried all our meager household goods, our cows, horses and dogs. It was to me a glorious trip. We covered a distance of probably two hundred or two hundred fifty miles, and it took us three or four weeks. We struck camp . . . twenty miles northwest of what is now Abilene, near a little hill called Truby Mound. My mother was an invalid. We took her out of the wagon on a bed, stretched our tent, built a little picket house and afterwards a log house and a dugout, and lived in there a number of years.[9]

Fort Phantom Hill was built in 1851 by the United States Army as one of a chain of forts extending across Texas to provide military protection for expanding white settlements. It was situated on a low hill between the Elm and Clear forks of the Brazos River, a mile and a half above the point where the streams joined to form the main Clear Fork. This was prairie country, with a clear view to the horizon obstructed only by low, stunted mesquite trees. On the north side of the Clear Fork was a dense, almost impenetrable, thicket of scrub oaks and green briars extending for several miles, called the Big Shinnery. The streams were edged by stands of elm, pecan, and hackberry trees. The prairie soil, covered by buffalo grass, was dry and thin, but near the streams it was more fertile and provided opportunity for cultivation. The area had been the camping grounds of Delaware and Caddo Indians and had been crossed by hunting parties of Wichitas, Tonkawas, and Comanches. In 1854 the army decided to reduce the number of frontier outposts in Texas and Fort Phantom Hill was abandoned.[10] Four years later the old fort was refurbished and established as Station No. 54 on the Butterfield Stage and Southern Overland Mail Line, which ran twenty-four hundred miles from Saint Louis to San Francisco. The Civil War made this route impossible to maintain as part of the mail service, and in 1861 the line was discontinued.[11]

Buffalo hunters established camps in Jones County during the years of the great buffalo slaughter. Headquartered at Fort Griffin, about forty-five miles northeast of Phantom Hill, in the middle 1870s the hide hunters virtually wiped out the great southern herd and with it the Indian commissary.

As the buffalo and hostile Indian disappeared from the area, the cattlemen moved in. First to establish in Jones County were the Roberts brothers, Dick, John, Creed, and Emmett. They brought a herd of two thousand cattle to the Clear Fork from Eastland County in April 1873 and set up a base camp east of the Big Shinnery. They did not erect permanent buildings but moved their camp every few weeks as precaution against Indian attack. Horse thievery was their major Indian problem. Emmett Roberts recalled only one Jones County confrontation with Indians in which shots were fired. "Some Indians chased us into the creek bed," he said. "About that time an old Indian buck came riding down a buffalo trail to the creek. Just as I took good aim at the Indian he saw me and reined up his mule. Instead of killing the Indian I shot the mule right in the forehead and killed him. The boys had a good laugh at me. But the Indians didn't come here to kill the white man. They were looking for horses."[12]

Soon other cattle raisers followed the Roberts boys into the new country. J. G. and Mode Johnson, Nick Eaton, John Merchant, J. B. Carpenter, and Rufus McKinney arrived early and established ranches.[13]

Emmett Roberts remembered some salty characters who came into Jones County in those very early days:

> Sol Jackson . . . lived in a little picket shack covered with dirt.
> . . . There was a man named George Gilland, who lived at the fort, and a man named Williams who had his tongue shot out in a saloon in Abilene by a man named Howard Jung, who was shooting at Judge Hammond. A fellow lived in the commissary at the fort named George Kaiser. He harbored two bad men up there in the Shinnery. Those fellows killed our calves until we got tired of it and finally posted a notice giving them so many days to clear out of the country. The bluff worked. They posted a counter notice, but left the country.

A little community developed at Phantom Hill and a man named Pretty Smith opened a hotel there. "Pretty Smith was the ugliest fellow I ever saw," Roberts said, "but his wife was a portly, handsome lady, and she was smart and a hard worker. Their hotel, a boxed and stripped two-story building, was moved to Anson when that place was made the county seat."[14]

Joe T. McKinney, a New Mexico peace officer in later years, worked cattle near Truby Mound in 1878:

> There were some few buffalo in the country at the time we went there," McKinney recalled, "bunches around in what is called the 'Shinnery,' on the north side of the Clear Fork. There were lots of antelope and wild turkey and deer and plenty of the finest catfish. . . .

It rained a great deal that year and there was the finest grass and water holes all over the country. I will incidentally add, too, that there were mosquitos galore. They punished the horses greatly. Around the campfire at night I have known the horses to come and stand in smoke to avoid the mosquitos, and of mornings to be specked with blood from their bites.[15]

Operating just a few miles away from the Scarborough settlement was an outfit called the Sawed-Horn Cattle Company, owned by Billy Barry, Capt. Pete Hatchett, and Ben Calhoun. These partners had purchased longhorns in Southwest Texas and sawed off their horns before turning them out on the Clear Fork ranges. Joining them as a fifteen-dollar-a-month cowhand that year was a lad fresh from Florida and eager to experience life in the Wild West. Jeff Davis Milton, sixteen years old when he came to Jones County, was youngest of the ten children of John Milton, governor of Florida during the Civil War. In the years to come, Jeff Milton would share with George Scarborough some exciting experiences and some difficult times. They would face gunfire together and stand side by side before the bar of justice charged with murder. Jeff Milton would become the best friend Scarborough ever had.[16]

The rugged life in Jones County seemed to help Martha Scarborough's health, and that first Christmas in their rude dugout home she invited all the county residents, all sixteen of them, to a celebration and feast. The country was thick with wild turkeys and the parson and his sons were able to bag many of the birds as well as other game. But the meat was all hauled to Fort Griffin to trade for other necessities and no turkey carcasses were available for Martha's dinner. Undaunted, she cooked enough turkey gizzards and livers in the iron wash pot mounted over the camp fire to feed the entire assemblage.[17]

A story of those very early days passed down in the family is recounted by Mrs. Ada Phillips, a granddaughter of the parson and Martha:

> They had a dugout to live in. Once when the rains lasted a week, the sod roof leaked. My grandmother had buckets under the drips. She sat by the fire mending a shirt. Grandfather sat quietly reading his Bible. She went to empty the buckets, sat down and reached for her pipe to the utter disgust of my grandfather. As she picked her

Martha Rutland Scarborough, George's mother.
Courtesy Mrs. Evelyn Linebery.

sewing up, a wet clump of dirt fell from the ceiling, knocking her
pipe out of her mouth and scattering hot ashes. She cleared up the
mess, threw her pipe in the fire with a "Drat that pipe," and never
smoked again.[18]

Rough and primitive as the household was, it was never without
reading materials. Foremost of these, of course, was the Bible. There
were songbooks and the published works of Baptist clergymen the
parson admired: B. H. Carroll, R. C. Buckner, J. B. Hawthorne,
J. P. Boyce, John A. Broadus, J. R. Graves. Parson Scarborough
subscribed to two newspapers, the *Tennessee Baptist* and the *Baptist
Standard,* which appeared in bundles when someone made the more
than three-hundred-mile round trip to Fort Worth to get the mail.[19]

"I cannot remember when we did not have a family altar," Lee
Scarborough said. "Many a time in our dugout . . . after supper the
children and the visitors who were present would gather around the
family altar and Father would read tenderly some passage of Scripture

and then lead a song. He had taught music, and had a splendid voice and a good knowledge of music for that day. My mother had a beautiful voice and could sing treble."[19]

It is doubtful young George Scarborough stayed with his parents and siblings to enjoy that Christmas dinner with the entire county. Mollie was expecting and the time was close. He returned to McCulloch County to be by her side when their first child entered the world. On January 12, 1879, Mollie gave birth to a boy, christened George Edgar, always to be called Ed. Another baby came into the family on November 19, 1881, when a girl, Martha Ann, was born.[21]

While primarily employed as a cowboy in McCulloch County during these years, George made frequent trips to Jones County to see the family. Parson Scarborough and C. B. were running a small herd of cattle on the public lands, and George helped them as he could. These were the years of the great cattle drives, and both George and C. B. also took employment as trail hands for cattlemen moving herds into and out of Jones County.

George Scarborough . . . was the bravest man I ever saw.

—EMMETT ROBERTS, AUGUST 24, 1933

-3-

The Bravest Man

Jones County was created by a special act of the Seventh Texas Legislature on February 1, 1858. The first white permanent settlers, buffalo hunters and a few hardy cattle ranchers, began arriving in 1873, and the following year the county was attached to neighboring Shackelford County for judicial purposes. Under the law, provision had been made for organization when seventy-five free white male inhabitants over twenty-one years of age petitioned the presiding judge of an adjoining organized county. In April 1881 a petition was circulated, signed by 185 residents, and presented to the Shackelford County Commissioner's Court. The court granted the petition and divided Jones County into four precincts. Elections were ordered to choose county officers and select the site of a permanent county seat.

Officers were chosen in a series of special elections that summer. The first sheriff and tax collector was James Polk Cole. At an election held on November 14, 1881, Jones City, a tiny hamlet of twenty residents, was made the seat of the new county, and on January 1, 1882, the sparse books and records of the new county were formally moved from the temporary seat at Phantom Hill to Jones City. Shortly thereafter the name of the town was changed from Jones City to Anson, so that the full name of the last president of the Republic of Texas, Anson Jones, could be memorialized in the new county.

The first courthouse was a twenty-four-by-thirty-two-foot plank structure built by Sheriff Polk Cole and J. M. Anderson with lumber hauled from Abilene. Including the courthouse, the little village had no more than a half-dozen buildings in January 1882. But by year's end the town had shown rapid growth and boasted seven business

24

houses, two hotels, two livery stables, a blacksmith shop, a church, a schoolhouse, and thirty private residences.[1]

In 1879 the Reverend George W. Scarborough had preached the first sermon ever delivered in Jones County before an assembly of eight on the banks of the Clear Fork not far from his home.[2] Later he conducted outdoor services at Phantom Hill. By 1880 he was holding services under a brush arbor fronting a dugout church two miles southeast of Jones City. This, the first established church in the county, was organized as the New Providence Baptist Church of Christ and later became the First Baptist Church of Anson.[3] In 1880, Parson Scarborough also erected the first school building in the county, a small construction of poles and mud-daubed logs situated about a mile northeast of Truby. Later he built a larger schoolhouse, also of logs, on Clear Fork Creek three miles from the Scarborough home. Here his small children, Ada, Will, and Lee, were taught by the county's first full-time schoolteacher, twenty-four-year-old Emma Scarborough, eldest daughter of the parson's brother Andrew. Later on, Lee attended a new school built in Anson and stayed with his brother George, who maintained a home in town after he was elected sheriff.[4]

George had moved his growing family to Anson in early 1883. On August 5 of that year he and wife Mollie joined Parson Scarborough's church. Acceptance into this assembly was no small accomplishment; the parson's son and daughter-in-law were received as members of the congregation only after presentation of a letter of recommendation from the pastor of the Middle Bosque Baptist Church of McLennan County. When he was seventeen, Lee Scarborough asked to be excluded from the church because he had never been exonerated. His father accepted Lee's withdrawal and so stated in the minutes of a January 1887 meeting. Lee was later fully converted and became in his lifetime one of the most renowned ministers and teachers of the Baptist faith in the country.[5]

At a meeting on March 31, 1883, the church adopted a covenant, encompassing rules of decorum, which forbade members from engaging in dancing, drinking, or the use of profane language.[6] The influence of the Baptists, led by Parson Scarborough, was primarily responsible for keeping Anson free of saloons and dance halls with their attendant evils. Neighboring Haskell County and its seat, Haskell City, a town of comparable size and composition which had only one saloon, invites comparison. During its first fourteen years, 1885–99, Haskell recorded four killings; three victims fell in shootings within the saloon and the other while drinking just outside. During its first fifty years, Anson had only one homicide within its city limits, that by a criminal in the act of escaping from jail. As evidence that violence dogged the trail of George Scarborough, it should also be noted that he was directly or indirectly involved in three of the five deaths cited.[7]

In addition to building churches and schools and ministering to his growing congregation, Parson Scarborough in the early eighties was working his farm and ranch and still found time to take on other large projects. In 1883 he contracted to fence a farm northwest of Anson and a horse pasture for the larger Heart Ranch. Then he made a major contract: fencing the east line of the huge XIT Ranch in the Texas Panhandle. For this project he hired a number of Anson men, including sons C. B. and Will, and was gone for almost a year.[8]

Son George, now settled in Anson, took a job as town constable and deputy under Sheriff Polk Cole. Work as a lawman immediately appealed to him, and by the fall of 1884 he had decided to run against his boss for the office of sheriff and tax collector. On November 4 he defeated Cole by a vote of 190 to 166 and was elected to a two-year term at a salary of two hundred dollars per quarter.[9]

Assuming office as county attorney was twenty-seven-year-old J. F. Cunningham, whose boyish appearance soon earned him a sobriquet: The Kid. Although Sheriff Scarborough was two years younger, there is no record that from the day he first pinned on a badge anyone ever referred to him as a kid. Cunningham presented cases before Anson resident J. V. Cockrell, who held juridical responsibility for the Thirty-ninth Judicial District, a huge area encompassing more than thirty Texas counties. The Thirty-ninth extended 125 miles north to south and 150 miles east to west. Judge Cockrell, who stood well over six feet and weighed nearly three hundred pounds, was a big man for a big job.

"We had no form books in those days," recalled Cunningham, who in 1888 was elected district attorney for the Thirty-ninth. "There were no stenographers, no typewriters, everything was done in long hand—charges, indictments, facts, briefs, etc., had to be written out. We had nothing like Wilson's *Criminal Forms,* there was no *Southwestern Reporter.* We simply wrote out what we wanted and trusted that it would stand the scrutiny of the higher courts. The lawyers on the defense were in no better position than we. They did not know how to get up an appeal any better than we knew how to draw up an indictment."[10]

Frontier sheriffs like George Scarborough came to their jobs even less prepared than did the attorneys. Usually with no more than a grade-school education and with a knowledge of law and its enforcement limited to what might have been acquired on the job as a deputy, these men relied on courage and common sense to perform their duties as the chief law enforcement official in the county. Attorney Cunningham, after a fifty-year career in the Texas courts, had high praise for these early frontier lawmen. "There were great sheriffs in that day," he said. "Bill Standifer of Crosby County and George Scarborough of Anson were among the best—as game as any men I ever knew."[11]

As sheriff of Jones County, Scarborough was authorized to employ one deputy and one jailer. M. H. Rhoads was the new sheriff's first deputy, later succeeded by Lee Youngblood and Eb Poole. J. S. ("Doc") Ballard acted as jail guard. Later on, George employed his older brother, C. B., as permanent deputy but called on others, including his preacher father, for help when the situation called for an extra show of force. Emmett Roberts, who in a long frontier experience had known a legion of cool and daring men, stated flatly in 1933: "George Scarborough . . . was the bravest man I ever saw. I've seen him go right down in dugouts after bad men, and his daddy, old Parson Scarborough, would go right down with him with a pistol in his hand."[12]

Cicero Battle Scarborough, George's older brother, brought an imposing physical presence to the job of deputy sheriff. An inch over six feet tall and weighing 250 pounds or more, C. B. could physically intimidate unruly prisoners. But the work of a lawman did not really appeal to C. B.; he took on the deputy's assignment just to help his brother. After George left the sheriff's office, C. B. never again pinned on a badge. He was basically a genial, easygoing

Jones County, Texas, officials. Front row: F. T. Knox, druggist and first
county treasurer; W. H. ("Red") Smith, county clerk, alerted the town to
Add Cannon's escape; Howell Carr, deputy sheriff and second tax assessor;
W. H. Hollis, deputy and later sheriff; Sheriff George A. Scarborough,
holding a pistol; D. L. Flint, early county attorney; unknown; J. S. ("Doc")
Ballard, deputy sheriff. Back row: A. J. Carr, first tax assessor; J. V.
Cockrell, district judge, later congressman; A. H. Kirby, teacher; L. M.
Buie, county judge. *Courtesy Western Observer, Anson, Texas.*

man. Children adored him; his many nieces and nephews called him
Big Bud. But C. B. could be iron willed and tough when the situation
demanded it, as is illustrated by a family story.

When he heard that his bank in Abilene had closed, C. B. drove
the twenty-five miles to town in his buggy. The door of the bank
was locked and the shades drawn, so he went around to the back and
knocked. The door was opened a crack and he was told the bank
was closed. But C. B. jammed the toe of his boot into the opening,
leaned his great weight against the door, and muscled his way in.
Placing a pistol on the counter, he demanded his money and got it.
Then he demanded the deposits of all his hired hands. These he also
received. Picking up his gun and the cash, C. B. walked out. He

Left to right: Eb Poole and C. B. Scarborough,
deputies, and Jones County Sheriff George Scarborough. *Courtesy Dan Scarborough Abbott.*

was the only customer of the bank to salvage all his deposits. "Now
days," said the niece who recounted the story, "we would call that
a hold up, but then, it was a courageous deed."[13]

George Scarborough served a pair of two-year terms as sheriff
of Jones County. In November 1886 he was reelected, defeating
candidate John R. Moore 222 to 175.[14]

During his four years in office, Scarborough had to deal with a
number of hardcase criminals. Two of the worst were youthful
bandits named A. B. ("Add") Cannon and Joe Brown, who went on
a road-agentry rampage in several central Texas counties during the
fall of 1885. Scarborough got on their trail when they held up a
drummer's hack on the Anson-to-Abilene road on October 25 and

shot the traveling salesman. The next night, the Abilene–San Angelo stage was stopped and robbed by a pair of youthful highwaymen believed to be the same pair. On December 2 the desperadoes struck again, holding up the Fredericksburg coach near Comfort in Kendall County, some two hundred miles to the south.[15]

Scarborough had been dogging their trail since the crime in his county. He nabbed Cannon and on December 21 slapped him in a cell at Anson, but the outlaw made bail and fled the county. Working with Mitchell County Sheriff Dick Ware, a notable law officer with whom Scarborough would be closely associated in later years, George traced the fugitive to Nolan County, where he had again linked up with Brown. There the officers arrested both Cannon and Brown in early February 1886. Deputy U.S. Marshal William Van Riper claimed the prisoners, however, arguing that the case against them for robbery of the United States mails in the Fredericksburg holdup presented the best hope for conviction. The county officers released the prisoners into the custody of Van Riper, who took them to San Antonio for trial.[16]

On May 25 the two road agents appeared in federal court, but the jury could not agree on their guilt and they were returned to their cells in the Bexar County Jail to await a second trial. It took months for Cannon and Brown to raise the twenty-five-hundred-dollar bond set for each, but they were finally freed on July 13. However, Sheriff Scarborough, "a cruel and unfeeling officer," according to a tongue-in-cheek report in a San Antonio paper, was waiting at the jailhouse door. Scarborough clamped handcuffs on the pair and placed them under arrest for the Jones County holdup. "Brown and Cannon are very much crestfallen over this additional and unexpected bad luck," said the newspaper, "for they had labored long and patiently to secure a bond only to have their hopes of liberty again dashed to the ground. Truly, the way of the wicked is hard."[17]

On July 21, George and C. B. checked out of San Antonio's Southern Hotel and started back to Jones County with their manacled prisoners.[18] Cannon and Brown went into Sheriff Scarborough's lockup on the twenty-third, joining Ben Kirby, another hard character, who was being held on charges of murder, horse theft, and assault.

The Jones County Jailbook contains descriptions of the prisoners as set down in Scarborough's hand. Ben Kirby was a big fellow, six feet, two inches tall, with a dark complexion and black hair and eyes. Add Cannon, age twenty-one, stood five feet, ten inches and was also dark, with black eyes and hair. Joe Brown, only nineteen years old, was five feet, nine and fair, with blond hair and blue eyes. On August 12 these three were joined in jail by J. S. ("Sam") Boyd, a twenty-nine-year-old charged with murder.[19]

Shortly after Scarborough's election, funds had been appropriated for construction of a jail at Anson. Prior to this, prisoners were confined in jails in other counties and Jones County was burdened with board expense in addition to the fifteen cents per mile the sheriff collected for transporting the prisoners. Scarborough supervised construction of the new jail with "cages of P. J. Pauley improved make." Cells were six and a half by eight feet, with seven-foot ceilings. An eight-by-thirteen-foot prisoners' corridor separated the cells. There were six bars "of I-beams or old railroad iron" fifteen feet, four inches long. The floors, sides, and ceilings of cells were of jail-plate iron three-sixteenths of an inch thick.[20]

On August 18, Scarborough turned over the jailer's responsibilities to William C. Glazner, a thirty-year-old farmer. With six children and a pregnant wife, Glazner was enduring much hardship in the severe drought of 1886. The sheriff, in an act of compassion, took him on as temporary jailer although Glazner had no experience handling tough characters like those currently lodged in the Anson hoosegow.

On Monday, August 30, Scarborough and C. B. took Sam Boyd to Seymour, seat of Baylor County, for a habeas corpus hearing. The 160-mile round trip would take them two days.

At dusk the following evening, Will Glazner was moving his prisoners from the day cell to the one they would share for the night. As Add Cannon followed Kirby and Brown into the cell, he turned to Glazner and asked if he could have some cigarette papers. Glazner closed the night-cell door, locking Kirby and Brown in and leaving Cannon in the corridor separating the cages. He had turned to enter the jailer's office for the cigarette makings when Cannon struck him from behind with an iron bar wrapped in a towel.

Glazner fell to the floor and Cannon pounced on him, beating him unmercifully over the head with the bar. The jailer's few faint cries

for help before he lost consciousness were heard by Anson citizens
W. H. ("Red") Smith and W. G. Rhodes, who ran to the jailhouse.
Peering through the window they saw in the fast-gathering darkness
the body of Glazner on the floor and Cannon, in his underwear,
bending over him with a blood-soaked bludgeon in his hand.

Smith and Rhodes yelled for help and Smith ran to the Star Hotel
to secure a pistol. Cannon, who had been going through Glazner's
pockets in search of keys, heard the shouts and gave up any plans
he may have had to release the other inmates. Dropping his weapon,
an eighteen-inch, two-and-a-half-pound bar that he had wrenched
off the water box, he grabbed the jailer's pistol and rushed into the
office. Shoving a desk against the locked front door, he climbed on
top, and smashed out the transom with the pistol. He squeezed
through the opening, leaped to the ground, and sprinted off into the
darkness.

Within moments a large crowd gathered at the jail. The door was
forced and a physician summoned to attend to Glazner, who had
multiple skull fractures. The jailer was carried to the home of A. J.
Carr, where he remained in a coma for five days before dying of his
wounds on Sunday, September 5.

Some Anson citizens wanted to organize a party to pursue Cannon
immediately after the escape, but others were not particularly anxious
to chase an armed and dangerous fugitive in the dark. After some
discussion it was agreed that since all the horses in town had been
turned out to pasture for the night and much time would be lost
catching them and preparing for the hunt, they would await the return
of the sheriff, due back the next morning.

When George and C. B. rode into town, they learned of the attack
on Glazner and the escape of Cannon. Without pausing for rest,
Scarborough assembled a posse and set out after the outlaw. He was
still in the field when the local paper gave the details of the escape
under the headline "A Horrible Deed." The iron bar Cannon had
wielded so viciously was on display in the offices of the paper, where
all were invited to see it. "We hope to see the scoundrel caught,"
said the editor, "and would also enjoy seeing him dangling at the
end of a rope, and hope that if he is caught, he would be dealt with
as he so richly deserves."[21]

Scarborough's posse was unsuccessful in its search. Cannon was tracked to the Big Shinnery, where his trail vanished. Barefooted and clad only in underwear, he had disappeared into the labyrinthine thickets.

A reward of one hundred dollars was posted for information leading to the arrest of Add Cannon and was still being offered fourteen years later. The 1900 List of Fugitives for the State of Texas included the name of Add Cannon, wanted for murder in Jones County. The one-hundred-dollar reward was noted, as well as additional information about the fugitive. His age was inaccurately given as thirty-three; his hair black; his eyes "very black and uncommonly wide between; his beard black, "what there is of it, but thin"; his mustache "not very much, but black"; his complexion dark. He was described as well built with a high and prominent forehead. His height was given as five feet, six inches and his weight as 160 pounds. He originated in Buffalo Gap, Taylor County, Texas, where his mother, father, and brothers still resided. "Not much to say. Does not drink. Smokes cigarettes. . . . May be in Mexico; last heard of was going in that direction."[22]

The murder of Will Glazner and the escape of Add Cannon were the most depressing events for George Scarborough in his tenure as Jones County sheriff. Even as his fame as a manhunter grew, his inability to locate and collar Cannon, the brutal killer of his friend and fellow officer, became particularly distressing.

Joe Brown and Ben Kirby were cleared on charges of complicity in the Glazner murder but convicted of their other crimes. In March 1887, Scarborough delivered Kirby to the state penitentiary at Huntsville, where he was joined the following December by Joe Brown.[23]

Although there is no record that Cannon was ever brought before the bar of justice, retribution may have come to him years later at the hand of Welborn Glazner, eldest son of Will. Welborn, nine years old at the time of his father's tragic death, was terribly shaken and swore he would avenge that crime. As a teenager he left home determined to find the killer of his father and worked as a trail hand during the last Kansas cattle drives. He returned to Jones County after an absence of several years but refused to discuss with anyone whether he had ever found Cannon. He took that secret to the grave with him when he died in 1952.[24]

A recurring source of trouble during Scarborough's term as sheriff was a gang of stock thieves operating in Jones County. Led by a desperado named A. J. Williams, the gang included Redmond ("Bud") Coleman, Nath Gatlin, and Tom Babb. On March 7, 1885, Scarborough arrested Gatlin for cattle theft and lodged him in the Jones County calaboose. Gatlin made bail on March 28 and was released.[25] Three weeks later Scarborough had warrants for the arrest of Williams, Coleman, and Gatlin on indictments for cattle theft. Based on information that the outlaws had been seen in Lincoln County, New Mexico Territory, Scarborough on April 20 requested extradition papers from the state of Texas.[26] Upon receipt of the papers, he went over into New Mexico after his quarry. According to the recollections of a Jones County old-timer Archie Jefferes, he had to make the trip twice:

> There was an outlaw named Williams that was considered one of the worst. [Scarborough] was notified that he was working on a ranch in New Mexico and George got orders to get him. He rode the train to a small town in New Mexico, rented a horse and headed for the ranch. Williams seen him coming and took off. George run him for several miles, but his horse was no match for Williams'. He come back to Abilene, turned in his report, and said he would git him the next time. . . .
>
> When he got word again he shipped his thoroughbred horse by train and rode the train with him. He rode out to the ranch and Williams saw him coming again. But this time he run him down. . . . Williams refused to stop [and] George shot his horse. Williams fell and George had him handcuffed before he could git up.[27]

Scarborough also nabbed Coleman and Babb and escorted his three prisoners by train back to Abilene where his feat was applauded in the local press and papers as far away as Arizona picked up the story.

> Sheriff Scarborough, of Jones County, arrived in the city tonight [May 22] with A. J. Williams, a noted Clear Fork cattle thief and desperado, and Bob [Bud] Coleman and Tom Bob [Babb], two of his principal assistants. The gang was captured in Lincoln County, New Mexico, after a dangerous search of several weeks. The gang have been a terror to the residents of Jones and surrounding counties, and their capture will be hailed with universal delight.[28]

Scarborough took Williams and Coleman to Anson and jailed them. Tom Babb apparently had been turned over to other authorities or released in Abilene. Scarborough described Williams in his jail-book as a man of thirty years, five feet, eight in height, with dark complexion, hair, and eyes. Coleman was twenty-three, six feet tall, with black hair, gray eyes, and a dark complexion.

Even the new Jones County calaboose with its I-beam bars and jail plate was considered inadequate to secure the dangerous outlaw pair, so it was decided to move them to Sweetwater to await trial. Scarborough passed through Abilene again with his prisoners on May 30 and the local press took note:

> A. J. Williams, the Clear Fork desperado and cattle thief, recently captured in New Mexico, and Coleman, another desperado, were brought to the city today from Jones county, the scene of their exploits. They will be taken to Sweetwater and confined in the Nolan county rock jail. The jail of Jones county is insecure, and it was feared they would be rescued by confederates on the outside, who have sworn to rescue them. A conviction on all the charges against Williams will send him to the penitentiary for life.[29]

Evidently the Sweetwater jail was no more secure than the Jones County lockup, for a little more than a month later Williams and Coleman were involved in a breakout. Besides Williams and Cole-man, the jail housed two convicted felons awaiting transfer to Hunts-ville, a boy named Fuller charged with theft, and W. J. Woods and Neil Bayett, indicted for the murder of a state detective. On July 5 as Sheriff Bardwell was bringing the evening meal to the inmates in the second-floor prisoner area, he was seized from behind by Wil-liams. Coleman ran downstairs to the sheriff's office and returned with a Winchester rifle, which he leveled at Bardwell. The sheriff, struggling in the grasp of Williams and Bayett, worked an arm free and struck Coleman in the eye. The enraged Coleman was prevented from shooting Bardwell only by the intervention of Bayett.

During this scuffle, the other prisoners piled out of the windows and fled. Woods stole Bardwell's horse from the jail stable and galloped out of town. By the time Bardwell was subdued, an alarm had been sounded and some fifty armed men surrounded the jail. Williams, Coleman, and Bayett were captured before they could escape the jail grounds. Three others were taken in the next day and Wood was recaptured three days later by a posse led by Bardwell.[30]

When Scarborough learned of the escape attempt, he went at once to Sweetwater. "Sheriff Scarborough, from Jones county, was in yesterday, and had Williams and Coleman heavily ironed to the floor," noted a Sweetwater news dispatch of July 8.[31]

Nine months later, on March 26, 1886, Scarborough had the Jones County outlaws back in the confines of his jail. According to the sheriff's jailbook note, Williams was in default of bond and Coleman was held on charges of attempting to bribe an officer. Details of this arrest are not available, but Scarborough had been hunting the two badmen for some time. Emmett Roberts remembered serving on a posse the sheriff enlisted to capture the pair. "One night a bunch of us, the Roberts brothers, John Bryan . . . Eugene Mayfield, Molair Mayfield, C. B. Scarborough, George Scarborough and old Parson Scarborough, met down at the old Jackson shack in Nugent to try to catch two bad men, A. J. Williams and Redmond Coleman. It was awful cold. Some other fellows were helping these men to escape the country. We did not get them that night, but later they were both captured."[32]

Coleman was released on bond on May 8 and Williams on June 3. The cases dragged on in the courts. Coleman evidently beat the many charges filed against him and disappeared from Jones County. "I understand that Coleman was under an assumed name, that he later turned out to be a good citizen," said Emmett Roberts in 1933.[33] But Williams was still a free man and a particular bur under Scarborough's saddle. The two were to meet in the town of Haskell with fatal consequences.

Haskell was the seat of Haskell County, which adjoined Jones County on the north. Its single drinking establishment, a two-story wooden structure on the south side of the town square, was owned and operated by J. L. Baldwin and W. F. Draper. Originally called the Q. T. Saloon, it later was quaintly tagged "Whiskey, The Road to Ruin Saloon."[34]

On Saturday, October 15, 1887, Sheriff Scarborough and his nineteen-year-old brother Will were in the saloon and George was writing a letter to his wife when A. J. Williams entered. According to Archie Jefferes, "George . . . was facing a mirror with his back to the door when he saw Williams come in. Williams drawed his gun. But George whirled and drew his gun and killed him."[35] We have no contemporary records to confirm this story; the newspaper files have been lost and the court records are meager, but it is certain that there was shooting and that when the smoke cleared, Williams was dead on the floor.

The killing of the notorious Williams generated much excitement in the town and triggered a reprise to the violence two nights later. W. M. Carter, while drinking in the saloon, accused J. L. Baldwin, one of the owners, of taking Scarborough's side in the dispute and being unfair to Williams. The argument led to guns being pulled, and Baldwin shot Carter dead.[36]

George and Will Scarborough were arrested by Sheriff R. H. Tucker and charged with murder. In March 1888 they stood trial in Haskell before Judge J. V. Cockrell.[37] "The jury in the case of G. A. and W. F. Scarborough, charged with the murder of A. J. Williams, were not out over five minutes before they returned a verdict of not guilty," reported the *Haskell City Free Press* of March 17. "We have

W. F. ("Will") Scarborough stood trial with his brother George for the killing of A. J. Williams and later became a very successful rancher and oilman. *Courtesy Mrs. Evelyn Linebery.*

heard many express themselves that this was the most clear case of justifiable homicide they ever saw and the defendants were properly acquitted."

J. L. Baldwin also came off clear in the shooting of William Carter. "The case was submitted without argument on the charge of the court," said the newspaper. "The jury retired long enough to write the verdict of not guilty and returned into court. This, like the Scarborough cases, was a very clear case of justifiable homicide."[38]

Judge Cockrell cleared his docket of another piece of business that week. In the matter of *State of Texas* v. *A. J. Williams,* charged with attempt to bribe an officer, the judge dismissed "on the ground of the death of the defendant."[39]

A sequel to the Williams story suggests that the badman's passing went unlamented, even by his family. Archie Jefferes told it as he got it from George's cousin, John Scarborough:

> After George killed the outlaw Williams, John was going through the shinnery north of Abilene heading for a job in Stonewall county [when] he got indigestion real bad; . . . thought he was going to die. But he rode into a small clearing and there was a shack of a house. . . . He hollered hello [and] a woman came out with several kids behind her.
>
> John asked if he could get a drink of water. [When] she asked his name, he told her it was John Scarborough.
>
> ". . . Are you any kin to the lawman George?"
>
> ". . . Yes, he is my first cousin."
>
> She said: "He killed my husband."
>
> John said it scared him, thinking she might shoot him, so he went to apologizing.
>
> She said: "Don't apologize. It was the best thing that could have happened. He was seldom here and we lived in fear all the time even when he was home."
>
> John gave her most of the money he had, which was very little, and rode on. . . . I think this was in 1890.[40]

Of course most of the work performed by George Scarborough as sheriff lacked the drama of the Cannon and Williams cases, but he was active and small items in the Texas press took note of that activity. The *Dallas News* of January 5, 1887, reported Scarborough's arrest of a suspect in a murder committed twenty-eight years earlier. George apprehended a man named S. S. Henslee, wanted for a murder in Nacogdoches County in 1859. The paper said Henslee's sixteen-year-old son admitted that his father had killed the man "to save his brother."

In April 1888, Scarborough nabbed a butcher named Thomas Suggs in Whitewright, Texas, and charged him with bigamy. Suggs, with a wife in Whitewright, protested that his former wife was dead, but the sheriff placed him under arrest, saying that wife number one was alive and well in Jones County, looking for her husband.[41]

In the midst of the terrible drought of 1886, when the Great Plains lay parched under the burning sun for months without a hint of moisture, former Sheriff Polk Cole showed up in Anson one day carrying a rain slicker under his arm. Soon he was accosted by Scarborough, who announced that he had a warrant for Cole's arrest. When the surprised former lawman demanded to know the charge, Scarborough answered for "unlawfully carrying a slicker, against the peace and dignity, dampness and future prospects of rain, in the free state of Jones." It was the custom in frontier communities for the victims of practical jokes to lead the way to the nearest gin mill and treat the crowd to a drink, but as Anson had no gin mills, Cole purchased a "good quantity of cigars [and Scarborough] restored the prisoner to liberty."[42]

One Sheriff Scarborough story that did not make the papers was told by C. B. to his son Moliere. According to this tale, George was taking a prisoner east on the train and had handcuffed him to a seat. When several women boarded the train and stood in the aisle because all the seats were filled, he uncuffed the prisoner and told him to stand up and let a lady sit down. The man refused to get up. Starborough jerked him to his feet, snapped the cuffs on his wrists, and pushed him down the aisle and out between the cars. There he opened the door and shoved the manacled prisoner off the train. "Just kicked him off the train!" related Moliere in wonder. "He just did it because that fellow wasn't polite enough to the women."[43]

An economy move in February 1888 reduced the pay of the Jones County sheriff and tax collector from $200 to $170 a quarter.[44] During his years serving the county, George's family had grown by two more daughters, Georgie May in April 1884 and Ethel in March 1887. With increasing family responsibilities and a declining income as sheriff, Scarborough lacked enthusiasm for reelection. His name was on the ballot for sheriff in 1888, but he did not actively campaign. On November 6 he was defeated by Ed M. Tyson.[45]

A problem relative to Scarborough's term in office surfaced in June 1889. The Commissioner's Court Minutes for June 29, 1889, allege that "during the year 1887 . . . George A. Scarborough collected taxes for said year in the amount of $300 from M. O. Lynn by virtue of a certain levie [sic] by him made upon the property of M. O. Lynn, sold said property for the sum of $300 to William Hittson and collected same and made report of same to the county clerk, but failed to report same to the Commissioner's Court of said Jones County, or turn same into the treasurer of said county." The court ordered Scarborough "to appear before this court at its regular term in August 1889 and show cause why he should not pay same or any other moneys he ever collected over to said county or why he should withhold same from said county." Judge C. P. Woodruff ordered the clerk to charge Scarborough with the amount cited. But the minutes of the August meeting and subsequent meetings make no further reference to the discrepancy. Evidently the matter was cleared up to the satisfaction of the court.

I'd rather run men than cattle.

—GEORGE SCARBOROUGH, JUNE 1893

-4-

Running Men

After turning over his badge and jailhouse keys to newly elected Sheriff Tyson, George Scarborough went back to the cattle range. A. P. Black, a twenty-two-year-old cowboy for the F Diamond R outfit, worked a general roundup with him in 1889. "George Scarborough," Black recalled, "was running a wagon for the HIT outfit on the Double Mountains. I worked with him from Jones County up to the Salt Fork of the Brazos. He was a very fine man."[1]

Scarborough was employed during this period as a protection man or association man, whose duties included resolving disputes over cattle ownership at roundup time. "Not a day passed at one these roundups," said Black, "but what there was some argument about burnt cattle." It was the responsibility of the protection man to maintain order and be the final arbitor in these disputes. "He wasn't allowed to gamble with any of the cowpunchers and had to keep his head clear and his gun on the danger side. I've never seen one at the roundup with both gloves on; he always had his gun hand bare."[2]

Arguments at roundups sometimes led to shootings, and Scarborough's intervention in the 1889 roundup described by Black may have saved the young cowboy's life. "I'd gathered some 4TX cattle that the F Diamond R's had bought from a road outfit down south," Black wrote, "when this big Texas gunman and LIX man rode up and tried to take them away from me." Poke Berryhill, the LIX gunman, claimed an LIX brand on the cattle had been altered to a 4TX. "He cut the cattle away from me a couple of times and I cut them back again." Scarborough was nearby and, "when I explained everything to him, he told me to get out my Winchester and tell

41

[Poke Berryhill] . . . that I'd kill him if he tried to take those cattle. The tough boy just rode off. He wasn't afraid of me but [Scarborough] made him squirm."

The incident and Scarborough himself made a deep impression on young Black. Scarborough was, he said, "a square, law-abiding man if I ever saw one. . . . I can still see [him], a wonderful picture of a man, especially when he sat on a horse. Always wore a big Stetson hat, weighed about a hundred and eighty or ninety pounds, had a big flowing black mustache and a goatee. A real man in every sense of the word. Always backing up law and order and never killed anybody but hard eggs trying to run over somebody."[3] Looking back almost a half-century, Black's lens of memory was a bit distorted. George Scarborough was not a big man, perhaps weighing 150 or 160 pounds. His hair was sandy brown and not black. He did sport a mustache and goatee during these years, later eliminating the goatee, but the youthful Black perceived him as a big man in 1889 and that was the way he remembered him.

Between roundups the protection man acted as a cattle detective and was paid to protect his employer's herds against rustlers. He was to the rancher "just as important and necessary as the bronc buster and the herder. . . . [He] carried his only authority in his holsters and . . . had but one great mission in life—to patrol the ranges, find as many rustlers as he could, and kill them where he found them," according to one rangeland chronicler.[4] Undoubtedly, rustlers (or suspected rustlers) were dispatched by protection men in this wild, unsettled country during these years, but no evidence has been found to indicate that George Scarborough participated in any killings.

Another young cowboy whose trail crossed Scarborough's also remembered him many years later as larger than life, "more than six feet tall." Will H. Roberts, nephew of noted Texas Ranger Capt. Dan Roberts and a former ranger himself, was working as a trail hand in the late eighties when he encountered Scarborough at Doan's Crossing on the Red River. Back in the 1870s, C. F. Doan had established a store at the Red River crossing on the Western Cattle Trail, a wide, hoof-beaten road stretching almost nine hundred miles from Bandera, Texas, to the railheads at Dodge City, Kansas, and Ogallala, Nebraska. By 1889 a tiny community had grown up around the store where the drovers rested and outfitted before fording the Red and plunging into Indian Territory on their long trek north. According to Roberts, interviewed in 1952 when he was ninety-one, Mollie Scarborough was running a hotel at Doan's when he went through with a herd. Sent back alone by his trail boss with a message for a following herd, he stopped at the hotel for the night. Mollie fed him and then insisted he accompany her to church. It was a hot night and after returning from church Roberts said he would prefer to sleep on the hotel gallery rather than in a bed inside. He had not yet fallen asleep on the gallery when George Scarborough, "a fine looking man more than six feet tall" and wearing a six-shooter, approached, noticed the recumbent cowboy, and moved toward him warily. "He walked over to me and peered down and looked me over very carefully," Roberts said. "I reckon he satisfied himself because he went on inside. He thought I was asleep, but I wasn't." The incident must have given the young cowboy a real scare to be recalled so vividly sixty-three years later. Roberts remembered Scarborough as "a fine man and a fine officer, one of the very best we ever had in this country."[5]

During these years Scarborough maintained a close friendship with Richard C. Ware, six-term sheriff of Mitchell County, who had worked with him in the apprehension of Add Cannon and Joe Brown. In 1889, Ware was in Crosby County, range country where Scarborough was operating, and got involved in a post-office holdup. Temporarily serving as postmaster for the newly formed and sparsely populated county, Ware was held up and his mail robbed by cowboys John Harvey and George Spenser, who stole two horses in escaping. The infuriated Ware, who had been jabbed in the head by a six-gun in the hands of Harvey, got on the trail of the robbers, captured them, and took them before a justice of the peace to be tried for horse theft. Lawyers at the hearing got into a fight and started throwing chairs. Deputy Sheriff Joe Sherman, hearing the commotion, came running with a rifle. Thinking the prisoners were escaping, he shot Harvey in the chest. The cowboy recovered, stood trial with Spenser before Judge Cockrell for robbing the mails, and was convicted. Cockrell gave Harvey fifteen years and Spenser eleven, explaining that the additional four years for Harvey was "to ease the outraged feelings of Dick Ware."[6]

In the summer of 1890 the Wichita Valley Railroad built into Seymour in Baylor County and the end-of-track town was booming. The excitement drew cowboys from ranches far and near. It was probably at Seymour that Scarborough first met several riders whom he would come to know intimately in coming years. Fred Higgins, who as a deputy U.S. marshal and sheriff rode with Scarborough on several New Mexico manhunts, was there, as was a cowpuncher going by the name of Williams who later became a prime outlaw target for Scarborough in New Mexico, where he was known as Broncho Bill Walters.[7]

Whenever George returned to Jones County after one of his cowboying junkets, his brother C. B. would try to talk him into settling down and making a permanent home for himself and his growing family. George's wife presented him with two more daughters during these years—Mary Ada Elizabeth, who, like her mother, was called Mollie, in April 1889, and Eva Hollis, more commonly called Emma, in September 1891—so there were now six youngsters around the house. In 1886, Parson Scarborough had moved to Merkel, a small town west of Abilene, where he devoted more of this time to preaching. C. B. was managing the family farm, running a small herd of cattle, and keeping a store at Truby. He offered George a 160-acore parcel of the family land and George may have made some desultory efforts at farming, but the quiet agrarian life was not for him.[8] The excitement of the chase was now in his blood, and he was happiest on a good horse with a warrant in his pocket and the trail of a badman stretching out before him.

On April 25, 1893, Richard C. Ware assumed office as U.S. marshal for the Western District of Texas, having received appointment by President Grover Cleveland.[9] When Scarborough heard the news, he contacted his old friend, and requested appointment as deputy marshal. Upon receipt of a letter from Ware directing him to report to El Paso to await official papers naming him deputy U.S. marshal, George walked into his brother's store and slammed his six-gun down on the counter.

"C. B.," he said, "I am leaving."

"Leaving?" his brother said.

"Yeah. I'd rather run men than cattle."[10]

Arriving in El Paso in late June 1893, George found a city of more

U.S. Marshal Richard C. Ware appointed
George to the deputy's post at El Paso. *Courtesy
Jim Baum.*

than ten thousand that had been in constant boom since the arrival
of the first Southern Pacific train in 1881. Tucked away in isolation
in the extreme western corner of Texas, with the New Mexico
Territory on its north and west, Old Mexico to the south, and no
cities of comparable size within hundreds of miles, El Paso was
unique in the American West, retaining much of its frontier character
even as it was fast developing into a modern city. Special features
peculiar to El Paso were its isolation, its border sharing with the
Mexican frontier town of Juárez across the Rio Grande, and its
location on a geographical funnel, El Paso del Norte, which chan-
neled east-west traffic along the southern boundary of the nation and
north-south international commerce through the city.

It was a city of stark contrasts. Three-quarters of the population was Hispanic, but political and economic control was solidly in the hands of the Anglos. Generally recognized in the 1890s as the most progressive of southwestern cities, it retained many elements of its frontier origins long after they had disappeared or had been outlawed in other expanding western communities. Even as modern, socially accepted recreational diversions for young men—bicycle clubs, baseball teams, racing events—were introduced and greeted with enthusiasm, the established frontier sports of gambling, whoring, and gunfighting went on unchecked. As a gambling mecca, the town was known as the Monte Carlo of the United States; the red-light district, concentrated on Utah Street just off the central commercial district, was one of the nation's largest and most notorious; and in the decade of the nineties the small army of celebrated gunmen on hand gained for the town yet another title: Sixshooter Capital.[11]

Headquartered in El Paso, Scarborough would be more than 500 miles away from his boss, Marshal Dick Ware, in San Antonio. With the possible help of one other deputy, Baz Outlaw, stationed at Alpine, over 200 miles away in Brewster County, Scarborough would be responsible for the enforcement of federal laws in all of those large, sparsely populated Texas counties lying southeast of El Paso between the Pecos River and the Rio Grande: El Paso, Reeves, Jeff Davis, Presidio, Brewster, Pecos, and Val Verde. It was an area almost 400 miles long and as much as 170 miles wide. Dry and windswept, it was ridged by rugged mountain ranges and dotted with widely scattered little cattle towns, railroad watering stops, and tiny county seats. Arteries through this great open wilderness were the Southern Pacific Railroad, which ran southeast from El Paso to San Antonio and beyond, and the Texas Pacific, which joined the Southern Pacific at Sierra Blanca, 100 miles southeast of El Paso.

Towns Scarborough would frequent in his work included those lying along the track of the SP: Ysleta, home of Company D of the Frontier Battalion of the Texas Rangers; San Elizario and Fort Hancock in El Paso County; Valentine and Marfa in Presidio County; Alpine and Haymond in Brewster County; and Langtry, lair of the celebrated Judge Roy Bean, and Del Rio in Val Verde County. Toyah and Pecos in Reeves County were on the Texas Pacific.

Accessible only by horseback or stagecoach were Fort Davis, county seat of Jeff Davis County, and Fort Stockton, seat of Pecos County. While waiting in El Paso for his official papers to arrive from Ware's office in San Antonio, Scarborough participated in a law-enforcement operation that caused much excitement in the town and gave him an opportunity to learn something of the area and the type of criminals with whom he would be dealing.

Along the Rio Grande north and south of El Paso lay two dense thickets in the river bottoms called bosques. Like the Big Shinnery in Jones County, the bosques sheltered outlaws who preyed on ranchers in the surrounding open lands and then disappeared back into their thicket strongholds. Operating out of the northern bosque was a gang of horse thieves and cattle rustlers. South of El Paso was a larger area called the Island, almost ten miles long and five miles wide in places, which harbored several hundred criminals and their sympathizers. The area, created by a natural rechanneling of the Rio Grande forty years earlier, had since become a kind of no-man's-land in which outlaws flourished. Smugglers were also active along the border and used the bosques as places of concealment. Outlaws were able to follow the river and move from one bosque to another without detection. Three years before, Deputy U.S. Marshal Charles H. Fusselman had entered these outlaw precincts in search of horse thieves and was killed for his trouble. His murderer was known, but such was the elusiveness of the brigands that he still had not been brought to justice.[12]

On June 29, 1893, Capt. Frank Jones and four other Texas Rangers rode into the lower bosque with Deputy Sheriff R. E. Bryant of El Paso County. Bryant had arrest warrants for Jesús-María Olguín and his son Severo, members of the notorious Olguín clan, who had pursued criminal activities along the border through three genera-tions. As the laymen approached a tiny settlement of four jacales, or shacks, deep in the thicket, they were fired upon. In the ensuing gunfight, Captain Jones was killed and the other lawmen were forced to withdraw. Bryant wired his boss, Sheriff Frank B. Simmons, in El Paso for assistance, and Simmons issued a call for volunteers to go after the body of Captain Jones. Within two hours he had signed up sixteen possemen, including George Scarborough.

Riding in this posse were some of the men with whom Scarborough would work closely during his years at El Paso: Bob Ross, later to be captain of the city police department; J. C. Jones, county jailer; Peyton F. Edwards, Jr., customs inspector and son of an El Paso judge; Tom Bendy, a deputy sheriff and city policeman; and Frank McMurray, who would become a staunch supporter of Scarborough and provide bail-bond sureties for him in the most difficult days lying ahead.

The Southern Pacific furnished a special train with a coach for the possemen and a stock car for their horses. Simmons's forces, combined with a party of Mexican officers led by Lieutenant Martínez of Juárez, not only successfully recovered the body and effects of Captain Jones, but also cornered and arrested Jesús-María Olguin and his sons Severo and Antonio. The arrest was made in Mexican territory, so Martínez claimed the prisoners and took them to Juárez.[13] Scarborough returned to El Paso, received his papers of authority, and on July 6 left for Jones County to get his family.[14]

Within two months, Mollie's young brother, twenty-three-year-old Frank M. McMahan, followed George Scarborough to the El Paso district and also embarked on a career as a lawman. On September 1 he joined the Texas Ranger company of Capt. John R. Hughes, who had replaced the fallen Captain Jones. Within a year McMahan would move into the Scarborough family home at 1116 San Antonio Street in El Paso and, while still retaining his ranger status, join his brother-in-law as a deputy U.S. marshal.[15]

Meanwhile, George energetically tackled his new responsibilities. The apprehension of illegal Chinese aliens became a major component of those duties, and the papers took frequent note of his activities:

> Deputy Marshal Scarboro [*sic*] and Deputy Sheriff [J. C.] Jones to-night captured nine Chinese that had just reached the country. They were in an opium joint and are the toughest looking outfit ever seen in town.[16]
> A Brilliant Capture. Deputy U.S. Marshal Scarborough made a successful capture last night of six Chinamen and their escorts who were attempting to evade the exclusion act. Scarborough got on the track of the proposed smuggling expedition and was prepared for the

Company D, Texas Rangers, at Ysleta, Texas, 1894. Deputy U.S. Marshal
Frank McMahan, in light-colored vest, stands at far left behind shackled
Mexican prisoner. His position as captain entitles John R. Hughes, at right,
to the only chair. *Courtesy Western History Collections, University of
Oklahoma Library.*

party. A "pilot" was sent over ahead and he was promptly gathered
in by the officers. Billy Davis and his driver, Charles Richards, were
in charge of the Chinese and as the carriage reached American soil it
was taken in by Scarborough, and the two white men and six Chinese
were captured. The coach, horses and harness were confiscated and
the prisoners lodged in jail.[17]

Four Chinese were caught this morning at 3:30 by Deputy U.S.
Marshal Scarborough while endeavoring to cross the line three miles
below the city.[18]

Deputy Marshal Scarborough this morning arrested L. S. Irwin on
the charge of aiding and abetting in the smuggling of Chinamen into
the United States. Four Chinamen were arrested at the same time and
other arrests will be made within a day or two. Irwin has been special
agent of the treasury department in this city till last summer when he
resigned. He has been for several months looked upon here as the
representative of the Chinese "Six Companies" in the smuggling of
Chinese and the customs officers and Special Agent Wagstaff have
been watching him. Both the deputy marshal and Special Agent

Wagstaff say that they have all the proof needed to convict Irwin.
. . . It is a very important arrest.[19]
Deputy Marshal Scarborough yesterday brought up five Chinamen
from Midland, charged with being unlawfully in this country. Three of
them were tried yesterday before Commissioner Edwards and ordered
deported and the other two will be tried today. These two will be joined
in their trial by another that Mr. Scarborough picked up yesterday.[20]
U.S. Marshal Scarborough and his assistant F. M. McMahan arrested three Chinamen yesterday.[21]

Scarborough was called into another case involving certificates of
registration, which all Chinese nationals were required to carry.
Two Chinese arrested on suspicion by Federal Inspectors Davis and
Gaither in July 1894 presented certificates when taken before Internal
Revenue Deputy Collector Kaughman. Scarborough, who was responsible for the issuance of all certificates in the district, was
summoned and asked to confirm that he had indeed issued the
two in question. He took one look and declared them forgeries.
Scarborough told an *El Paso Times* reporter:

> In the first place, Collector Kaughman never signed these papers.
> Then, too, the blanks themselves are forged. You see, all these blanks
> are printed in Washington and sent to the internal revenue collectors
> in different parts of the country. They are uniform in size and style
> and are numbered consecutively. Therefore, no two certificates in the
> United States have the same number. But one of these has the same
> number that I delivered to a Chinaman in El Paso. I have no doubt
> that the whole thing is a forgery and the forger will probably be
> discovered.[22]

Contraband smuggling operations also took up a large share of
Scarborough's time:

> Deputy Marshal Scarborough has arrested P. Desota on a telegram
> from San Antonio, charging him with selling smuggled opiates in that
> town.[23]
> Deputy Marshal Scarborough returned to the city yesterday, having
> in charge two Mexicans . . . whom he had captured at Fort Hancock
> charged with smuggling mescal.[24]
> Lacadio Apadacs, arrested Wednesday by Deputy Marshal Scarbor-
> ough on the charge of smuggling mescal, was yesterday bound to
> appear before the next federal grand jury.[25]

> Deputy Marshal Scarborough yesterday arrested two Chinamen
> . . . charged with smuggling opium.[26]
> Deputy U.S. Marshal Scarborough came up from San Elizario
> Sunday with three Mexican smugglers.[27]
> U.S. Deputy Marshal Scarborough brought in Anastacio Vegas
> this morning from 300 miles southeast of here. He is charged with
> smuggling and other crimes and is said to be the man who killed a
> Mexican guard some years ago.[28]
> Last night Deputy U.S. Marshal George Scarborough and Officer
> Frank McMahan caught Jose Martinez, a Mexican, with 143 smuggled
> opals, one diamond and an opal ring in his possession.[29]
> Ben Taylor, who was indicted by the federal grand jury for horse
> smuggling, was captured down at Big Bend by Deputy Marshal Scar-
> borough the other day and is now in the El Paso jail.[30]

In September 1894, Scarborough, working with Captain Boone
of the U.S. Mounted Inspectors, assisted in a major seizure of
contraband opium. The officers suspected Joe Rogers, an El Paso
saloonkeeper, and his brother, Steve, a Wells Fargo wagon driver,
with opium smuggling and, acting on an informant's tip, raided the
homes of the brothers. At Joe Rogers's residence, they discovered
112 pounds of narcotics, and an additional 129 pounds was found at
the home of brother Steve. The officers went on to search the old
customhouse near the Rogers saloon and added ninety-four one-
pound cans to their haul. Both brothers were arrested and charged
with smuggling.[31] They were convicted, and five months later Scarborough took them in chains to San Antonio, where they were turned
over to other officers for conveyance to the federal penal facility in
Brooklyn, New York.[32]

Less than a month after the arrest of the Rogers brothers, another
major seizure was made by Scarborough and Customs Officers Davis
and Boone. One hundred pounds of opium was turned up in a
warehouse near the railway yards. The officers then arrested George
Sauer, a cigar manufacturer, and charged him with smuggling.[33]

One of the duties of the deputy marshal was the disposal of
contraband. How Scarborough got rid of some part of his confiscated
opium is indicated by this item: "This afternoon Deputy U.S. Marshal
Scarborough sold one hundred and twenty cans of opium to the
highest bidder from the custom house steps."[34]

Less-frequent arrests were made by Scarborough for such federal offenses as illegal liquor sales, passing of counterfeit money, robbery of a federal facility or the United States mails, and violation of the Edmunds Act. The latter, passed by Congress in 1882 as an attack on polygamous practices in Mormon Utah, made a man's living with more than one woman in marital relations a misdemeanor. Officers found it a handy instrument to use in the arrest of sporting men and women whose adulterous lifestyle was notorious.

When Scarborough collared peddlers of illegal liquor, it was usually as part of a smuggling investigation, but on occasion he made an arrest on suspicion of unlicensed sale, as in January 1894 when he brought in an unidentified Mexican for selling mescal without a license.[35] Several months later he nabbed a man who was wanted in Albuquerque, New Mexico Territory, for unlicensed liquor sales.[36]

In March 1895, Scarborough arrested J. M. Hughes for having counterfeit money in his possession. Hughes was released when it was shown that he only had one bogus coin and had been carrying that for a number of years.[37]

The following January, Scarborough arrested a man on the basis of a telegram from Phoenix, Arizona, stating that he was wanted there for counterfeiting, but soon released him when it was learned that the telegram was a hoax.[38]

A more productive counterfeit arrest was made a few months later when Scarborough bagged confidence man H. M. Gage, called by the *Times* "the old stag of the cons." Gage was charged with defacing United States legal tender by raising one-dollar bills to appear to be fifties. The trick was done with figures cut out of a cigar stamp. "George Scarborough had been laying for Gage for a long time," said the *Times*. Later, Scarborough nabbed William Laughman, a Gage confederate, and brought charges of possession of forged checks and defacing U.S. currency.[39]

Robberies covered by federal statutes were few and rather mundane during Scarborough's tenure. In June 1894 when the postmistress at Ysleta requested his assistance in the apprehension of a stamp thief, he quickly made an arrest.[40] Two weeks later he was called in to investigate a series of burglaries of officers' houses at nearby Fort Bliss because some of the valuables taken were government property. Scarborough collared a suspect and brought him before the U.S.

commissioner.[41] The following January he arrested a man on a charge of breaking into a government building at Fort Bliss.[42]

In his travels through western Texas, Scarborough sometimes encountered men wanted by county authorities and made the arrest for them. This was the situation in April 1895 when he nabbed a man named Ed Ramsey who was wanted for cattle theft.[43]

The papers noted one arrest by Scarborough for violation of the Edmunds Act. In February 1894 he brought in D. F. Newell and Mrs. Wilson and charged them with illegal cohabitation.[44]

Much of the deputy marshal's time was spent in the routine work of delivering subpoenas and seeing that witnesses appeared in court as scheduled, and even this activity was often noted in the papers:

> Deputy Marshal Scarborough returned yesterday from Midland County where he went to serve 21 citations in civil cases pending in the district court.[45]
> Deputy U.S. Marshal Scarborough is as busy as six men, gathering in witnesses for the federal grand jury.[46]
> Deputy Marshal Scarborough returned yesterday from a trip four hundred miles east of here after witnesses.[47]

Scarborough played a part in a story that filled many column inches of space in southwestern newspapers in 1894. It centered on Victor L. Ochoa, an American citizen and resident of New Mexico Territory, where he had edited and published Spanish-language newspapers and had held a number of county offices. Ochoa was also a leader in a group dedicated to the overthrow of Mexican President Porfirio Díaz. In October 1893, Ochoa mounted a vitriolic underground press campaign against the incumbent government of the Mexican state of Chihuahua and succeeded in defeating the Díaz minions in some districts. He followed up this victory by taking over the customhouse at Palomas, across the line from Columbus, New Mexico Territory, and issuing a manifesto calling for the deposition of the Díaz government.

At the urging of the Mexican consul in El Paso, United States officials on November 30 issued a warrant for Ochoa's arrest, charging that he had violated the neutrality laws. He was said to have taken a commission under Santa Ana Pérez, a Mexican revolutionary, and hired gunmen in the United States to cross the border and make war against the government of Mexico. Scarborough made the arrest and brought Ochoa before U.S. Commissioner Gibbs, but evidence supporting the allegations against Ochoa was lacking and he was released.[48]

Ochoa went into Mexico and resumed his antigovernment activities. In January 1894 a massive Mexican army attack on Ochoa's dissidents resulted in their defeat. All were killed except Ochoa and three others. Ochoa escaped by donning the uniform of a soldier he had killed and slipping over the border into the United States.

His flagrant violations of the neutrality acts were now evident, and Scarborough was again looking for the editor. In February he took in a Mexican national named Cercas who was believed to have helped Ochoa escape.[49]

It was as a fugitive in his own country that Ochoa made his way across Brewster County. Along the way he was joined by a Mexican desperado, wanted in San Angelo for murder and jailbreak. One night Ochoa's companion killed Jeff Webb, an Alpine cowboy. This was unfortunate for Ochoa as it put the Texas Rangers, as well as Scarborough, on his trail. But the fugitive had the support of the Mexican community throughout West Texas, and for ten months he managed to stay hidden and beyond the reach of lawmen.[50]

In August 1894, Captain Hughes received a report that Ochoa was in El Paso and dispatched Cpl. E. D. Aten and two other rangers to help Scarborough find him. The officers went through the city's barrios thoroughly but failed to find their quarry.[51]

Then, on October 11, Texas Ranger J. W. Fulgham and Pecos County Sheriff A. J. Royal, rounding up suspected horse thieves in Fort Stockton, took into custody a man who claimed to be W. C. Blode but whose papers indicated was the fugitive Victor Ochoa. Scarborough was notified of the capture on October 13, but because of the press of other business, he was unable to go after the fugitive for a week. Meanwhile, Ochoa was in the custody of Sheriff Royal, who had plans for this prize catch other than to turn him over to the federal officer.

Andrew Jackson Royal, sheriff of Pecos County, was in the middle of a very bitterly contested political battle in October 1894. He saw Ochoa as the means by which he could swing the November election in his favor. Ochoa's immense popularity among Mexican-Americans was as strong in Pecos County as elsewhere. Royal reasoned that if he could persuade Ochoa to speak to his Hispanic constituents and give his blessing to the Royal candidacy, he might ensure victory in the election. He held a powerful persuader: the key to Ochoa's cell. On October 16, Royal promised a group of Hispanics in the Pecos County Courthouse that in return for their support in the coming election he would assure them of Ochoa's release.[52]

On Saturday, October 21, George Scarborough took the train to Haymond. At three o'clock Sunday morning he went on "by special conveyance and reached Fort Stockton before noon . . . having previously made all arrangements to return to Haymond on the same day with the prisoner."[53]

Royal initially refused to turn over his prisoner, muttering something about a possible reward for Ochoa being offered by the Mexican government. Finally the sheriff agreed to relinquish custody to Scarborough, but not until the next morning. That afternoon the sheriff conducted a political meeting at the courthouse and invited Ochoa to speak, which he did in eloquent Spanish before "the entire Mexican population." The speech "brought forth the wildest applause [and] the candidates were highly pleased at what they supposed was an enthusiastic approval of their desires for office," but Ochoa later said that his talk was devoted to the recent revolt and had nothing to do with who wore the badge in Pecos County.[54]

That evening a grand *baile* was held in Fort Stockton and large quantities of mescal were consumed. "Royal proceeded to shoot up the town unmolested," reported County Judge O. W. Williams.[55] Ochoa celebrated with everyone else and was not taken back in his cell until "long after midnight."[56]

Shortly thereafter a band of men armed with Winchesters held up the jailer and released the prisoner. Provided with a fast horse, he quickly vanished into the night. The alarm was spread and pursuit was mounted with dawn's first light. The officers thought the fleeing Ochoa would try to reach a train; Fort Stockton lay midway between the two railway lines and he might have headed for either. Scarborough and Ranger Joe Sitters elected to scout southwest toward Brewster County, while Rangers Fulghum and Schmidt headed northwest. Scarborough and Sitters returned to Fort Stockton empty handed after two days and eighty miles in the saddle but Fulghum and Schmidt had better luck. Circling north, they cut a trail that led to

Toyah in Reeves County. There they captured Ochoa and took him
to Pecos for jailing.

Scarborough, who had returned to El Paso, was notified of the
apprehension by wire and on October 24 went to Pecos, secured his
prisoner, and returned on the evening train. Ochoa attracted much
attention all along the track. "When he arrived [in El Paso]," according to a news dispatch, "he was met by a larger crowd than
greeted Governor Hogg a week ago."[57]

Both Scarborough and the rangers believed that Royal had been
involved in Ochoa's breakout from the jail at Fort Stockton, and a
week later Scarborough was back in that town with arrest warrants
for Royal and three others, charging them with assisting a prisoner
to escape. He found the town in an even bigger furor than it was
when he left it a week earlier. Obsessed with the approaching election
and with mounting fear that he would be deposed, Royal was openly
threatening the lives of his adversaries; the town was primed to
explode in violence. How the arrests were handled became crucially
important. Scarborough enlisted the aid of Ranger Sgt. Carl Kirchner
and Privates Fulgham and Schmidt and formulated a plan.

It was felt that the first order of business was to remove the most
volatile element in the powder-keg atmosphere. That meant Barney
Riggs had to be locked up first. Riggs, a deputy under Royal, was
a dangerous gunman who had been sentenced to a life term in Arizona
Territory's infamous Yuma Prison for murder but had been pardoned
after assisting prison officials in breaking up a mass escape. It was
Riggs's boast that he had gone to prison for killing one man and had
got out for killing two.[58]

On November 1, Scarborough and the rangers took Riggs into
custody and jailed him. The next day they collected Royal, and on
the third they rounded up Camilio Terrazas and John P. Meadows,
Ochoa's brother-in-law. All four were held on the charge of complicity in the escape of a prisoner.

Furious, Royal claimed that the whole proceeding was nothing
but a trick on the part of his political enemies to get him and his
friends out of the way until after the election. From a prison cell he
struck back quickly, lodging a complaint with Scarborough that four
of his leading political adversaries, Judge O. W. Williams, Jim and
Morgan Livingston, and Shipton Parke, had dealt in smuggled stock

in 1890. Jim Livingston was not in town and his whereabouts could not be determined, but Scarborough arrested Williams and Morgan Livingston and picked up Parke at Haymond on the way to Del Rio, where he had decided to take all seven prisoners. It was obvious that under the circumstances an impartial hearing was impossible in Fort Stockton on either set of charges, so Scarborough and the rangers set out with the seven to face a Val Verde County justice of the peace.

It was over two hundred miles to Del Rio by stagecoach and train. Every moment of that trip was fraught with tension as the bitter enemies sat glaring at each other, but Scarborough and the rangers maintained control and prevented violence. At the hearing the justice of the peace released each of the prisoners on his own recognizance and the officers left them all to fend for themselves after advising Williams, Livingston, and Parke to arm themselves against a likely attack by Royal and Riggs.[59] But the embattled Pecos County seven returned home without incident. At the polls the next day, Royal and his entire slate of candidates were defeated. R. B. Neighbors was the new sheriff.[60]

Two weeks later, on the afternoon of November 21, as A. J. Royal sat at his desk in the courthouse with two other people in the room and many more people, including Texas Rangers, in other parts of the building, he was shotgunned to death. Those in the room saw nothing, they said, except the barrel of a gun extending into the room from the doorway. No one in the building came forward to testify regarding anything of material value. The killer apparently had vanished as mysteriously as he had appeared and no one was ever arrested or charged with the crime. Andrew Jackson Royal was dead; folks in Fort Stockton and Pecos County seemed satisfied.[61]

Sixteen months later George Scarborough was brought into yet another case of alleged neutrality-act violations by enemies of the Mexican government. This time, in the discharge of his duty, he was wounded.

On Monday, March 9, 1896, Scarborough received instructions from Marshal Ware's office in San Antonio to keep an eye on two men named Lauro Aguirre and Flores Chapa. This was in response to a request from the Mexican government's emissary in Washington, who believed the two were preparing to publish an inflammatory

Spanish newspaper calling for revolution in Mexico and then raise an invasion force in Nogales, Arizona Territory, both acts in violation of United States law. On Tuesday, Mexican Consul Mallen at El Paso discussed the situation with Scarborough and asked him to place Aguirre and Chapa under arrest. Scarborough agreed on the condition he would be provided the proper warrants. The consul promised to swear out the warrants but insisted that the deputy act at once because Aguirre and Chapa were preparing to leave the city that night. He asked Scarborough to round up the two and take them to the consulate until the warrants could be issued the next morning. Scarborough said he would apprehend the men but would hold them overnight in his office in the Federal Building rather than deliver them to the consulate.

The consul concurred in this arrangement and Scarborough took charge of Chapa, who was at the consulate, removed him to the federal offices, and detained him under guard. Then, with Mallen and Will McMurray, he went in search of Aguirre, who was found in a house on Stanton Street. An old man named Antonio Viscarra answered the deputy's knock and confirmed that Aguirre was staying there. But when Scarborough asked him to bring Aguirre out, Viscarra suddenly stepped back and slammed the door in the officer's face.

Scarborough promptly kicked the door in, but "as he did there was a deafening report, a blinding flash, and the officer staggered back, the hot blood spurting from his chin and jaw." Viscarra had shot him in the face.[62]

Jerking his pistol, Scarborough "started in to make a killing [when] he remembered that the consul had not yet furnished him with a warrant. . . . The officer swallowed his wrath and waited until Senor Aguirre could be taken from the house peaceably."[63] Scarborough dispatched a messenger for local police assistance. He sent Will McMurray around to watch the rear door while he guarded the front until Officers Frank Carr and John Pinkney arrived.

> Then Aquirre agreed to surrender, but without waiting on him Officer Scarborough, seeing his man in the room, rushed in and grappled with him and pulled him out of the house. After landing Aguirre and the old Mexican who fired the shot in jail, Officer Scarborough, who had bled like a cut pig for over an hour, but was still dead

game, went to the office of Dr. J. J. Dooley . . . and had his wound examined and dressed. The ball entered his chin on the right side and came out under the right jaw bone, inflicting an ugly and painful wound.[64]

The next morning, Scarborough brought Aquirre and Chapa before Judge Sexton to answer Consul Mallen's charges. Sexton continued the hearing for a week, set bail at fifteen hundred dollars each, and the two were returned to jail.

A reporter for the *Times* interviewed Scarborough, who, "aside from a little soreness in his jaw, said he was feeling all right. He ruined his best suit of clothes by having it drenched in blood from his wound while waiting the arrival of Chief Carr. . . . Antonio Viscarra . . . was released yesterday as Officer Scarborough said he did not intend to prosecute him for shooting him."[65]

This incident belies the characterization of Scarborough put forth by some of his enemies and later writers as a bloodthirsty, hair-triggered killer. Although dripping in blood from a painful gunshot wound, Scarborough exercised restraint and demonstrated his professionalism in subsequent actions. His decision not to press charges against the old man who had shot him also shows a surprisingly forgiving nature for one who was fast developing a reputation among transgressors as a man to be feared.

-5-

The Man with No Soul

Of all the storied towns of the wild and woolly West—Bodie, Dodge City, Deadwood, Leadville, Tombstone—those legendary cattle centers and mining camps where first strode forth the gunfighter, that uniquely western American figure who captivated the imagination of people all over the world for a hundred years, none compiled a roster of renowned gunslingers comparable to the galaxy of six-shooter celebrities who paraded through El Paso in the mid-1890s, the years of George Scarborough's residency. The list included names that were familiar throughout the land during the period and some that are still commonly recognized, but all were names that inspired fear and awe in that place and time.

They came to El Paso because it was the largest community, geographically centered, in a band of territory stretching from the Big Bend country of Texas through the southern counties of New Mexico and Arizona territories to Tucson. This was a land of deserts and mountain ranges and great sweeping cattle spreads. It was sparsely sprinkled with dusty cow towns and remote horse camps. Perched in the mountains were raw mining towns—Tombstone and Clifton in Arizona, Silver City in New Mexico, Shafter in Texas—with their transient populations and inevitable sporting crowd. It was a land tied together by the twin steel ribbons of the Southern Pacific and the shining hub of activity in the middle of this great expanse, the City by the Pass.

From 1890 until 1910, the two decades bracketing the century's turn, this vast land became the last refuge of the western gunfighting outlaw, and hard on his trail came the gunfighting lawman. Some of the six-shooter celebrities filled both roles, for all stepped close to the dim line separating outlaw from lawman and many crossed it.

El Paso, with its streetcars, electric lights, and telephones, its sumptuous parlor houses featuring some of the most beautiful women in the West and opulent gambling halls offering any game for any stake, was the beckoning playground for the hardened denizens of the fast-vanishing frontier who roamed this wilderness.

Gunslingers of renown who appeared in El Paso during George Scarborough's years, 1893–96, included Mannie Clements, John Denson, Les Dow, Bill Earhart, Bud Frazer, Pat Garrett, John Wesley Hardin, Oliver Lee, Bat Masterson, Jim Miller, Jeff Milton, Baz Outlaw,[1] Commodore Perry Owens, Barney Riggs, John Selman, Tom Tucker, Ben Williams, and a host of quick-triggered Texas Rangers, perhaps the most well known of whom were Captains John R. Hughes and Bill McDonald. Before Scarborough's days in El Paso were over, his name would become a high-ranking addition to any list of El Paco's most famous and adroit gun wielders. Twelve of those mentioned would die violently, half of them by a gun in the hand of another of the dozen.[2]

Given the caliber of personnel, bloodletting by the mankillers within the city during Scarborough's residency was surprisingly infrequent. There were four fatal encounters in El Paso involving the six-shooter hierarchy in those three years; George Scarborough was a direct participant in two, John Selman in three of the four.

John Henry Selman, whose trail cut Scarborough's at El Paso, forever changing Scarborough's life and his memory, brought with him a history of violence unsurpassed by any among that violent El Paso coterie. Fifty-four years old in 1893, he had seen and actively participated in more violent frontier episodes than the composite experiences of many considered gunsmoke veterans. By all odds he should have filled a space on some lonesome Boot Hill years before, but by a combination of luck, skill with weapons, absolute lack of scruples, and a highly developed sense of self-preservation, he had survived to a very advanced age for one in his profession.

John P. Meadows, who had worked as a cowhand for Selman back in the 1870s and was well acquainted with him again at El Paso in the nineties, described him thus: "Sellman [*sic*] . . . was the most cold blooded, heartless man I ever knew. I never knew of him having

more than two . . . fair fights. . . . He was [responsible for] 20 or
more deaths, but the other fellow had no chance. . . . He was about
6 ft. high, weight 180, complexion sandy, cold gray eyes set deep
back in his head, large mouth, and no soul whatever."[3]

Frank Collinson also had known Selman for twenty years. "He had
served as a sharpshooter in the Confederate Army," said Collinson. "I
saw him shoot a gun or pistol several times. He never closed an eye,
just looked straight down the barrel, both eyes open." Those eyes
were very unusual, Collinson recalled. "They were such a light blue
that it was hard to see where the blue began and the white stopped."[4]

Selman was born in Arkansas and moved to Grayson County,
Texas, with his father in 1858. He served in the Confederate army
during the Civil War but deserted in 1863. His father had died, and
Selman moved his family, a mother and several younger brothers
and sisters, to a homesite near old Fort Davis on the east bank of the
Clear Fork of the Brazos, where he joined the state militia and was
elected lieutenant.[5]   —FORT PHANTOM HILL ?

In 1869 he moved to Colfax County, New Mexico, but Indian
attacks decimated his livestock and threatened his family and in a
year or two he was back on the Clear Fork, located on a ranch some
eight miles from Fort Griffin. It was here that he was first recognized
as an outlaw, although his criminal activities remained hidden for
several years and Selman added to the confusion by wrapping himself
in the cloak of an officer of the law.

While serving as a deputy to Shackelford County Sheriff John
Larn, Selman and Larn ran a rustling operation. At the same time,
Selman was a conspicuous leader in a vigilante organization formed
to control the outlaw element, but under his guidance it became a
tool to help him destroy his enemies. Said Frank Collinson: "I cannot
say how many were hanged, but there were a good many. I was out
on the buffalo range, and every time we heard from Griffin, we
learned someone was found hanging to a tree on the Clear Fork of
the Brazos. Lawreen [Larn] and Selman, with the aid of the Vigilantes, were making a clean sweep." Collinson recounted one instance
in which Selman and his vigilantes had rounded up three suspected
horse thieves at buffalo hunter George Causey's camp and it was
only through the intercession of Jim White, a well-known hunter

around Fort Griffin, that Causey did not share the fate of the three others who were found later with their throats cut.[6]

Selman emptied his pistol at a man in Fort Griffin and then, as his victim fell, "exultantly offered to bet a hundred dollars that he could cover ever one of the holes with a silver dollar." Since only one bullet had hit its mark, he would have won his bet had there been any takers.[7]

It was during this period that John Meadows worked at the Selman and Larn Ranch and was cheated out of his back pay through intimidation by Selman. Meadows was furious but so in awe of Selman's fearsome reputation as a mankiller that he decided to shoot him down from ambush. He loaded both barrels of a shotgun and lay in wait for his quarry, but a friend who knew of the plan sought him out and convinced him to leave the country instead.[8]

There were other attempts to bushwack Selman. Once he was riding with John Larn when a hidden rifleman fired at them, knocking off Larn's hat. On another occasion a shotgun blast tore off Selman's saddle horn as he worked cattle in the brush. Selman fired blindly into the bushes and was luckier than his intended murderer, managing to hit and kill the bushwacker.[9]

By June 1878, Larn and Selman were no longer officers and the Shackelford County citizenry, bellies full of their high-handed actions, turned on them. A posse under the new sheriff, William R. Cruger, rode out to take the two into custody. Selman was warned by a Fort Griffin prostitute named Hurricane Minnie and, with his usual luck, slipped away in the night. Larn was captured and taken to the Albany jail, where a mob shot him to pieces in his cell.

With a sheriff's posse on his heels, John Selman traveled hard and fast to get out of the country, leaving ranch, wife, and children behind. In October a grand jury indicted him on nine counts of cattle theft, and the Texas Rangers added his name to their wanted list.

Selman's sudden departure from the Fort Griffin country prevented a meeting between Selman and young George Scarborough, who in the fall of 1878 was helping his father and family establish a homestead up the Clear Fork in neighboring Jones County. Parson Scarborough and sons C. B. and George often traveled to Fort Griffin in those early days to sell wild game and purchase food staples. No doubt the lynching of Larn and the escape of his partner were hot topics of conversation around the potbellied stoves in the Fort Griffin stores that fall and winter, so George must have heard a great deal about John Selman, but there is no evidence that the two ever met before their paths crossed at El Paso in 1893.[10]

Selman rode fast and hard for several hundred miles from Fort Griffin before he struck the cow camp of Charlie Siringo on the Canadian River. He lay over there two days, resting his jaded horse and fabricating ammunition with the help of Siringo's reloading outfit. When he moved on, he headed southwest across the Staked Plains toward New Mexico.

Siringo, a Texas cowboy who later worked as a Pinkerton detective for many years and studied the ways of badmen, wrote that Selman came across a pair of young Mexican boys driving a flock of two thousand sheep and that he killed the boys and drove the sheep to El Paso, where he sold them for a dollar a head. He said Selman admitted as much when Charlie ran into him in El Paso several years later. Siringo summed up the Selman character succinctly: "John Sellman [sic] would kill and steal through pure cussedness."[11]

With what his biographer has called "his sure instinct for finding trouble spots,"[12] Selman next turned up in Seven Rivers, New Mexico Territory, where several outlaw gangs were headquartered. Taking advantage of the turmoil caused by the Lincoln County War then raging, these gangs embarked on a vicious campaign of murder, plunder, and pillage unprecedented even in Lincoln County, a district notorious for its history of bloodshed and violence.

Selman quickly maneuvered for a position of leadership among the cutthroats of Seven Rivers. Recognizing that his main rival was a gunman named Ed ("Little") Hart, who had been active in the county since the Horrell War five years earlier, Selman dealt with his challenger in typical fashion. As the two sat across from each other at a table, awaiting a meal, Selman surreptitiously slipped his revolver onto his lap and fired up through the table at the unsuspecting Hart, the top of whose head was torn off by the impact of the heavy slug.

Selman's Scouts, as the Seven Rivers outlaws now called themselves, swept the countryside, leaving death and terror in their wake. Led by John Selman, the man one Lincoln County historian has characterized as "a particularly vicious specimen of border scum,"[13] the gang was composed of other Texas desperadoes and some of the worst elements of the New Mexico outlaw bands of Jessie Evans and John Kinney. Members included Tom Cat Selman, younger brother of the leader; Gus Gildea; Reese Gobles; John Gross; Rustling Bob Irwin; Charles Snow; John Nelson; Bill Dwyer; Bob Speakes, V. S. Whitaker; Jake Owens; and Marion Turner.

On September 28, 1878, Selman's Scouts went on a particularly brutal day-long rampage. For a warm-up they virtually demolished Will Hudgens's saloon, just outside Fort Stanton. Smashing glassware and furnishings, they threatened and insulted Hudgens's wife and sister and pistol-whipped a bystander who objected to this treatment of the women. Riding on to Lincoln, they ransacked houses but were repulsed by gunfire when they attempted to take over the store of Issac Ellis. At the Bartlett Ranch they dragged two women out into the brush, stripped them, and raped them. Continuing down the Rio Bonita, they came upon a hay cutter and two young boys and shot all three down in cold blood. Later, on the Hondo, they pumped three bullets into the young son of rancher Martin Sanchez, mortally wounding him.[14]

By October an outraged citizenry had organized against such depredations and a large posse led by Juan Patron, a leading Lincoln resident, chased the outlaws up the Pecos and killed several in a series of running gun battles that lasted almost to the city limits of Fort Sumner. As honest men mobilized, the brigands found few sanctuaries and little rest. Like cornered animals, they turned on each other; at Dead Man's Crossing on Rocky Arroyo, a tributary of the Pecos River, two of the gang were cut down by gunfire, reportedly at the hand of John Selman.[15]

In March 1879, New Mexico Gov. Lew Wallace gave Capt. Henry Carroll of Fort Stanton a list of the most-wanted outlaws in the territory, a rogue's gallery containing some three dozen names. John Selman and brother Tom were third and fourth, respectively, on that list, which included other former gang members Reese Gobles, Bob Speakes, Gus Gildea, Jake Owens, and Rustling Bob Irwin. Also appearing were such legendary figures of six-shooter lore as Billy the Kid, Tom O'Folliard, and Charlie Bowdre, all of whom would be hunted down and killed by Pat Garrett; John Slaughter, afterward

a respected rancher and sheriff of Cochise County, Arizona; Henry
Brown, who would become city marshal at Caldwell, Kansas, and
would be lynched after a foiled bank-robbery attempt; Doc Scurlock,
who would die in a gunfight at John Chisum's Seven River Ranch;
and John Middleton, Fred Waite, and Jessie Evans.[16]

Selman, under the name of John Goss, one of the aliases he used
during this period (others being John Gunter, Gunther, and Gross),
was indicted in April 1879 for the murders committed on that bloody
September day the previous year. Also named in the indictment were
eight other members of the now disbanded gang. None ever came to
trial.[17]

Before the indictments against him were returned, Selman left
New Mexico and soon was busily engaged in signing up recruits for
a large-scale rustling operation in western Texas. He was said to
have lined up about 175 renegades in a criminal enterprise that was
to extend from the Panhandle to the Rio Grande. But even before it
got rolling, this grand rustling scheme began to fall apart. Gang
members squabbled and broke association, lost interest and drifted
off, or ran into angry, determined cattlemen and ended up in lonely
graves on the prairie. Then their leader came down with Mexican
black smallpox and almost died in an isolated tent outside Fort Davis.
By the time he recovered, the great Selman rustling operation was
dead.[18]

His face badly pitted and his body wasted by the smallpox ordeal,
Selman assumed the name Capt. John Tyson and stayed on at Fort
Davis. He opened a butcher shop, always a good means of disposing
of rustled cattle, a commodity he was interested in again after or-
ganizing with Jessie Evans yet another outlaw band. Soon the gang
members were expanding their operations from rustling to holdups,
and the local residents, unable to cope with this new wave of lawlessness, called on the Texas Rangers for help.

Despite his alias and changed appearance, the Fort Davis butcher
was recognized by Ranger Sgt. L. B. Caruthers as John Selman, a
wanted fugitive from Shackelford County. On June 28, 1880, Caruthers arrested Selman and slapped him into the bat-cave underground
jail at Fort Davis. Evans and other gang members were captured after
a running gun battle in which one outlaw and a ranger were killed.

The other members of the Selman-Evans combine were tried,

convicted, and sentenced to the Huntsville penitentiary on murder and robbery charges in October 1880, but Selman himself was not brought to trial. He was to be returned to Shackelford County to answer for his crimes there.

Folks in Shackelford were not anxious to have old John back, however, as evidenced by a letter from Sheriff William Cruger to Ranger Maj. John B. Jones in which Cruger said that it was likely the charges against Selman could not be sustained in court and that "the indictments were probably found in order to keep him out of the country, as he is such a great thief and scoundrel and withal so sharp that he cannot be caught in his rascality." He added that he "could not answer for John Selman's life" if Selman were taken to Shackelford.[19]

Disregarding Cruger's objections, the rangers took Selman in irons to Comanche County in August to await court action in Shackelford County. He was later moved to Albany, but there his guards, by prearrangement, removed his manacles, gave him a horse and saddle donated by George Reynolds, a shirttail relative of the late John Larn, and told him to make tracks, emphasizing their point by firing their pistols in the air. Selman, aware that his luck had not deserted him, needed no urging and made lots of tracks. He did not stop until he reached Old Mexico, although he slowed down a little in Fort Davis to gather up his second wife, whom he had married two days before his arrest. He settled in San Pablo in southern Chihuahua and for the next few years did a little prospecting but engaged primarily in the saloon and gambling-hall business.

John Selman's name has been linked by some to a particularly brutal double murder in Sierra Blanca, Texas, in May 1885. A cattleman named Tom Merill and his wife were savagely slashed and stabbed to death and their bodies hacked into pieces. Back in Shackelford County in the 1870s, Merill had bested Selman in a poker game, pulled a gun, and humiliated him before witnesses. Selman had gone off muttering threats of retribution. Later Merill was said to have been one of the leaders of the mob which lynched Selman's old partner, John Larn. A veteran of those Shackelford County days claimed that Selman hired two Mexicans to murder the Merills, simply out of a thirst for vengeance. No one was ever charged with the crimes.[20]

John Selman and young son John, Jr., about
1880. This photo was discovered in the album
of El Paso madam Alice Abbott. *Courtesy R. G.
McCubbin Collection.*

Learning in April 1888 that the old charges against him in Shackelford County had been dropped for lack of evidence, Selman moved
to El Paso with his two sons, William ("Bud") Selman, seventeen,
and John Selman, Jr., thirteen. There he took a series of jobs with
a smelting company, the Mexican Central Railway, and the Wigwam
Saloon.[21]

In the fall of 1892, Selman ran for the office of constable of
Precinct 1 in El Paso and on November 8 the old bushwacking
murderer, rapist, cattle rustler, and horse thief was elected by a 88-

vote majority out of 1,486 votes cast.[22] He became a fixture in the job, holding it until his death. He also became something of a local celebrity in El Paso and soon was being referred to affectionately in the papers as Uncle John.

Selman had brought a well-worn six-shooter to his lawman's position. A writer for the *El Paso Herald* handled this weapon and described it in an article:

> I got a look the other day at Uncle John Selman's young howitzer. . . . The pop is quite an oldtimer, the owner having carried it for 23 years. It is a Colt's .45 and when he got it Uncle John removed the ivory handles and put on walnut ones taken from a Colt's revolver that he carried through the war and naturally they are much worn. This young gun formerly had a long barrel and Uncle John says he has killed many an antelope with it, while he could shoot off a squirrel's head fifty yards away. There is no doubt about Uncle John's good marksmanship and that trusty pop of his hits where it is aimed.[23]

The reporter mentioned no notches in the grips of Selman's weapon, but Tom Bendy, who was on the city police force during these years and had handled Selman's pistol many times when the officers practiced firing together, stated flatly: "He was the only man I ever knew who indulged in the practice so often related in Western stories notching his gun." Bendy, interviewed in 1921, considered Selman a glory seeker and said that to his best recollection the weapon "had at least seven and perhaps nine notches."[24]

This was the six-shooter that dispatched two gunmen in much-publicized El Paso shootings and was the key ingredient in the mystery surrounding Selman's own death. The first shooting occurred on April 5, 1894. Federal court was in session and El Paso was stocked even better than usual with gunfighters, many of whom were in town to attend court proceedings. Representing the Texas Rangers were Pvts. Joe McKidrict and Frank McMahan, up from Company D headquarters at Ysleta for the court session. U.S. Marshal Dick Ware and several of his deputies, including Baz Outlaw, Bufe Cline, and Scarborough, were on hand.

Baz Outlaw, the officer with the unlikely name, was an enigma. A native of Georgia from a good family, he was intelligent and exhibited social graces and an educational background which set him apart from most of the rough frontier types with whom he associated after moving west. He joined the Texas Rangers in 1885, displayed skill and courage under fire, and advanced quickly to the rank of sergeant in Company D, but a weakness for the bottle and a propensity for belligerence while drinking forced Capt. Frank Jones to dismiss him. He subsequently accepted an appointment as deputy U.S. marshal and in April 1894 was also a special ranger attached to Company D.[25] Outlaw was small, standing about four inches over five feet, and perhaps suffered from the sense of inferiority and resulting overaggressiveness that afflicts some diminutive men. The six-shooter, that old equalizer, made him as big as any man, how-

Baz Outlaw. His death added the next-to-last notch on Selman's pistol. *Courtesy R. G. McCubbin Collection.*

ever, and Outlaw practiced with it until he had attained a level of dexterity and accuracy that amazed his fellow rangers, all of whom were skilled in the use of weapons. It was said that with nothing more than his .45 he could provide quail for an entire ranger camp.[26]

The story went that he had killed a man in Georgia, necessitating his departure, and had participated in several shooting scrapes involving the rangers and outlaws, but there is no record that he had ever been tested in a stand-up man-to-man gunfight. On several occasions when on the prod he had backed off when his bluff was called. Brewster County Sheriff Jim Gillett faced him down in Alpine when Baz went to town and raised hell after being thrown out of the rangers.[27] The *El Paso Herald* said that in 1893 "he made a play in McLane's saloon and was called down promptly, whereupon he went to the rear of the saloon and fired off his pistol. He is not known to have killed anybody in close quarters but has always been a source of uneasiness."[28]

Frank Collinson, the old buffalo hunter who was now ranching in West Texas, was also in town to attend court. On Utah Street he ran into Outlaw, well fortified with alcohol and loudly proclaiming that he intended to kill Dick Ware before sundown. In addition to his load of red-eye, Outlaw was carrying a heavy burden of enmity toward Ware because the marshal had sent Deputy Bufe Cline into the Alpine country with papers to serve and Outlaw had lost out on some lucrative fees. Collinson accompanied Outlaw into Ernest Bridger's saloon, where the undersized deputy marshal continued to drink and voice threats against his boss.

Leaving the saloon, the two ran into Selman. Collinson, who was trying to get Outlaw to go to his room in the Lindel Hotel and sleep it off, signaled for Selman to help him. "Come along, we're going to Bass's room," he said.

"I'm going to show you my girl at Tillie Howard's first," Outlaw said, staggering toward Tillie's resplendent parlor house at 307 South Utah. Collinson and Selman trailed along.[29]

"Bass . . . and myself and an Englishman that I have known for many years [Collinson] walked down to Tillie Howard's where Bass has a girl—Ruby I think her name is—and went in," Selman later told a newspaperman.[30]

In 1893, Tillie Howard was El Paso's leading madam. Born to

parents named Weiler in Pennsylvania in 1869, she had been or-
phaned early in life and raised by a neighbor to the age of twelve,
when she ran off and rode the rails, living off the generosity of
trainmen. As an adolescent, she became a caboose girl, a prostitute
working the railroad lines. Later, Willie Sells, owner and star trick
horseback rider of the Sells Circus, took her as his mistress. When
Sells deserted her in San Antonio in 1890, she came to El Paso and
as Tillie Howard leased, and later purchased, the bagnio of longtime
madam Alice Abbott. Twenty-five years old in 1894, Tillie was a
beautiful woman despite her rough history.[31] Texas Ranger Alonzo
Oden visited her place in 1893 and noted in his diary:

> Went down to Tillie Howard's Sporting House. I've been anxious
> to visit Tillie. She is the talk of the border. . . .It is a regular saloon,
> and sort of hotel and dance hall combined, but Tillie makes the place
> different. She is tall and I imagine she doesn't need these artificial
> bosoms the ladies are using now; hers look natural enough—I'll ask
> her when I know her better. . . . She has the blackest hair, and she
> is one of the most beautiful women I've ever seen.[32]

Outlaw, Selman, and Collinson entered Tillie's place and Outlaw
found his girl and brought her around to show her off to the others.
"Bass was drunk," Selman said, "but I did not think he particularly
wanted to fight. He started out of the parlor with his girl, and my
friend and I sat down to talk over old times."[33]

After only a short time—Collinson said a few minutes and Selman
said less than a minute—a shot rang out in the back of the building.
"Bass has dropped his gun," Selman remarked casually. Tillie Howard ran through the house, frantically blowing a police whistle.
"Don't do that," Selman warned her. "All the police in town will
soon be here." Tillie ignored him and ran out the back door into the
yard, still blowing the shrill whistle which seemed to enrage Outlaw,
who pursued the madam into the yard tried to take it away from
her.[34]

The alarm was indeed attracting lawmen. By the time Selman and
Collinson reached the rear of the house, Texas Ranger Joe McKidrict
and Constable Leon Chavez had jumped the back fence into the yard.
Tillie Howard's cathouse was now literally aswarm with lawmen:
two constables, Selman and Chavez; a deputy U.S. marshal and

special ranger, Outlaw; and a Texas Ranger, Joe McKidrict. Soon they would begin shooting each other.

"Joe had beat me there without knowing what the matter was," Selman said. "Joe was saying that there must be no more shooting as that would call the police down there. I spoke up and said that Bass shot his pistol off by accident and that there would be no more."[35]

Outlaw still held his pistol in his hand and when McKidrict persisted in demanding to know why a shot had been fired, he suddenly pointed the weapon at the ranger, snapped "You want some, too?" and began shooting.

"Outlaw threw his gun almost against Joe's temple and fired," said Selman. "He fired another shot into the boy's body." Collinson said that "Selman then shot Outlaw above the heart. . . . Although mortally wounded, Outlaw shot twice, hitting Selman in the thigh."

"The first shot," said Selman, "was so close to my face that my eyes were powder burnt till I was blind, but I pulled on him at random, and I think I got him. I know that if I could have seen his bulk I would have got him, for I can't miss a man with that gun of mine."[36]

During his rampage, Baz Outlaw fired all six rounds in his pistol: the first shot, which had started all the trouble; two into the body of Joe McKidrict, killing him instantly; one past Selman's head, blinding him; and now, as he reeled backward, mortally wounded, he pumped his last two into Selman, one slug striking just above the right knee, the other passing through the thigh, cutting an artery.

Outlaw, clutching his chest, wandered out onto Utah Street and weaved his way for almost a block before encountering Ranger Frank McMahan, running to investigate the disturbance. McMahan took Outlaw's empty pistol and placed him under arrest. Outlaw believed a mob was gathering to attack him and begged for protection. McMahan helped the deputy into Barnum's Show Saloon at Utah and Overland streets. There, stretched out on top of the bar, he was examined by a physician, who found his situation hopeless. Outlaw was taken to the rear of the saloon and placed on the bed of a prostitute, where he died about four hours after the shooting.

During those hours of agony, Outlaw kept repeating, "Oh God, help! Where are my friends?" Will Burges, who was present, said that Outlaw, whom he called "a human wolf," was the only man he ever saw "who died in mortal terror."[37]

Despite the testimony of Selman, Collinson, Ranger Captain Hughes, who filed a report of the affair the following day, and the newspaper stories, all of which are in basic agreement regarding the events at Tillie Howard's parlor house, lawyer Burges always insisted that Selman deliberately murdered Outlaw. "There is no question in my mind that he was killed in cold blood," Burges said in 1945. "Tillie, the prostitute, showed me where Selman stood behind a fence and shot him down. Selman just wanted another notch on his gun barrel." Tillie had a good deal more credibility with Burges than did Selman. "I believed every word of it," he said. "Further, I'll argue her case in the hereafter if I can, though I do not expect to be called as counsel."[38] Burges does not explain how in Tillie's version Selman received the damage to his eyes and bullet wounds in his leg that afflicted him for the remaining two years of his life.

Selman had gone by carriage to the offices of Dr. Alward White for treatment after the gunfight. White confined him to bed and it was two weeks before he was back on his feet. Collinson visited him the day after the shootings and found the old gunman cheerful. "It doesn't take my flesh long to heal after a gunshot," he said.[39]

Dr. White's son, Owen, in later years a New York newspaperman and frequent contributor to popular magazines, was a fifteen-year-old schoolboy in El Paso at the time of the gunfight. In his autobiography he said he was on his way to the Howard parlor house to present some of his father's medical bills to her girls and was "not two hundred feet from Tillie's place . . . when the bombardment began." He "heard a fusillade of shots, a police whistle [and] a few more shots."

According to White's colorful but garbled account, Outlaw, "Kid McKittrick," and another unnamed companion, bent on shooting up Tillie's establishment, had "yanked out their guns and cracked loose at the bric-a-brac and the chandeliers. . . . Miss Howard . . . ran out on her back porch and began blowing a police whistle. Hearing that whistle Constable John Selman, who was playing seven-up in the Monte Carlo near by, responded by running into the alley and starting to climb over Tillie's back fence. . . . As Selman threw his leg over the fence, Bass Outlaw . . . saw it and just for the hell of the thing put a bullet in it. No one bullet had ever yet stopped John Selman and this one didn't." Now, with "a personal interest in what was going on," Selman limped across the yard and into the back hall, "where he was instantly shot at, and unanimously missed, by the three celebrators. When Selman returned the fire he didn't miss. With his first shot he got Outlaw, who dropped in the hall, with his second he destroyed McKittrick in one of the parlors."

White says he saw the third man, "the unknown," run out of Tillie's front door and across the street into an Italian saloon. "Behind him, with a gun in his hand, limping badly . . . came Uncle John Selman. Uncle John crossed the street, pushed open the swinging doors of the Italian's saloon," and, with his third shot, "demolished the stranger." White's summation: "Obviously this was fine shooting." It would have been indeed had it ever happened. He says "the unknown" was "promptly buried and forgotten," apparently to be remembered only in the clouded recollections of Owen P. White. He titled his memoirs *The Autobiography of a Durable Sinner,* one of those sins evidently being a lack of respect for the truth.[40]

The body of Joe McKidrict was taken to Austin for burial. Although John Selman had referred to him as a boy, McKidrict, whose real name was Joe Cooly, was about thirty years old and had worked on the San Antonio police force before joining the Texas Rangers. Outlaw was buried by friends in El Paso on April 6.[41]

In the aftermath of the shootings, Marshal Dick Ware was subjected to censure. "There has been much criticism of U.S. Marshal Ware for his appointment of such a man as Outlaw . . . to so important an office as deputy marshal," said the *El Paso Times* of April 7. Ware responded in the same issue:

> When I came into office I found Outlaw with a deputy marshal's commission. The people about Alpine in large numbers petitioned me to retain him and I did so out of deference to the public wishes. He was never my style of man, for I want sober men in office. But I thought if he pleased the people of that section he should please me. At the last court here I told him that he knew if he got drunk again he need not wait for me to ask for his resignation.

Selman was charged with the murder of Outlaw and went on trial in October 1894. After presenting the evidence, the district attorney asked for a directed verdict of acquittal and Judge Buckler obliged:

"There being no evidence before you that the defendant John Selman is guilty of the crime of which he is charged in the indictment in this case—you are therefore instructed to find the defendant not guilty."[42]

George Scarborough's thoughts on the whole affair have not been recorded. But whatever his opinion of the character of Baz Outlaw, the plain facts must have weighed heavily on him: Outlaw carried the commission of a deputy United States marshal; John Selman had killed him and put another nick on his gun. Two years to the very day after the shootings at Tillie Howard's parlor house, Scarborough would feel threatened by that same Selman six-shooter. In the microsecond he had to react, the ghost of Outlaw may have flickered across his mind and influenced his response.

The day for man killers in this town has passed.

—EL PASO TIMES, APRIL 2, 1895

-6-

The Day of the Mankillers

In the year following the shootout at Tillie Howard's, there arrived on the El Paso scene a group of characters destined to play vital roles in George Scarborough's life. Joining John Selman, the quick-triggered constable with the dark, unsavory past, and Scarborough, the deadly serious career lawman, the new arrivals formed as colorful a cast as ever enlivened a western novel of romance and action. The clash of these personalities was to set in motion a chain of events that would involve Scarborough in a tangled web of greed, passion, and violent death.

First to appear was Jefferson Davis Milton, whom Scarborough had known as a sixteen-year-old cowboy on the Clear Fork in 1878. Milton left Jones County after the spring roundup of '79 and drifted down into the Huntsville area, where he took a job overseeing a convict work gang from the penitentiary. Young Milton yearned for a life of adventure, and appointment to the Texas Rangers seemed the quickest way to achieve that goal. In 1880, at the age of eighteen, he joined the rangers, giving his age as twenty-one, a minimum requirement. In due course he was assigned to Capt. Ira Long's Company B, Frontier Battalion, stationed at Hackberry Springs, near the site where Colorado City would soon sprout. Sergeant of Company B was Dick Ware, still a Texas celebrity for his role in closing the career of bandit Sam Bass two years before; he was generally credited with firing the shot that brought down the notorious outlaw. Ahead were his years as sheriff of Mitchell County, service as U.S. marshal, and close association with Scarborough.[1]

At San Angelo, Milton assisted in the arrest of Emmanuel ("Man-

77

nen") Clements, a hot-tempered, hair-triggered cattleman and erstwhile associate of an outlaw cousin, the legendary John Wesley Hardin. Clements resisted until young Milton jammed a pistol into his midsection and in his soft Florida drawl ordered him to behave or die. A flint-hard determination in the dark eyes of the teen-age ranger convinced the old gunfighter it was no bluff and he submitted.[2]

When Mitchell County was organized in January 1881, Dick Ware was elected sheriff, defeating a local cattleman named W. P. Patterson. The county seat was the tent town of Colorado City, which had blossomed along the tracks of the Texas and Pacific Railroad, then building across West Texas. Ranger Company B was assigned to maintain order in the riotous new community, and it was there on May 16, 1881, that Jeff Milton engaged in his first gunfight.

Investigating sounds of gunfire near the Nip and Tuck Saloon, haunt of the town's rowdier elements, Ranger Cpl. J. M. Sedberry, Pvt. L. B. Wells, a new recruit, and Milton encountered recently defeated sheriff candidate W. P. Patterson. The rangers asked to examine his six-gun to see if it has been fired recently. When Patterson refused to hand over his weapon, a scuffle ensued and the gun went off. No one was hit by the bullet, but Sedberry suffered powder burns. Jeff Milton fired once, dropping Patterson, and the excited and inexperienced Wells pumped another round into the dying man as he lay on the ground. Patterson had been popular with the cattlemen. An angry mob formed and a lynching was threatened. But Sheriff Ware controlled the potentially explosive situation and took the three rangers into his custody. Two and a half years later, in November 1883, Milton, Sedberry, and Wells stood trial at Abilene for the killing of Patterson and were cleared.[3]

Jeff Milton served three years in the rangers, much of the time in the El Paso and Big Bend country, territory that would be roamed by Deputy Marshal Scarborough a decade later. After leaving the rangers Milton remained in the Fort Davis area and took appointment as deputy sheriff under Presidio County Sheriff Charles L. Nevill, a former company commander in the rangers.

In 1884, Milton wandered up into New Mexico Territory, cowboyed for a time, and then took another deputy's job, working for Sheriff Charlie Russell of Socorro County and as a detective for the cattlemen's association. Here he was wounded when he and a companion were bushwacked as they rode up the Gila River Valley. A bullet struck Milton in the leg above the knee, exited through his calf, and continued on, killing his horse. He managed to jerk his Winchester from its scabbard as his horse collapsed under him. "Then," Milton would say in his laconic style, "there was a lot of shooting." When it was over, three dead Mexicans lay scattered in the brush. Milton wrapped a rag around his wound and rode two days on a pack horse to his homestead in the San Mateos. There he poured turpentine through the hole in his leg and soon recovered completely.[4]

Driven by a restless nature, Milton drifted on into Arizona Territory, working briefly as a deputy for Sheriff Commodore Perry Owens of Apache County before receiving an appointment as mounted inspector along the Arizona–New Mexico border. In 1889 he settled down on a horse ranch he had established near Tucson. A year later he was on the move again, taking employment on the Southern Pacific Railroad, first as a fireman and later as a conductor.

He was thus engaged when El Paso Mayor R. F. Johnson wired him in Saint Louis, offering him the position of chief of police. Johnson was struggling with a problem endemic to a developing frontier town like El Paso: the attempt to balance the well-established business concerns of the liquor, prostitution, and gambling interests against the demands of the reformers, who wanted to break out of the wide-open frontier cow-town mode and develop a cleaner town.

By 1894 the entrenched gambling element had the upper hand in this ongoing battle, and vice and corruption of police officers were rampant. Juan Hart, owner of the *El Paso Times* and a leader of the reform element, inveighed against the gamblers daily in the columns of his paper. Many, including Mayor Johnson, himself in the liquor business, agreed that it was time for a crackdown. What was needed was a firm, courageous lawman to come in and bring the forces of vice back into line. Thirty-two-year-old Jeff Milton, tough and vigorous, was the man for the job. On August 10, 1894, he was sworn in as chief of police.[5]

It was during this period that George Scarborough and Milton renewed their acquaintanceship, formed sixteen years earlier in Jones County, and established their strong bond of friendship. The two had much in common. Only two years apart in age, they were both

Twenty-six-year-old Jeff Milton in 1888. *Courtesy Nita Stewart Haley Memorial Library, Midland, Texas.*

products of a proud southern heritage. Medium-size men of pleasant, fair-complexioned features and fashionable long, bushy mustaches, there was nothing in the general appearance of either that a casual observer would find imposing. In the eyes alone could be seen the steely determination and unflinching courage that characterized both men. Scarborough's eyes were pale blue, his hair straight and sandy; Milton had dark, wavy hair and piercing, jet-black eyes.

Former cowboys, Milton and Scarborough were outdoor types, men of the trail who knew cattle and horses, could read sign like an Indian, and were most comfortable in a saddle. Both seemed to thrive on danger and the hazards inherent in frontier law enforcement.

Each had killed a man in line of duty under circumstances that necessitated a trial for murder. It wouldn't be the last time for either. Both would be shot more than once in the line of duty. In marital status was their difference most pronounced. Milton was a bachelor and would remain so until the age of fifty-seven. Scarborough had been married for seventeen years and was the father of a large family. His seventh child, Ray, was born in September of 1894, a month after Jeff Milton came to El Paso.

Of course, in his capacity as deputy U.S. marshal, Scarborough had no responsibility for the enforcement of city ordinances and could take no official part in Milton's campaign to clean up El Paso. But as a resident of the city and a family man with many small children, he doubtless was supportive of his friend's efforts. George Scarborough was a saint by no means. Although he was an active member of the strict Baptist Church, he frequented saloons and gambling halls, the masculine meeting places of the period. He may have taken an occasional drink, although Tom Bendy said he was known in hard-drinking El Paso as "almost a total abstainer."[6] There is no record of his being seen inebriated, nor was he known to be an habitué of El Paso's famous parlor houses. He did gamble, however, and had the reputation of being a skilled poker player. John Selman, Jr., recalled a memorable session in the Ruby Saloon where were gathered "some of the best poker players together at one sitting" he had ever seen. Taking hands in the game were Scarborough, John Selman, Pat Garrett, Judge Roy Bean, and Judge Farrel. "It was draw poker for high stakes," young John said, "and the players were masters of the art of bluffing. It was well worth watching."[7]

Milton's efforts to clean up the town brought him into conflict with constable John Selman, and it is clear that he despised the man. He had known of Selman's rustling activities back at Fort Griffin when Milton was working cattle in nearby Jones County and had cut Selman's trail again at Fort Davis as a member of the Texas Rangers when Selman was arrested and returned to Shackelford County for trial. In El Paso, Selman was popular with the sporting crowd, the saloonmen, gamblers, pimps, and whores, whom Milton had been brought in to control.

J. Evetts Haley, who interviewed Milton over a long period in the 1930s and 1940s and in a biography of Milton faithfully reflected the old lawman's views on people he had known, called Selman "the most degenerate of the bunch" of hard cases Milton had to deal with in El Paso. "He had drifted west to El Paso with twenty dead men to his acknowledged credit."[8] According to Milton, Constable John Selman, "the most depraved gunman in Texas, [was] levying ten dollars a month on the many fancy houses" in the city.[9]

When Selman, who may have had a yen for the police chief's job himself, heard that Milton had been appointed with instructions to clamp down on such nefarious activity, he announced that he would take the new chief's pistol away from him, stick it where it hurt, and kick the handles off. Hearing this fighting talk, Milton called on the constable and asked him if he was ready to try that trick right then. Selman laughed it off as a joke.[10] Later Selman and a pal plotted to catch Milton off guard and kill him, but Milton got wind of the scheme, called Selman's hand again, and the old gunman once more backed down.[11]

That is the extent of Milton's association with Selman as represented to Haley by Milton. In his biography of John Selman, Leon Metz disputes this, pointing out that nothing in the records confirms the charge that Selman was shaking down prostitutes and that Milton is the sole source of the other confrontation anecdotes.[12]

When a Selman deputy, J. N. Schoonmaker, was convicted of taking illicit money from one of the soiled doves and fined twenty-five dollars, the old bushwacker and cattle thief claimed to be unaware of the graft and outraged at the revelation. "No deputy of mine shall unlawfully hold up any person in El Paso," Selman fumed to a newspaperman, "and I intend to camp on this trail until every person mixed up in the affair is singled out and I want you to know that Schoonmaker is no longer my deputy."[13] Metz points out that Milton hired John Selman, Jr., as a city policeman, suggests that this was probably done upon the recommendation of Uncle John, and concludes: "It looks as if the two gunmen got along quite well. . . . If Milton and Selman were never the best of friends—neither were they the worst of enemies."[14] Milton, however, told Haley that he had fired the entire police force because "they were worthless" and had taken on young John with his new recruits because "he was the best boy to have the sorriest daddy" that he had ever seen.[15]

Milton couldn't fire old John; the office of constable was elective and therefore Selman's position was more secure than that of Milton, who served at the pleasure of one man, the mayor. Milton worked with and tolerated Uncle John Selman because of his position but did not change his opinion of him as a man. That he was not able to prove Selman had been shaking down chippies does not mean he was not convinced of the truth of the charge. "I never killed a man that didn't need killing," Jeff Milton used to say.[16] John Selman, who represented everything Milton detested, certainly would have qualified. An understanding of the Selman-Milton relationship is important for a proper evaluation of events to come.

Next to arrive on the scene was an unlikely character who might have provided comic relief had not his role in the unfolding drama been so deadly serious. Martin Mroz was a cowboy who spoke English with a strong Polish accent, wore brogans instead of boots, and no underwear at all. Blond and blue-eyed with broad Slavic features, he had departed Saint Hedwig, a Silesian settlement east of San Antonio, about 1880 to become a cowboy.[17] He could not speak English when he met fourteen-year-old Dee Harkey, who was breaking broncos at a horse camp in Live Oak County. Harkey spent several years with the young Polander, teaching him how to handle horses and helping him with the language. One day Mroz mounted a gentle sorrel belonging to his employer, rode off, and was never seen in those parts again. Mroz pushed his stolen pony all the way to the Pecos country of southern New Mexico Territory, where he struck the VVN ranges of the Eddy-Bissell Cattle Company, managed by Tom Fennessey, who took a liking to Mroz and signed him on as a hand.[18]

Fennessey was trail hardened and tough as leather. In the spring of 1881 he and eight others had taken a herd of seven hundred horses from Goliad, Texas, up through Indian Territory for delivery to ranchman D. R. Fant at Ogallala, Nebraska. At Dodge City, Fennessey met C. B. Eddy, who was buying saddle horses for his big Seven Rivers spread. When Eddy returned to his ranch, Fennessey went with him.[19] A top hand with both horses and cattle, Fennessey was soon bossing the outfit. But, like many of his kind, he was a hard drinker who became extremely dangerous when in his cups and was reputed to have been involved in several gunplays. At Seven Rivers he took on a load, quarreled with saloonkeeper John Northern, and

Martin Mroz and Tom Fennessey. *Courtesy Nita Stewart Haley Memorial Library, Midland, Texas.*

shot him dead. He vanished from the country for about a year, and when he returned, he was not arrested for the killing. While he was gone, Martin Mroz bossed the operation.[20]

A. P. Black, the young cowboy who had been so impressed by George Scarborough at the general roundup on the Salt Fork of the Brazos in 1889, worked cattle with Mroz for the VVN in 1891–92. "Tom Finecy [sic] was general manager. His office was in Eddy. Martin M'Rose [was] never taking orders from the ranch board. It seems . . . Finecy killed a man and M'Rose was with him and there was a great friendship between the men." Fennessey was moving VVN cattle and horses to northern ranges owned by the Eddy-Bissell company and usually assigned Mroz as trail boss on these drives. "The company had a steer ranch in the Black Mountains of Colorado," Black recalled. "M'Rose was trail boss. He drove the first herd to the Black Mountains in the spring and came back and took a second herd from Liberty, New Mexico. He worked very little on the ranch, mostly on the trail. He was a good cowman and a good cowboy and everybody liked him."[21]

These drives could keep the VVN boys away from the home ranch for long periods. "We were gone nine months," VVN cowboy Nib Jones said of one such trip. "We celebrated my sixteenth birthday at Walsenburg. We went to a saloon and I saw Bob Ford, who claimed he'd killed Jesse James. There was a lot of drinkin' an' he an' Martin Merose matched, but there was plenty of men and they separated them."[22]

A. P. Black also remembered a Mroz-Ford set-to which he placed in 1891:

> Marose . . . had the first herd and I trailed a few weeks behind. When his herd got to Cripple Creek most of the boys rode into town for a little amusement. Bob Ford run a "honkey-tonk" and dance hall in Cripple Creek at the time, so Marose decided he'd ride in to take a look at the man who killed Jesse James. I guess he never thought a hell of a lot about Mr. Ford, for after taking one look at him, he whipped out his six-shooter and chased Ford down the middle of his own dance floor and ran him into a room in the back of the building. Just as Ford slammed the door, Marose slammed a couple of shots through the middle of it, but the victim escaped. When Marose told me about that he said he figured Ford was "still a runnin."[23]

It is clear that Black did not personally witness this incident and it became garbled in the retelling. Probably both the Jones and Black stories relate to the same occurrence, but it is possible that Mroz and Ford tangled twice, once in Walsenburg with no gunplay and again at Creede (not Cripple Creek) with some shooting.[24]

The significance of the event is its implication that Mroz held some standing as a badman. In the era of the frontier gunfighter, reputations compounded and reinforced reputations; hence someone who had backed down the man who put out the lights for Jesse James, one of the best known of frontier badmen, must necessarily be someone to be watched closely and feared. Mroz's emerging reputation, deserved or not, was to play a part in the events to follow in El Paso.

While working for the Eddy-Bissel Cattle Company, Mroz was building a herd of his own. How this was accomplished he explained to Dee Harkey in some detail after Harkey met the Polish cowboy again in Eddy in 1890. On Mroz's first trail drive for the VVN he had helped Tom Fennessey take a herd to Dodge City. "After we got our herd sort of broken in," said Mroz, "Tom would let me take three other men every morning, and we would gather all the cattle we could find and turn them in the trail herd. When we got to Dodge City, Kansas, we had as many cattle as the VVN's had, maybe more. We sold these cattle and then divided the money." Mroz returned to Texas and went up the trail with General McKenzie, with whom he started up a "partnership road-brand." Said Mroz: "When we got to Dodge City we had more cattle that we had picked up than McKenzie started with, so we sold them and divided the money."[25]

With this stake Mroz returned to Seven Rivers and set out to build a herd by means of rustling. He recorded 4X as a kept-up or ranch brand. For a road brand, or holding brand, as it was called in New Mexico Territory, he recorded what he called the Golden Ladders.

Vic Queen, an associate of Martin who would later play a strong supporting role in the El Paso drama, told family members he was present when Mroz invented his ladder brand. Queen and Mroz had roped and tied a steer, had a running iron heating in a fire, and were discussing how to brand the animal so as to obliterate the brand already on its hide:

> When the iron was hot Martin said: "I show you," and proceeded to burn two long, sloping lines up the steer's ribs, then connected these with several horizontal bars. The iron was reheated, the steer turned over and the lines repeated on the opposite side. "Dere she is," declared Martin, "The Golden Ladder—oop one side und down de udder!" Martin was said to have been very proud of his creation, for, said he, no matter what the original brand had been, he could cover it by simply adding a few more cross bars to his ladder.[26]

Dee Harkey also remembered that Mroz took pride in his idea and quoted him without attempting to approximate Martin's accent:

> I put my Golden Ladders brand all criss-crossed over the original brand that was on the cow I wanted to steal, and I would use as many

marks as was necessary to burn the original brand out. Then I would put my 4X brand on the cow, my kept-up brand. I branded all the calves I could get, anyway, with my 4X brand, and that is the way I built my herd of cattle.

When Harkey asked whether ranchers had objected to the thefts, Mroz said, "Well, I had to kill a couple of the gents and shoot another's hat off before they would leave me alone. When I told them to get to their hole, they would leave, and that is the way I got by."[27]

Through such bragging talk Martin Mroz contributed to his reputation as a bad man, and when he at last arrived on the El Paso scene, he was regarded as a dangerous desperado. Black states flatly that a murder precipitated his flight from New Mexico: "Martin killed a man at Seven Rivers . . . and was forced to leave the country. He gathered up fifteen thousand dollars that he'd made rustlin' and escaped to Mexico."[28]

An unidentified friend of Mroz was quoted in the contemporary press as saying that Martin left home after "he stole two carriage horses and was arrested, but succeeded in escaping the officers." He fled to the frontier counties of Texas, where "he killed a man and afterwards waylaid and killed the main state's witness. . . . He then went to New Mexico where he killed two more men. About eighteen months ago he killed his fifth man on Seven Rivers, New Mexico. . . . During his whole life he has been a horse, cow and hog thief, and there are a number of indictments hanging over him from New Mexico and the panhandle counties of Texas."[29]

A deputy U.S. marshal named Phillips who had cowboyed with Mroz argued that most of the notoriety was unwarranted. "Every person in [Eddy] County knows that M'Rose was never tried for any crime, let alone the killing of a man at Seven Rivers," he said. Phillips claimed he was in daily association with Mroz on the VVN from 1884 until 1891 and "there never was a charge of murder or any other crime made against [him]." Explaining Mroz's rustler reputation, Phillips said that "during the year when cattle were of no value in this country, when a big steer was sold as low as six dollars, many people did not pay any attention to their cattle and M'Rose then branded as many cattle as he could find." Like many, Mroz "burned brands and did a wholesale stealing business, but he was not near the thief as were others against whom nothing has been said."[30]

It is true that as a cattle rustler Martin Mroz was by no means a rara avis in Eddy County. Most of the small ranchers had built their herds by stealing from the large cattle companies. Their operations were so open that when Dee Harkey, acting in the interests of the Cattle Raisers Association, began a crackdown, he was invited to a meeting attended by some twenty rustlers and the county sheriff. Mroz, spokesman for the rustlers, offered to match Harkey's salary and brand a thousand calves for him in the coming year if he would back off. Harkey refused.[31]

Mroz was living at this time in Phenix, a sin town just outside the city limits of Eddy where were offered the liquor, gambling, and prostitution enticements that had been banned in Eddy by edict of its founder, Charles B. Eddy. During its three years of life, Phenix attracted a hard crew of cutthroats, tinhorns, and flesh peddlers. Mroz became a leader and avid participant in the continual bacchanal Phenix provided. He and his cowboy pals Vic Queen and Tom Fennessey caroused with a gang of notorious saloon gunmen that included Dave Kemp, Walker Bush, Lon Bass, and Walter Paddleford and were considered part of this tough crowd.[32]

Deputy Marshal Phillips believed that Mroz's downhill slide began when he met and "married a prostitute in the saloon town of Phenix" early in 1895, and this view was echoed by Sheriff J. D. Walker, who said that "the step Martin took when he entered into a matrimonial contract was the prime cause of all his trouble."[33] Mroz is said to have taken his bride at a ceremony in "the sheriff's whore-house" at Eddy. Blonde with blue eyes and described as an outstanding beauty, Helen Beulah Mroz was to play a prominent part in the events to follow.[34]

In the fall 1894 roundup cattle inspector Dee Harkey cut out a number of the Polish cowboy's burnt-brand cows and brought indictments against him for cattle theft. W. H. Mullane and W. J. Barber went his bond, but as the time approached for a court appearance in March 1895, Mroz sold his cattle to Barber for two thousand dollars in cash, promising to release the sureties by putting up part of it as his bond.[35]

Mroz, however, had no intention of either appearing in court or losing five hundred dollars. He rode with Vic Queen to the VVN range and, with a display of ingratitude for the ranch that had nurtured him, stole a herd of horses. The two then drove the stolen horses to another ranch and disposed of them. Queen headed for Juárez, Mexico, and Mroz, with ranchman Stem Daugherty, rode on east to Midland, Texas. There Mroz gave Daugherty a bill of sale to the horses and twenty-five hundred dollars in cash to hold for him. There he also met Beulah, who had, by arrangement, staged from Eddy to Pecos and then come on east to Midland by train.[36] Beulah later

Vic Queen fled New Mexico with Mroz and was locked up with him in the Juárez *juzgado*. *Courtesy Lee Myers.*

claimed that at Midland she and Mroz divided up the money she carried with her, keeping two thousand dollars in cash for herself and giving him a check for twenty-five hundred dollars.[37]

Mroz's eastward course would indicate he had intended to continue his flight in that direction, but his plans were changed when the duped bondsman Mullane trailed him to Midland and had him placed under arrest. The likable rustler was able to convince Mullane that he would return to Eddy with him, and Mroz was "put on parole" and allowed to stay in a hotel with his wife. "When Mullane went to look for him to start back home, the prisoner had made his escape . . . and Mullane came home without his prisoner."[38] Mroz lit a shuck for Old Mexico on a fast horse.[39] Beulah boarded a train to El Paso with the small child whom she had brought with her when she first came to Phenix from South Texas. At El Paso she crossed over to Juárez, hunted up Vic Queen, and waited to hear from her husband.

Queen was a big, gruff, tough-talking cowman-turned-outlaw with raven-black hair and mustache and piercing black eyes who loudly proclaimed that he backed down to no man. Because of his bluster and his hardcase associates, he was considered a dangerous man to cross, although, unlike most of those associates, there is no record of his ever having killed anyone. Rumor later had it that Mroz and Queen planned to purchase a ranch in Mexico. There may have been some truth to the story, for when Beulah next heard from her husband, he was deep in Mexico, scouting out the country.

Warrants were now out for the two horse and cattle thieves, with posted rewards of one thousand dollars for Martin Mroz and five hundred dollars for Vic Queen. But for the moment they remained in the wings while the final major player in the forthcoming tragedy stode upon the El Paso stage.

His arrival was first announced on March 30, 1895, in a simple two-sentence note in the *El Paso Herald:* "John Wesley Hardin, at one time one of the most noted characters in Texas, is in the city from Comanche County. It is reported that John Wesley is now studying law."

John Wesley Hardin! It was a name out of the past, a name that twenty years before inspired fear and awe throughout Texas and much of the Southwest. In a state which had become famous for producing top-quality gunfighters, so famous that cattle barons from northern territories came to Texas to recruit fighting men for their range wars, no more fearsome name was known.

Born in Bonham, Fannin County, in 1853, Hardin was a member of a proud Texas family which could boast of many illustrious forebears, including a signer of the Texas Declaration of Independence, a veteran of the Battle of San Jacinto, congressmen, and judges. Like George Scarborough, he was the son of a minister. Hardin's Methodist circuit-rider father had named his son after the founder of his church in the hope that one day the boy would also take up the ministry.

But Hardin was a product of the violence of the Civil War and its Reconstruction aftermath, a period which produced bloody racial clashes like the Colfax affair in Louisiana; spawned outlaw gangs typified by those of the James and Younger brothers of Missouri, which preyed on the hated bank and railroad interests; and Texas gunfighters and mankillers like Bill Longley and Ben Thompson. Hardin displayed a tendency to violence at an early age; while still in school he severely stabbed another boy in a schoolyard squabble. The boy survived, but the pattern of violence which was to guide the life of young Hardin had been firmly established. In 1868, when he was only fifteen, he shot and killed a former slave. Three blue-clad soldiers took his trail, but Hardin ambushed and killed all three. Barely beyond puberty, he already had four dead men to his credit and became the fugitive he was to remain for the next nine years. John Wesley Hardin was never outlawed for cattle rustling or horse thievery, as were contemporaries of the stripe of Dutch Henry Born or Doc Middleton; he was not a train or bank robber of the Sam Bass or Jesse James ilk; he was simply a reckless young man with an overblown sense of the chivalric code of the South and a complete disdain for the worth of human life. He considered the least slight or insult justification for a shooting, and as a shootist he had few equals. His dexterity and accuracy with pistols soon became legendary, as did his willingness to use them.

Estimates of the number of men who fell before Hardin's blazing six-shooters vary greatly. There were deadly encounters on lonely prairies with victims buried and the incident unrecorded; there were multiparticipant gunfights in which men died but no one determined then or later whose weapon fired the fatal shots. In an account of his life written shortly before his death, Hardin modestly admitted to some fifteen killings, but most chroniclers of frontier mayhem follow the lead of Eugene Cunningham, who set the figure at forty.[40]

Hardin drove cattle up the trail to the Kansas railheads and downed victims in Indian Territory and Kansas en route. He claimed to have backed down renowned pistoleer James Butler ("Wild Bill") Hickok in Abilene, Kansas. He played an important role as a top gun in Texas's sanguinary Sutton-Taylor feud. Along the way he shot down assorted soldiers and lawmen bent on terminating his bloody history.

In 1874, Hardin celebrated his twenty-first birthday in Comanche, Texas, by killing Deputy Sheriff Charles Webb. The state posted four thousand dollar rewards for his capture and the Texas Rangers listed him as their most-wanted fugitive. The pressure by the man-hunters became so intense that Hardin took his family to northern Florida, where he lived for three years under the name J. H. Swain, Jr.

A Dallas bounty hunter and detective named Jack Duncan traced Hardin to Pensacola, Florida, in 1877. There a trap was set at the railroad station and on August 23, Duncan and a squad of officers effected the capture of the notorious gunman. Hardin was taken back to Texas and tried at Comanche for the murder of Deputy Webb. Convicted of second-degree murder, he was sentenced to twenty-five years' imprisonment at Huntsville. Hardin spent more than a year in the Travis County Jail awaiting trial and sweating out appeals. Finally, all appeals were rejected and on October 5, 1878, the steel doors of the penitentiary slammed shut behind him.

He was a troublesome inmate in his early convict years, defying guards and constantly plotting escape, but after several severe flog-gings and isolations, he accepted his fate, became a model prisoner, and began to study law. In November 1892 he received word that his wife, Jane, who had supported him steadfastly throughout his ordeal, had died.

After sixteen years Hardin was released from prison on February 17, 1894, and received a full pardon a month later. He settled on a friend's ranch near Gonzales with his son and two daughters, at-tended church regularly, applied for and passed a law examination, and was admitted to the Texas bar. At the age of forty-one he seemed to have achieved a complete reformation, to have put Wes Hardin, gunfighting desperado and mankiller, behind him, and converted himself into an upstanding, reputable citizen. He spent long hours with pen and tablet, writing the story of his life. On January 8, 1895, he married a girl half his age named Callie Lewis, but shortly after the wedding the young bride left him, returned to her parents, and refused to see him again.[41]

Partly because of the pain of this rejection and partly because of his inability to attract clients to his law offices, Hardin began to backslide. He started to gamble and drink heavily. He frequented saloons instead of churches. When under the influence of alcohol, he became belligerent and overbearing. He took his pistols out of the trunk and practiced with them daily. The Wild Wes was reemerging.

Hardin was at this point in his ill-spent and troubled life when, in March 1895, he received a call for his legal services from a shirttail relative. Jim Miller, husband of a Hardin cousin, was coming to El Paso from Pecos for the trial of G. A. ("Bud") Frazer, charged with the attempted murder of Miller. Hardin was asked by Miller to assist in the prosecution. By recruiting Hardin, Miller was also adding another expert gunhand to his camp. Hardin's gunslinging expertise would be welcome should the Frazer-Miller case explode in gunfire on the streets of El Paso. Miller and Frazer had been feuding in Pecos for a long time and both had lined up a coterie of quick-triggered fighting men to back their leaders' play.

Hardin went to El Paso, where his arrival triggered much excitement in the saloons. "Hardin had an immediate following wherever he showed up," said John Selman, Jr. "A crowd would gather and beg for the honor of buying the great gunman a drink. Hardin took this hero worship as a matter of course." With the others, John, Jr., was closely watching the newcomer, whose legendary exploits had been recorded before the young policeman was born:

> I caught my first glimpse of Hardin on San Antonio street. He was across the street from me and I could not help but note the brisk and alert manner in which Hardin carried himself. He seemed to be a human dynamo of action. Hardin dressed in black, soft black Stetson hat and black bow tie. He was heavily built and a little under six feet in height. At a short distance he gave one the impression that he was smiling but at close range his face showed a certain hardness. One

had only to look into his keen brown eyes to see that Wes Hardin was
a bad man with whom to fool.[42]

Despite the furor raised in the saloons by Hardin's arrival, the
newspapers chose to low-key his appearance. The *Herald* gave him
two lines as noted; the *Times* waited a week to remark on his presence
and then published what amounted to an advertisement, composed
and paid for by Hardin himself:

> Among the many leading citizens of Pecos City now in El Paso is
> John Wesley Hardin, Esq., a leading member of the Pecos City bar.
> In his young days, Mr. Hardin was as wild as the broad western plains
> upon which he was raised. But he was a generous, brave-hearted
> youth and got into no small amount of trouble for the sake of his
> friends, and soon gained a reputation for being quick tempered and a
> dead shot. In those days when one man insulted another, one of the
> two died then and there. Young Hardin, having a reputation for being
> a man who never took water, was picked out by every bad man who
> wanted to make a reputation, and there is where the "bad men" made
> a mistake, for the young westerner still survives many warm and
> tragic encounters. Forty-one years has steadied the impetuous cowboy
> down to a quiet, dignified peaceable man of business. Mr. Hardin is
> a modest gentleman of pleasant address, but underneath the modest
> dignity is a firmness that never yields except to reason and the law.
> He is a man who makes friends of all who come in close contact with
> him.[43]

The paper had noted with some apprehension a few days earlier
the arrival in the city of Miller and Frazer gunmen, including Hardin.
"It is understood," said the *Times,* "that a lot of the people interested
in the Frazer-Miller case from Pecos come to El Paso armed to the
teeth and they will no doubt be taught that El Paso has her own peace
officers. The day for man killers in this town has passed."[44] Perhaps
Juan Hart of the *Times* was engaged in wishful thinking. He and the
people of El Paso were to learn that the sun had not yet set on the
day of the mankiller in the city at the Pass of the North.

After I fired the third shot, he said, "Boys, you've killed me"
And I said: "Stop trying to get up then and we'll quit."

—GEORGE SCARBOROUGH, JUNE 30, 1895

-7-

"Boys, You've Killed Me"

With the arrival of John Wesley Hardin, the cast of characters was complete. Hardin, at forty-two, and John Selman, now fifty-five years of age, were considered by some to be quaint and romantic relics of a violent frontier way of life that had given way to progress and a new civility. After all, Hardin had not been tested in a six-gun confrontation for two decades, and most of the six-shooter exploits of the man fondly known in El Paso as Uncle John dated back to that period of ancient history. The passage of arms with Baz Outlaw was shrugged off by these folks as an aberration, a footnote to the history of Selman's violent past. But these two grizzled gunmen, together with George Scarborough and Jeff Milton, tough lawmen in their prime, and the outlaw Martin Mroz and his voluptuous wife, were to play leading roles in a drama that would leave three of the six dead by gunshot within the year. Supporting players would include Scarborough's brother-in-law Frank McMahan, Mroz's pal Vic Queen, and John Selman, Jr., son of the old gunman.

Events moved fast after Hardin appeared on the scene in March. That month, officers from New Mexico Territory filed a complaint in El Paso, charging Mroz and Queen with bringing stolen goods into the city, thus enabling any local officer to arrest the rustlers if they should venture across the river. The Juárez authorities also were notified that two fugitives from American justice had taken refuge in Mexico and an official request was filed to arrest and hold them while extradition papers were being prepared. Dee Harkey filed horse-theft charges against Vic Queen in Juárez, and on March 26,

Queen was taken into custody by Mexican police and lodged in the Juárez *juzgado*.[1]

Although Beulah and her child were in Juárez, Mroz could not be found. Santa Fe Railroad detective Beauregard Lee heard of the reward offered for Mroz and decided to take a hand in the game. He kept an eye on Beulah and when she purchased a railroad ticket to Magdalena, Sonora, some three hundred miles to the southwest, he went to Juárez Chief of Police Haro and suggested they follow in the hope that the woman would lead them to Mroz. Haro agreed and the officers took the train, seating themselves where they could watch Beulah.

On April 6, Mroz boarded the train at Magdalena and greeted his wife, whereupon Lee stuck "a big sixshooter up under M'Rose's chin, called on him to throw up his hands or be blown in two, as he had a warrant for his arrest. M'Rose did not comply, when suddenly, ere the officer carried out his threat, Chief Haro rushed up behind M'Rose, and grabbing his arms, shoved them into the air, exclaiming, 'Don't shoot! For God's sake, don't shoot!' " Mroz submitted without further resistance and was cuffed, but Beulah "made a dive into her bosom for a gun which, however, was immediately snatched from her by a passenger and Mr. Lee, although some force was necessary." Lee searched Beulah and found that she was carrying a bankroll totaling eighteen hundred eighty dollars. Captors and captured returned to Juárez on the next northbound train.

Interviewed later, Lee said that "but for the quick action of Chief Haro he would have killed M'Rose then and there." It would have been necessary, he said, "because he knew of him as a most desperate character, a man with whom he would take no chances whatever. The officer laid considerable stress on this last statement."[2] Mroz's delay in raising his hands, even with the muzzle of a six-gun under his chin, is significant in light of subsequent events.

Jeff Milton said that "a Santa Fe detective," who was undoubtedly Beauregard Lee, coveted the reward money and had tried to lure Mroz across the line with a promise of official protection. Mroz had agreed to come, saying, "If the Chief will give me his word that I won't be bothered, I'll come over." But when Lee approached Milton with the scheme, the police chief refused to be a party to a double-cross "and the detective left in high dudgeon."[3]

Beulah later claimed that her bankroll and jewelry had been taken from her in Magdalena and, although she was released by the Juárez authorities the next day, her property was not returned. "I came over to this side of the river and secured counsel," she said. The counsel she employed was John Wesley Hardin, attorney at law.

Mroz had joined Vic Queen in the Juárez jail. Sheriff J. D. Walker of Eddy County, New Mexico Territory, and former Ranger Capt. George Baylor, now representing the New Mexico cattlemen, were working to procure extradition papers to get the two rustlers back across the line. Dee Harkey obtained the agreement of Mexican authorities to turn Mroz and Queen over to him once the papers were issued.[4]

On April 18, Walker and Baylor presented requisitions for Mroz and Queen, but these were rejected by the Mexican authorities as being improperly drawn. The *Times* reported on the twenty-third that the matter was still being argued:

> Martin M'Rose and Vic Queen . . . are making a hard fight against extradition from Mexico and from release from the Juarez jail. Their friends have rallied around them and declare that they (the prisoners) will never be brought to this side of the river alive. A writ of habeas corpus or some similar proceeding was to have been resorted to today and Col. Baylor and another officer from New Mexico and Chief of Police Milton and George Herold of this city went over this afternoon to look after the matter. It is believed that a decision as to whether the authorities will surrender the prisoners or turn them loose will be reached under thirty days, but meanwhile another charge will be lodged against M'Rose for horse stealing, as the stolen horse which he is said to have ridden from Roswell [*sic*] has been found in this city.

A week later, on May 1, the *Times* indicated the extradition problem had been resolved and that Walker and Baylor had been notified by Governor Ahumada of Chihuahua that the prisoners would be turned over to them the next day. It never happened. Dee Harkey alleged that Gene McKenzie went to Juárez and gave Mroz four thousand dollars to distribute judiciously among the Mexican authorities. Consequently, when Walker and Baylor arrived with the extradition papers, the Mexicans refused to honor them, saying that Mroz and Queen had applied for Mexican naturalization and therefore the papers were incorrectly drawn.[5]

Mroz was still badly wanted in New Mexico. Harkey went to George Scarborough. "I took up the Morose case with him and told him the Cattle Raisers' Association would pay him a reward of five hundred dollars if he would deliver Martin Morose to me on this side of the river." Walker later raised the ante, offering an additional five hundred dollars from the sheriff's office for the body of Mroz, dead or alive, delivered on the American side of the border.[6]

His duties as deputy marshal had Scarborough on the go at the time. On April 6 the *Times* had noted that he was "as busy as six men" scouring the countryside for witnesses scheduled to appear before the federal grand jury. Court was in session and two important trials were in progress, the Frazer-Miller case, which had brought Wes Hardin and a bevy of gunmen into town, and the Ochoa case, at which Scarborough would have to testify.[7]

While Mroz and Queen languished in the Juárez jail, Buelah in El Paso held lengthy conferences with her attorney, Hardin. Although he had come to El Paso to help in the prosecution of Bud Frazer, Hardin seems to have contributed little to that effort. After appraising the face and figure of the beauteous Beulah and learning that she also had substantial financial assets, Hardin assured her that his time was very much available. For him it was lust at first sight, and the former prostitute was not accustomed to resisting ardor. The two got their heads together; soon their contiguity would become more intimate. After expenditure of two hundred-fifty dollars for Hardin's services, seven hundred dollars for a Mexican lawyer, and the intervention of the American consul at Juárez, Beulah got most of her money and jewelry back.[8] Hardin was then retained by Beulah to represent her husband's interests in his extradition fight. Meanwhile, friends of Mroz and Queen were congregating in Juárez to offer support and to help prevent their being taken back into the States. Tom Fennessey was there, as was Sam Kaufman and a man identified only as Lightfoot, among others. All were regarded as fighting men.

When Mroz got wind of Beulah's contact with Hardin, he was not at all pleased. He did not trust Hardin and felt instinctively that the old gunfighter's interest was directed more toward Beulah than the welfare of her husband. He also suspected that Hardin was working with the officers trying to get him across the border. From his jail cell he directed his cronies to force Hardin out of the game. Messages were sent to Hardin "to the effect that he would never be allowed to get M'rose [across] the river and that he better make himself scarce in Juarez."[9]

On Sunday evening, April 21, Hardin was in Juárez and Fennessey, Lightfoot, and others braced him on the street and "tried to bulldoze him and grew quite saucy in their talk when they saw he did not want to have a row." Hardin, not liking the odds, accepted the harassment, but "the little Sabbath day collision did not sit well on his good-natured stomach."[10]

The next night, Hardin was back in Juárez again, this time accompanied by a friend.[11] There they met, probably by design, Jeff Milton and George Scarborough. Hardin invited the two officers into Deiter's and Saur's saloon for a drink and led the way past the bar to the back room. There they found five of the New Mexico crowd engaged in spirited discourse with Mrs. Beulah Mroz. Fennessey, Kaufman, and Lightfoot were present. Two of the men the officers didn't know. The four new arrivals seated themselves and were soon involved in the conversation.

The *Times* reported what then transpired: "M'rose's case was brought up and hot words passed between Hardin and Finnessey. Both men sprang to their feet. In an instant Mr. Hardin had slapped Finnessey's face and had his gun at his breast. In another instant Fennessey would have been a dead man, but quick as thought Chief Milton grasped the pistol and was struggling with Mr. Hardin."[12]

Scarborough and Hardin's friend both had their guns out covering the rest of the crowd. At Milton's request, Hardin put his weapon away, "but his blood was up and, remembering the occurrence of Sunday night, he walked up to Lightfoot and gave him a slap in the face that could be heard for a block. Chief Milton, as cool as if he had just stepped out of a bath, placed his back to the door of the room and stated it was best to settle the little problem right there and then if it was to have a continuance in the future." The New Mexico gunmen, "though game themselves, saw that they had four cool, brave men to deal with and it was quickly agreed the matter should be dropped."[13]

Back in El Paso, Milton told Will Burges about the tense confrontation and how impressed he was by Hardin's speed with a gun. "We are booked for trouble with Hardin," he said. "It was perfectly evident to my mind that Hardin was trying to pick a row, and I decided I'd stand on my feet, so if I had to act, I could act as quick as anybody. I was wrong about part of it. Hardin is the fastest thing I ever saw in my life with a gun. There is nobody that is a match for him as far as that is concerned. Before I could get my gun, he had pulled his and had it in Finnessey's belly."[14]

Milton had accomplished what he had been brought to El Paso to do—put pressure on the vice element—but now the pendulum of fickle public opinion was swinging the other way and the citizenry wanted a respite. On April 9, antireform candidate Poker Bob Campbell was elected mayor and on May 1, Milton was relieved of his duties as police chief in favor of Ed M. Fink, a man Milton had fired off the force.[15] Milton remained in El Paso and was not long without status as a peace officer; a month later he received a commission as a deputy under U.S. Marshal Dick Ware.[16]

Through the month of May there were no new developments in the Mroz case. The fugitives remained in the Juárez jail and a half-dozen or more New Mexico and Texas officers still tried to figure out a way to get them out and across the border. By midmonth the *Eddy Argus,* closely watching the developments in the case, noted that "the friends of M'rose [had] scattered, some to Arizona, and some to the interior of Mexico."[17] Beulah was spending less time in her room at the Wellington Hotel and more in Hardin's quarters at the Herndon lodging house on East Overland Street.

Early in June, Sheriff Walker made one last effort to dislodge the rustlers from their Mexican sanctuary. Reported the *Herald:* "Sheriff Walker is in town from Eddy and went over to Juarez this noon on business in connection with the extradition of the alleged cattle thieves."[18] His lack of success was announced a week later: "In accordance with instructions from the supreme court at the city of Mexico, the Juarez authorities have released M'Rose from jail, and he will not be extradited."[19]

Scarborough and Milton still wanted Mroz, but during early June had little opportunity to work on the problem as both were out of town much of the time. The El Paso papers noted their return together on Saturday, the twenty-second of June, after extensive travel throughout the state: "Ex-Chief of Police Milton and Deputy Marshal Scarborough returned this morning from the east. Mr. Milton had been in San Antonio and other parts of the state and will now remain in El Paso."[20] Scarborough had returned "from a trip four hundred miles east of here after witnesses."[21] While in Austin, Milton had secured appointment as a special Texas Ranger. He and Scarborough, with the thought of that reward for Mroz always in mind, were still working on a way to lure the outlaw across the border where they could nab him. If successful, they needed authority to serve the local warrant sworn out against Mroz in El Paso. As federal officers they lacked that authority, but as a special Texas Ranger Milton could make legal arrests anywhere in the state. During the long train trip back to El Paso, the two lawmen hatched a scheme to collar the rustler.

Meanwhile, in Juárez, Mroz was fuming. Reports of the Beulah-Hardin liaison furnished by busybodies infuriated him, but also sticking in his craw was the knowledge that Beulah held a large chunk of his bankroll. She refused to come to see him and because of the waiting lawmen and their warrants, he feared to cross and see her. Scarborough had somehow gained Mroz's confidence and the

Jeff Milton and George Scarborough in El Paso. *Courtesy Nita Stewart Haley Memorial Library, Midland, Texas.*

outlaw began sending letters to the lawman, asking him to come to Juárez to discuss the impasse and help seek a solution.

On Monday, June 24, two days after his return to town, Scarborough received another request from Mroz for a meeting. "I went over that evening," Scarborough said later, "had a long chat with him and delivered a message to a party on this side for him. He wanted a party on this side to meet him in Juarez and they refused to do so."[22] The party was, of course, Beulah Mroz. On Tuesday, Scarborough received another letter from Mroz. "Again he sent for me and asked me to make an appointment to meet him on this side of the river and Friday was agreed upon."[23]

Official business for Scarborough prevented the Friday meeting. "He had made arrangements to come over here Friday night," said Scarborough,

> but I went over and told him I could not be there, as I had to go to Sierra Blanca.[24] I told him on his asking me that I would be back Saturday morning at 10:15. He told me he was sorry I could not come that night as he and his two friends expected to leave Saturday morning. He asked me to come over when I got back and he said he would leave a letter for me stating when he would return. I got back from Sierra Blanca Saturday and between two and three o'clock went over the river to see M'rose. I met him on the street . . . and we went into Duchene's place and had a talk in his back room. When we got in there he told me he had decided not to come on this side the river. I told him that was all right—it was his business. I had never asked him to come over to this side.
>
> We went out on the street and Vic Queen came up and while we were talking I saw a person with whom I had some business and I left them and went to the Plaza with this party. I was gone about half an hour, got through my business, and started home. As I went down the street, M'rose, who was standing in a saloon door, saw me and followed me. We went down the street together. He told me he was very anxious to see a party on this side but was afraid to come over. I got on a streetcar and so did he and he said he believed he would come.[25]

Fugitive and officer agreed to meet in the middle of the Mexican Central Railroad bridge at eleven o'clock that night, or "about half an hour before the moon went down. [Mroz] wanted to come over before the electric light was lit."[26]

Scarborough and Mroz met in the center of the Mexican Central Railway Bridge spanning the Rio Grande. *Courtesy El Paso Public Library.*

Back in El Paso, Scarborough rounded up Milton and Frank McMahan and explained his plan for the taking of Mroz. "We met," said Scarborough, "about an hour or an hour and a half before the moon went down and went to the dump this side of the bridge about 300 or 350 yards. I left them there . . . and they understood I would be in front when M'rose and I came back and I had a certain place to stop near where they were."[27]

The officers hid in a patch of tall sunflowers near the Santa Fe dump. "When they received a signal from me," Scarborough said, they were "to order M'rose and myself to throw up our hands."[28] He said he also admonished them "to be careful and not hurt him if they could avoid it."[29]

Scarborough then walked out to the middle of the bridge and met Mroz. "He was waiting for me with a cocked revolver in his hand," said Scarborough, "and when I walked up to him he asked me to wait until he could uncock his gun, which he did with his back turned toward me."[30] While the two men talked, Mroz toyed with the revolver, which later was determined to have been Vic Queen's.[31] "He let down the hammer," Scarborough said, "and revolved the cylinder around several times and we sat down and talked for about ten minutes on the bridge."[32]

"I'm damn skittish about going across this river. They are watching for me on the other side," Mroz complained. Scarborough told him "he had better return to Juarez then, that there were no strings on him." Mroz asked if Scarborough had seen anyone hanging around the bridge when he came over and Scarborough answered that he had seen no one. Mroz "then jumped up and exclaimed: 'By God, I'll go over with you!' "[33]

The two men walked back toward the American side, Scarborough in front, Mroz trailing about six feet behind. "Reaching this side," Scarborough said, "he jumped down on the embankment and I climbed down after him and told him to keep out of the light and under the shadow of the bridge. . . . Even after reaching this side I told him if he was afraid, then to climb back on the bridge and return to Juarez. This he declined to do. When we reached a spot about twenty-five feet from where Milton and McMahan were concealed we stopped and I gave the signal."[34]

The lawmen in the sunflowers rose up with guns leveled and ordered Mroz to throw up his hands. "At that instant I was facing M'rose," said Scarborough. "I dropped my sixshooter on him—he was pulling his—and said, 'Don't make no play. We don't want to hurt you.' He didn't say a word but cocked his sixshooter and dropped it on me."[35]

Scarborough said he distinctly heard the "click click" as Mroz cocked his weapon. "I did not wait to hear any more," he said, "but commenced shooting. At my first shot M'rose fell but was instantly on his feet again, coming toward me."[36]

Milton, armed with a shotgun, and McMahan, holding a six-shooter, then turned loose their batteries. "I fired four shots and the others fired several," Scarborough said. "After I fired the third shot he said, 'Boys, you've killed me,' and I said, 'Stop trying to get up then and we'll quit,' He had been trying to get up with his gun in his hand. About that time he fell over and the shooting stopped."[37]

His intention had been to arrest Mroz, not to kill him, Scarborough said, adding, "I had been told he was a bad man, and he certainly died game."[38]

Moments after the firing had ceased, Woody Bendy and Pat

Martin Mroz carried this pistol, the property of Vic Queen, the night he met Scarborough on the bridge. It was kept by Sheriff Simmons, who later bought it from the county for one dollar. *Courtesy John Voliva.*

Dwyer, river-patrol guards on the watch for smugglers, came running with a lantern. Scarborough sent McMahan into town for a doctor and someone from the sheriff's office. At the county jail McMahan telephoned Dr. Alward White and then led Deputy Sheriff J. C. Jones back to the scene. "I took the light," said Jones, "and looked at the man's eyes and saw he was dead. He was lying on his back with his pistol cocked about an inch from his right hand. The pistol had one empty cylinder and one empty shell. The pistol had been recently fired."[39]

Dr. White soon arrived in hack driver Billy Guiberson's carriage and formally pronounced Mroz dead. His preliminary examination of the body disclosed eight wounds caused by pistol balls and buckshots. W. D. Howe, justice of the peace, and an undertaker were sent for. The body was taken to Powell's undertaking establishment at the Star Stables where Dr. White made a more thorough examina-

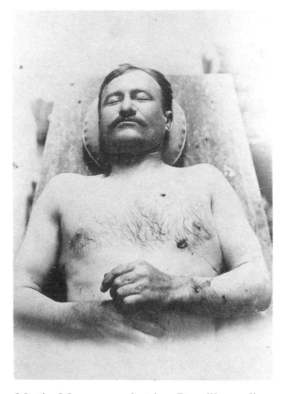

Martin Mroz on undertaker Powell's cooling
board at the Star Stables. *Courtesy John Voliva.*

tion. He found that Mroz had been killed by "seven penetration
wounds, all but two of which were made by bullets of large calibre.
Two of these large bullets passed directly through the heart. In
addition, there were six or seven shot wounds in the left arm."[40]
White believed that the fatal wound was "made by the first pistol
fired, which was fired by Deputy Marshal George Scarborough."[41]

Found on the dead man was a letter "directed to Miss Beula Mrose,
El Paso, Texas. The envelope was covered with blood and had been
struck by two of the pistol bullets." The letter was read and then
forwarded to Beulah.[42]

W. H. Burges was later to say in wonderment: "M'Rose was the
only case I have ever known where a man was shot through the heart,

got back up, and shot again, himself."[43] Burges, who would defend Scarborough, Milton and McMahan at their trial for the Mroz killing and who had intimate knowledge of the details of the affair, said the newspaper accounts at the time were fairly accurate.[44]

The following day, Sunday, June 30, W. D. Howe, acting as coroner, held an inquest in the matter of the death of Martin Mroz. Scarborough testified first and told substantially the same story he told a news reporter the same day. He made it clear that all his machinations with Mroz had been for the sole purpose of capturing the fugitive and collecting the reward. He had been armed, he pointedly reminded Justice Howe, with a warrant signed by Howe himself.

Milton's testimony largely corroborated Scarborough's. He added that he had wired Sheriff Walker at Eddy when Mroz was released from the Juárez jail, asking whether the reward money was still being offered, and had been assured it was. McMahan had been enlisted, Milton said, because "we thought it best to have another man, Mr. McMahan, to assist us, thinking it would avoid trouble, and he [Mroz] would give up quicker." All three officers had ordered Mroz to raise his hands, Milton said, and when he failed to do so immediately, "I told him a second time to throw up his hands and I think the others did too. . . . As he reached for his pistol Scarborough shot and I shot once. I was afraid one of us would get killed was the reason I shot. Several shots were fired. . . . I think Mrose fired. I saw his gun come up but couldn't say positively whether he fired or not."[45]

McMahan testified that he had been aware of the case for two months and had seen Mroz on the streets of Juárez frequently and knew him by sight. He said that as the two figures approached in the light of the descending moon, "from where I was stationed I could easily recognize the man believed to be Mrose." When commanded to do so, Mroz

made no move towards raising his hands but began drawing a revolver from the front of his pants. I saw the revolver and also heard the click as he was cocking it. About that instant there was a shot fired—I thought from Mrose's revolver, and I began shooting. I fired two shots and Mrose fell and then he got up and I fired two more shots. He fell back on the ground. . . . After the shooting was over I was

very much alarmed that either Scarborough or Milton had been shot
and asked them several times.[46]

Mroz's pistol was produced. "It was a forty-five caliber Colt, and
one cartridge had recently been fired as the powder in the barrel had
not yet dried from the explosion. . . . Mrose also had seventeen
forty-five caliber cartridges in his pocket and a small pocket comb."[47]

After hearing the testimony, Justice Howe found that "Martin
Mrose came to his death by gunshot and pistol wounds inflicted by
J. D. Milton, George A. Scarborough and F. M. McMahan, while
resisting arrest under a warrant for his arrest as a fugitive from justice
from New Mexico" and that said wounds were inflicted by those
named "acting as peace officers in the lawful discharge of their
duty."[48] Howe bound them over for action by the grand jury and
released them on bond of five hundred dollars each.

That Sunday a *Herald* reporter called on Beulah Mroz, who, "after
considerable persuasion," made a statement:

> Before Mrose was arrested at Midland, Texas, we divided what
> money I had. I took two thousand dollars and he took a check for
> twenty- five hundred dollars. He succeeded in getting away from the
> officers at Midland and skipped to Mexico. I arrived in Juarez in the
> latter part of March with two thousand-eighteen dollars. The first I
> heard of Mrose in Mexico was at Magdalena and I went there to see
> him.
>
> We were both arrested there and put in jail, [and] all my money
> and jewelry was taken from me. . . . I was released next day, but
> [the] authorities refused to give up my money or jewelry. I came over
> to this side of the river and secured counsel and after several days,
> through the assistance of my attorney and the American consul, my
> money was restored in part.
>
> While Mrose was in jail in Juarez I spent considerable money in
> trying to keep him from being extradicted. In fact the strain on my
> purse was so heavy that I thought I would be left penniless. The
> money I was spending all belonged to me, while Mrose had a check
> in his pocket for twenty-five hundred dollars, of which he was not
> using one cent. His friends also became a burden on my hands and
> fearing that I would be left penniless and having a child of my own
> to raise, I told Mrose that I would have to stop spending so much
> money and that he would have to use some of his own money.
>
> This enraged him and he threatened and abused me. His friends
> also abused me. When this occurred I notified Mrose that I could

stand it no longer and told him I was going to quit him. I then moved to this side of the river. The authorities at the jail also became so insulting that I could not visit him without being insulted.

I spent twelve hundred dollars of his own money trying to get him out of the trouble and felt that I had done my part in assisting him. After he was liberated he wrote me several letters for me to meet him, but I could not do so, knowing that if he came clear in this case he would soon be in other trouble.

The letter I received after he was killed was a request to meet him in a certain place in El Paso, but I did not get it until after he was dead. There was nothing more in the letter except in a private nature.

Beulah "felt badly about his sudden death, but could not blame the officers, as she felt sure there was no intention on their part to kill Mrose unless they had to."[49]

Martin Mroz did not remain long on undertaker Powell's cooling board at the Star Stables. Within sixteen hours after Mroz had gone down in a burst of gunfire by the light of the setting moon, his body had been examined by Dr. White, photographed for posterity, wagoned to Concordia Cemetery, and interred. No mourners appeared at the Star Stable and hack driver Billy Guiberson had to draft four young men off the streets to accompany him to the cemetery and help lay Martin Mroz to rest. At Concordia two figures stood quietly watching the burial: Mrs. Beulah Mroz and John Wesley Hardin.

News of the Mroz killing touched off a storm of controversy in El Paso and public opinion generally came down hard on the officers. There was no groundswell of sympathy for the outlaw Mroz, but something about the way Scarborough had enticed him over the bridge at night to meet death in a hail of gunfire ran counter to the people's sense of fairness. On Tuesday, July 2, the *Times* said the shooting "was the talk of the town Sunday and yesterday. Public opinion condemned the killing." In conversations with many people Sunday the writer had heard only one person—and that a peace officer—speak up in support of the action taken by the lawmen.[50] "In Juarez feeling ran high against the three officers. Many conservative people in El Paso declined to express an opinion, saying they were not willing to commend or censure the officers without having been present when the tragedy was enacted to see just how it happened." The officers, said the paper, "are taking public criticism very quietly.

They regret that the public should be so ready to criticize without fully understanding all the circumstances, but they say they are perfectly willing to wait until a thorough investigation vindicates them. The three have always been good and honest officers and feel that they can afford to await a full investigation."

In an editorial in the same edition, Juan Hart tried to remain objective:

> The officers who killed M'rose were either right or wrong. The Times admits that the present appearance of the affair is anything but complimentary to the officers. Yet, when the excitement is over and the testimony all in, the affair may appear in a totally different light.
> . . .
> The M'rose killing Saturday night is being severely criticized by a large number of the good people of El Paso. The officers who did the killing claim they did it in self defense, that they thought M'rose would surrender when he saw he could not escape, and as those officers are to be thoroughly investigated in the courts, the Times does not believe the press of the city should try their cause at the bar of maudlin sentimentality.[51]

Of course the rumor mill was churning around the clock. The *Times* had stated in its first story on Sunday, June 30, that while in Juárez "M'rose had made several threats that he would kill John Wesley Hardin, but said he was afraid to come to this side as the officers might get him." Based on this, it was easy for many to jump to the conclusion that Hardin, in the interest of self-preservation, must have somehow been involved in the elimination of Mroz, an idea that would be seized and expanded upon in the days to come.

Another rumor concerned the aborted designs of Mroz and his partner, Queen. Mroz had told Scarborough that he and two friends, presumably Queen and another, had planned to leave Juárez Saturday. On Sunday the talk in the Juárez saloons was "that M'rose and a party of his friends had arranged to leave Juarez Saturday night to go down the river some distance and then cross over to this side and hold up the G. H. & S. A. train."[52]

From his sanctuary across the river, Vic Queen added to the controversy with a calumnious letter to the *Times* attacking the officers, Scarborough in particular:

About six or eight days since George Scarborough began a systematic course of deception to inveigle Martin M'rose to going across the
river on the pretense of getting a division of the community money
that his wife had in her possession.
  Scarborough represented to M'rose that Mrs. M'Rose was willing
to divide the money, but was afraid to come into Mexico. He also
represented to M'rose that he had arranged a meeting between them
to take place in the middle of the railroad bridge. Mr. M'rose advised
with some friends on the subject and they one and all told him not to
trust Scarborough, but Scarborough had so worked on his confidence
that at the last moment he slipped away and kept his ill-fated appointment with his sacrificer. Scarborough represented to M'rose that his
wife had nearly fourteen hundred dollars of their money left and
[Scarborough] was willing to effect a settlement between them for
one half of whatever M'rose would receive from his wife, and in
consideration for said one half of his share of the funds Scarborough
was to arrange the settlement and see M'rose through safely and back
to Juarez from the middle of the bridge.

Queen then recounted a tale portraying the officers in the worst
possible light. "After I missed M'rose," he said, "I started to hunt
him up. I went to the Santa Fe bridge, then toward the railroad
bridge, just as the shooting began. Two men came running over the
railroad bridge. I stopped them and asked who was shooting; they
were afraid to talk to me." Later that night, after he heard that Mroz
had been shot, Queen said he crossed the river and attempted,
unsuccessfully, to see his friend. On his way back to Juárez he
encountered the same two men, Mexican smugglers, who had run
over the bridge previously. They were returning to Mexico again,
this time carrying sacks. Queen said he accompanied these men to
a house, where they told him what they had seen at the time of the
shooting.
  "We were talking over a few things to make a little money,"
Queen quoted one of the smugglers as saying.

When we were going up the track in the shade of the dump we saw
some men coming, and laid down in some weeds so they might pass,
but they stopped and talked for awhile, and then one of them, a tall,
slim man, went towards the bridge.
  In about half an hour he returned, followed by a big, heavyset man
who was walking five or six steps behind. When the first man got past

the two who were hiding he coughed . . . and one of them that was crouching down shot twice at the big man. He staggered and fell; at that moment the man in front that went to the bridge, turned and ran back and as the big man tried to rise the tall man fired a shot into his breast. The big man fell back but sprang to his feet like a cat and pulled his gun. Then the fat man with the long gun let fly and the other two at the same time began firing; then the big man fell but kept trying to get up; then one of the men went toward the street car and another lighted some matches and found the dead man's pistol and took it and laid it close to his hand on the ground. Then the man that was shot tried to rise again and the fat man put his foot on him and held him down 'till he died. The two men that were left were talking very fast, but there was not a word said by anyone until after the shooting. By this time there was a man coming with a light and we dragged our sacks away about one hundred yards and hid them and then crossed the bridge back into Mexico and in about two hours went back for our sacks and brought them back to Mexico.

"Now," said Queen, "I propose to see what can be done among our friends to protect those two men against being sent to jail for smuggling, and if this can be done then they will be witnesses for the prosecution of these high handed murderers in the guise of government officers."[53]

Because of a series of continuances, it would be almost two years before Scarborough, Milton, and McMahan would come to trial for the killing of Martin Mroz. During that time Vic Queen's Mexican smugglers were never produced. With nothing to substantiate their story or even their existence other than the heated mind and acid pen of wanted fugitive Victor Queen, little credence can be given to this tale.

*I made a talk . . . that I had hired Scarborough to kill M'rose.
. . . The statement was absolutely false . . . super induced by
drink and frenzy.*

—JOHN WESLEY HARDIN, AUGUST 10, 1895

-8-

Drink and Frenzy

As the Martin Mroz affair was building to its sanguinary climax, John Wesley Hardin was also keeping El Paso astir with his unpredictable antics, all of them edged with potential explosive violence.

Jeff Milton stepped down as chief of police on May 1, and that evening the city's professional gamblers, jubilant at the loosening of municipal restraint, opened their games. However, having rid themselves of the pesky Chief Milton, they now found they faced a new kind of problem in the person of Wes Hardin. On the very first night gambling resumed, Hardin flashed his famous gun and held up a crap game.

The next day the *Times* chose to tell the story in a tongue-in-cheek fashion without identifying Hardin. El Paso "Has Lost Her Nerve" and "Is No Longer Bad Medicine" read the headline.

> Last night a quiet game was opened in the Gem Building and the game was moving smoothly when a visitor to the city dropped into the game and commenced losing and was behind a nice little sum when a dispute arose between the dealer and the stranger [who said] 'Since you are trying to be so cute, just hand over the money I have lost here,' [and] placed the muzzle of a ferocious looking pistol in the dealer's face. . . . The dealer winked his other eye at the muzzle of the savage looking gun and . . . proceeded to count out the money. When he had counted $95 the stranger raked it into his pocket and strolled leisurely out of the room.

Groaned a witness:

> El Paso has lost her nerve and she can't play tough any more. Two years ago no man on earth could have walked into a house in this city

113

and held up a game in that style and got out of the house alive. No sir, El Paso is no good any more. She is cornered, and I wouldn't at all be surprised to see the stranger hold up the entire police force.[1]

The following day the paper identified the stranger, noting that "the all-absorbing topic of conversation on the streets was . . . the 'hold up' of the crap game the night before by John Wesley Hardin."[2] Later a similar scene was enacted at the Acme Saloon when Hardin, showing neither winning cards nor artillery, scooped up a large poker pot and brazenly walked out.

Publication of these indiscretions prompted a letter from Hardin which exemplifies the man's peculiar, outsized sense of honor and manhood. "To the people of El Paso and to everyone to whom it may concern," he began,

> I have noticed several articles in the *Times* and *Tribune* reflecting on my character as a man. I wish to announce right now that in the past my only ambition has been to be a man and you bet I draw my own idea, and while I have not always come up to my standard, yet I have no kick to make against myself for default. My present and my future ambition is no higher than it has been in the past and I wish to say right now that whether in a gambling house or a saloon, and El Paso seems to be crowded with these places, my own aim is to acquit myself manly and bravely. And as to the Acme jackpot, I would not stand a hold out and got the pot without ever threatening violence or drawing a gun. As to the Gem hold-up on craps, after I had lost a considerable sum, I was grossly insulted by the dealer in a hurrah manner, hence I told him he could not win my money and hurrah me too and that as he had undertook to hurrah me he could deliver me the money I had played and you bet he did it. And when he had counted out the $95 I said that is all I want, just my money and no more. He said all right, Mr. Hardin, and when I left the room and had gotten half way downstairs I returned, hearing words of condemnation of my play. I said to everyone in the house and connected with the play, I understand from the reflective remarks that some of you disapprove of my play. Now some one has asked for my pedigree. Well, he is too gross to notice, but I wish to say right here, once and for all, that I admire pluck, push and virtue wherever found. Yet I contempt and despise a coward and assassin of character whether he is a reporter, a journalist or a gambler. And while I came to El Paso to prosecute Bud Frazer and did do it on as high a plane as possible, I am here now to stay.[3]

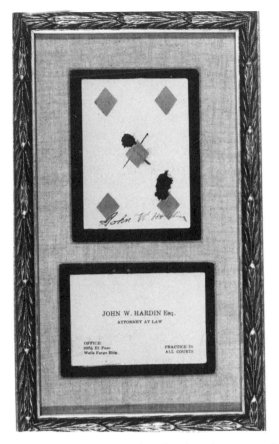

Hardin's business card and a signed target card
said to have been shot at five paces by Hardin
with his Colt double-action .41-caliber Thun-
derer. *Courtesy Jemison Beshears Collection.*

As proof that he meant to remain in El Paso, Hardin announced
that he had purchased a half-interest in the Wigwam Saloon, a
popular resort in the center of the city's commercial district.[4] Hardin's gambling and investment funds were being drawn from the
Mroz bankroll held by Beulah; small wonder that across the river
Mroz gnashed his teeth.

On May 6, Hardin was arrested on a gun-carrying charge stemming

from the Gem Saloon incident.[5] Released on a one-hundred-dollar
bond, he was indicted by the grand jury three days later for robbery.
"Sheriff Simmons served the warrant . . . on Mr. Hardin in his
saloon and all the astute gentleman said when he read the paper was,
'Well, I swear!' Then he went out with the officer and rustled up Ed
Bridges and E. J. Symes who went his bonds in fifteen hundred
dollars. Mr. Hardin thinks that some people in this world have
considerable nerve."[6] In county court on May 16, Hardin was found
guilty and fined twenty-five dollars.[7]

Hardin's notoriety as Texas's premier gunfighter led to a bizarre
episode in the Wigwam a week later. Charles C. Perry—deputy U.S.
marshal, sheriff of Chaves County, New Mexico Territory, and a
well-regarded lawman at the peak of his fame, having recently
assisted in the capture of the celebrated outlaw Bill Cook—came to

Charles Perry came to El Paso gunning for Hardin. *Courtesy Larry Ball.*

El Paso for the express purpose, he said, of shooting it out with Hardin. Dee Harkey, who innocently accompanied Perry on this trip, characterized him as a "shooting sheriff [who] had a mania to kill people that posed as bad men and killers."[8]

Well fortified with red-eye, Perry entered the Wigwam the evening of May 23 looking for Hardin. George Gladden informed the visitor that Hardin was out but that he was a friend of Hardin's and asked if he could be of help. Perry, primed for combat and reasoning through an alcoholic haze that if Hardin was not available a friend of Hardin's would have to do, retorted: "Mr. Hardin has sought an introduction to me on several occasions, and I want nothing to do with him or you, for you and Hardin have murdered my friends."

"I desire no row. I am unarmed," said Gladden quickly.

Producing two revolvers, Perry placed them on the bar. "Here are two pistols," he said. "Take your choice." He stepped back, gripping the butt of yet another six-gun.

Gladden refused to accept the challenge and Perry struck him twice in the face and cursed him for a coward. Warning that he would return to the Wigwam at nine o'clock the next morning and if Gladden were a man he would be armed and there to meet him, Perry took his leave.

When Hardin returned and learned of the visit of the pugnacious Perry, he reacted for once like the responsible businessman he was trying to become and had Perry arrested on charges of carrying a gun, rudely displaying a pistol, threatening to take life, and assault and battery.[9] The next morning, instead of confronting Gladden or Hardin in the Wigwam, a chastened Perry was standing at the bar of Judge Harvey's court, where he entered a plea of guilty to two of the charges and was fined five dollars on each.[10]

In the light of events less than two months in the future, the remarks of an unidentified observer regarding this unconsummated gunfight are interesting. "[Perry] tanked up on whiskey and allowed John Selman to persuade him to go to the Wigwam after Hardin," this informant was quoted as saying. "When Perry called for Hardin at the bar that morning John Selman was standing on the stairs with his gun in his hand. After taking a nap Perry realized that he had run a big risk, so he sent word to Hardin that he would be around to apologize in a few minutes; and I heard him make the apology."[11]

This incident took place more than a month before the death of
Martin Mroz, and the significance of the story, if true, is that Selman
was plotting to murder Hardin before Mroz was killed, which does
much to explode a theory later floated to explain the Hardin assassination.

In the days that followed, Hardin slid deeper into dissipation and
paranoia. His landlady at the Herndon House, Mrs. Annie Williams,
interviewed shortly after his death, has provided an intimate description of him in his last days.

It is difficult to describe how Mr. Hardin's presence influenced me.
I did not hesitate to talk saucy to him when he got drunk and damaged
my furniture, and yet I know I feared him, for I would feel my very
bones chill when he looked at me with his darting little serpentine
eyes. He would bring his whiskey up here by the gallon and I could
hear him at all hours of the day and night stirring his toddy. But I
never did see him staggering drunk and could only tell he was drunk
by his extreme politeness and the peculiar snake-like glitter of his
eyes. . . .

He frequently talked to me about his book—the history of his life
he was writing. One day I walked in and asked: "What are you doing
now, telling how you killed a man or stole a horse?" He replied that
he was stealing a horse just then. He commenced talking about his
history and said he had just one more man to kill. He said that there
was living near here a man who had assisted in lynching his brother
at Comanche and that he had intended to go to that man's house, call
him to the door and kill him and no one would ever know who did
it.[12] He said that hereafter he intended to do his work on the sly, as
other people did. He declared to me that he had no confidence in
human nature; that the human heart was rotten and that everything
living was deceitful and he made me shudder when he said, "I would
not trust my own mother but watch her just as I watch everybody
else."

. . . Hardin would walk the hall for hours at night with a pistol in
his hand. I think he was crazy with fear, for no matter who knocked
at his door he would spring behind a table where a pistol was lying
before he ever said "come in," and he never allowed a living soul to
enter his room while he was sitting down.

. . . Mr. Hardin was certainly a quick man with his guns. I have
seen him unload his guns, put them in his pocket, walk across the
room, and then suddenly spring to one side, facing around and, quick
as a flash, he would have a gun in each hand clicking so fast that the

clicks sounded like a rattle machine. He would place his guns inside
his breeches in front with the muzzles out. Then he would jerk them
out by the muzzle and with a toss as quick as lightning grasp them by
the handle and have them clicking in unison. He showed me how he
once killed two men in that way. They demanded his guns and he
extended them, one in each hand, he holding the muzzle as if to
surrender, and when the men reached for the guns he tossed the pistols
over, catching the handles, and killed both men while their hands
were yet extended for the weapons. Oh, he was a wonderful man. He
practiced with guns daily, and I liked to see him handle them when
they were empty.[13]

Late in June, Hardin sold his interest in the Wigwam to "devote
himself to the task of writing his own biography," which would "no
doubt be an interesting book," noted the *Times*.[14] Out of the saloon
business, he had completely reformed, reported the *Herald:* "John
Wesley Hardin . . . says he has quit drinking and gambling and will
apply himself to the practice of law and to writing a history of his
life. Mr. Hardin is to be congratulated on this righteous resolve."[15]
But the very next day the paper reported that Hardin was fined ten
dollars and costs in county court on a gambling charge.

On Tuesday, July 2, three days after the death of her husband,
Beulah Mroz became violently ill in her rooms at the Wellington
Hotel and a doctor was called in. A rumor raced through the streets
that she had taken poison in a suicide attempt and reporters rushed
to the scene. Beulah granted no interviews, but her physician assured
the press that there was no truth to the suicide story and that she was
all right, "though a little the worse because of her condition of mind,
the natural result of Saturday night's experiences."[16]

From across the river, Vic Queen pleaded with Beulah to meet
with him. Beulah had become even cosier with Hardin after the death
of her husband and soon moved in with him at his quarters in the
Herndon. This infuriated Queen, who felt that Hardin would get the
remainder of Mroz's bankroll from the woman and that he, as Mroz's
partner, had a better claim on that money. A letter Queen wrote to
Beulah during this period has survived:

> July the 30th, 1895. Juarez, Mez. Mrs. Bula Mrose. Dear friend I
> will write you a few lines. I want to see you on some Business and
> I dont want anyone else to no anything about it. I have bin trying to
> get to see you for some time but have faled. Now Bula if you will

A cabinet-card photograph of Beulah Mroz and
child, taken in Juárez. *Courtesy Jemison Beshears Collection.*

come over let me no at once it is for your own Benefit it will save
you a grate Deal of trouble over there and there ant anything against
you over here for if you can come over and see me Please do so at
once. Sa no more for this time. as ever your friend Victor Queen.[17]

It is not known whether Beulah responded to Queen's entreaty
and met with him, but something set her off just two days later. She
went on a monumental drunk and was arrested by young Selman.
The *Herald* found humor in the incident:

> Mrs. M'Rose . . . drank too much Texas rabbit's foot last night
> and became decidedly bellicose. At the hour of murky midnight this
> goddess of war camped on Officer Selman's trail in front of Charlie's
> Restaurant on San Antonio street where she made a few cursory
> remarks in the way of general compliment and then invited the officer
> to pull his gun or be made a target of. Selman noticed the glimmer of
> a gun in madame's parasol and straightaway made a dive for the same.
> She was not quick enough and he got it away from her. Then she riz

right up in her wrath and turned her vocal batteries loose on the
officer's head until the air was of something more than a cerulean hue
and the paint scaled off the neighboring woodwork. Mrs. M'Rose
was locked up but is out on bond today. She will appear this evening
to the recorder on the charge of carrying a gun.[18]

John, Jr., designated the beautiful Beulah as "the queen" in his
account of the arrest, written almost forty years later:

> The queen went on a big spree and wound up down on San Antonio
> street in Billie Ritchie's restaurant. There she made a gun play. I was
> passing at the time and saw her through the large glass windows.
> Billie was standing facing the street with his hands up. The queen
> was holding a pair of guns on him. The door was open so I walked
> in very quietly and, stepping up behind her, I encircled her with my
> arms and squeezed her so hard she dropped the guns on the floor.
> They were a beautiful pair of matched forty-one pearl handled Colts.
> I took her to jail and had the jailor hold her in the office for a couple
> of hours and then release her on a cash bond.[19]

In court a sober Beulah apologized to everyone, particularly Officer
Selman, and paid a fifty-dollar fine. Hardin, on one of his frequent
trips out of town in search of a publisher for his nearly completed
autobiography, was absent when Beulah went on her binge and did
not return until August 3.[20] His drinking had not diminished despite
his professed reform, and his drunken arguments with Beulah made
life miserable for Mrs. Williams at the Herndon. Hardin was angered
by young John's arrest of Beulah and was particularly irate because
she had apologized to him. Mrs. Williams said she never heard him
speak ill of old John, "but he hated young John Selman and Officer
Chaudoin and frequently abused them to Mrs. M'Rose. I tell you
those two, Mr. Hardin and Mrs. M'Rose, made life a burden for me
and I tried in every way to get them out of the house before they
finally left."[21]

On Monday, August 5, Hardin tanked up at one of his watering
holes and made some enigmatic remarks about George Scarborough
which caught the ear of a *Times* reporter. "Hardin . . . expressed
himself as not pleased with Officer Scarborough and intimated that
he would tell something about the killing of M'rose." Scarborough
heard the loose talk and the following morning chased Hardin down
and demanded to know what was meant by the remarks. Hardin,

somewhat more sober, "explained the matter to Mr. Scarborough and apologized for any harsh language he might have used."[22]

His overdeveloped self-esteem bruised by the meeting with Scarborough, Hardin went home and started a violent row with Beulah; it culminated in his arrest. Said Mrs. Williams:

> Mrs. M'Rose carried a gun also in some kind of a stationary pocket in the folds of her dress and I tell you she could pull it out in a hurry. The night I had Hardin arrested, I went into the room where they were quarrelling and she drew a gun on him, but I grabbed it and told her for God's sake not to have a killing in my house. Hardin would have shot her then and there but his pistol was on the table across the room and I believe he feared to attempt to reach it.
>
> Mrs. M'Rose then followed me out to my back steps and said: "Mrs. Williams, I hate to do it in your house, but I must kill that man tonight or he will kill me." I told her if she did not mind he would kill her whenever she attempted to shoot him. She said she would wait until he went to sleep and then put her pistol to his head and blow his brains out.
>
> He told me that night in her presence that he intended to kill her. Then she handed me a letter and he snatched it out of my hands. She said right there in front of him: "Mrs. Williams, that letter is one he forced me to write, saying that I had committed suicide. He wanted the letter found on me after he had killed me." I was so completely put out that I just told them to please get out of my house to kill each other.[23]

Beulah finally fled the Herndon and ran screaming through the offices of the *El Paso Tribune* below. Editor Lowe of that paper,

> an admirer of sensational drama in its proper place, but not caring to have his office transformed into a stage for blood curdling theatricals, . . . warned the lady to skip out into the alley. . . . In the meantime the landlady and lodgers of the Herndon house had quit the building without waiting on the order of their going, and were hunting hiding places. They created quite a commotion on Overland street.[24]

Annie Williams and Beulah swore out a warrant for Hardin's arrest. It was served in the Acme Saloon by Frank Carr and the two officers Hardin had been railing against, Chaudoin and young Selman. Hardin went along without trouble and the next day posted a peace bond of one hundred dollars.[25]

To all who knew him it was obvious that whiskey and terrors of the mind were tearing the formerly steel-nerved Hardin apart. The city waited for the pent-up violence within him to explode or for someone to kill him before that happened. It appeared to many during this torrid week in August that when the long-awaiting blowup finally came, Hardin would tangle with either George Scarborough or Jeff Milton. It was an eventful and tension-packed week that Hardin negotiated in his alcoholic haze. On Saturday, August 3, he had arrived back in town after his trip and had learned about Beulah's arrest two nights previously. This triggered an angry binge that built to full steam through the weekend and led to Hardin's cryptic remark about Scarborough on Monday. On Tuesday he made his apologies to Scarborough and then went home, had his house-emptying clash with Beulah, and was arrested. On Wednesday he posted his peace bond, and on Thursday he was back in recorder's court on the gun-carrying charge he had been fighting since May. On Friday he was confronted by Jeff Milton. Hardin's mouth was running again; he had bragged in the saloons that he had hired Milton and Scarborough to lure Mroz across the river and kill him so that he, Hardin, "could get his woman." Said the *Herald:*

> John Wesley Hardin . . . and a well-known officer had a rather stalwart interview last night on account of the former's having made a remark about the officer which he did not then care to father. The result has been what the Leadville papers back in the "good old days" would have said "trouble was feared" and citizens who are posted have been looking for a little impromptu target practice.[26]

Milton had braced Hardin on El Paso Street. Will Burges said he witnessed the encounter and his recitation of the Milton-Hardin exchange sounds like dialogue from a Grade B Hollywood oater:

> "Hardin," Jeff said, getting right to the point, "I hear you've been telling around town that you hired me to kill Martin M'Rose."
> "Well, what of it?" asked Hardin in an imperious tone.
> "I want you to tell these gentlemen here that when you said that you were a goddamn liar."
> Hardin looked into Milton's angry black eyes and hesitated. "Go on, Milton, I don't want to have any trouble with you. And besides, I am unarmed," he said.
> "That's a damn lie. You never go out without your gun," said Milton. "Hardin, I mean what I say. You tell these gentlemen that

you were a damn liar when you said you hired me to kill Martin
M'Rose, or I'm going to count three and when I get to three, you'd
better starting shooting, because I'm going for my gun."
    Milton started counting.
    "All right," growled Hardin. "When I said I hired you to kill Martin
M'Rose, I was a goddamn liar."[27]

For his part, George Scarborough was determined this time to put
at rest Hardin's not-so-subtle insinuations that had set off a new
wave of ugly rumor and vicious gossip regarding the Mroz affair. A
personal retraction and apology was not enough; all El Paso had to
know that Hardin had lied. On Saturday morning he collared Hardin
and marched him to the offices of the *Times* where he ordered him
to write and sign a retraction. It appeared the following day:

> Yesterday morning John Wesley Hardin accompanied by United
> States Marshal Scarborough, called at the *Times* office, where Mr.
> Hardin wrote the following card for publication: "To the public: I
> have been informed that on the night of the 6th while under the
> influence of liquor, I made a talk against George Scarborough, stating
> that I had hired Scarborough to kill M'rose. I do not recollect making
> any such statement and if I did the statement was absolutely false and
> it was superinduced by drink and frenzy. John W. Hardin." The above
> card is published at the request of Mr. Scarborough for whom it was
> written.[28]

Spurned by his paramour, evicted from his lodgings, chagrined
by his shameful behavior during the week, and humiliated by Scarborough, Hardin beat a hasty retreat from El Paso that same day. He
told people he was going to San Antonio but instead went over to
Juárez and huddled with Vic Queen, perhaps seeking solace by
communing with another pariah. He came back briefly Monday "to
get his grip fixed" and then returned to Juárez, reportedly to form a
partnership with Vic Queen and open a saloon.[29]
    Perhaps not coincidentally, the *Herald* that same day included a
long story concerning the simmering dispute between the remnants
of the Mroz crowd, "a gang of renegade Americans," in Juárez and
certain El Paso law officers:

> There is serious trouble brewing in El Paso and Juarez of which
> few people know anything. . . . Ever since the killing of Martin

M'Rose there has existed a bitter feeling between the friends and chums of M'Rose and the officers who killed M'Rose. The officers knew of this bitter feeling, but have continued . . . going over to Juarez when their business called them or when they felt inclined. . . . They have been told by different parties to be on the lookout, and at the same time parties . . . have spoken to friends of M'Rose and told them they had better not make trouble, as it would eventually result in them getting the worst of it. Vic Queen has been warned that it would be best for him to leave Juarez. Vic is not a mean man, although outlawed from this country, and, while he is strong-headed . . . he would leave Juarez if it was not for the gang of hangers-on who are always around him and keep continually urging him on to get revenge for the killing of [Mroz]. . . . These same friends . . . are his worst enemies [and] have worked upon him until now he is in a frenzy. . . .

This morning an officer went over the river and . . . as he dismounted from his horse a party stepped up and warned him to be on the lookout as several of M'Rose's friends were in town . . . and had been talking very strongly of revenge for the killing of M'Rose. The officer was in no way connected with the killing, but being a friend of the officers who did the killing, he was one of the parties on whom revenge was intended to be taken. The officer returned to this side and reported the matter to his friends. This state of affairs will ultimately result in someone being killed as all the parties are high-strung and fearless and should they meet a shooting scrape is sure to occur.[30]

Queen immediately fired off a letter to the *Herald* denying that his friends had urged him to stay in Juárez or seek revenge. As for being outlawed from the United States, he pointed out that a man was entitled to a trial before a jury of his peers, which he had not been afforded, and promised to "clear all this matter up in due time." He did not know who was referred to as "renegades" but said he did "not wish to associate with such," adding sarcastically, "As for the three officers of El Paso coming over the Juarez, I for my part cannot see why such bold, brave men should not come over. He took a final jab at those who seemed bent on whipping up a fight between the factions: "It seems to be their delight to keep up the agitation. If this . . . suits them I shall not attempt to moderate it for them. I shall keep right on attending to my old affairs and abide by the laws of this country, regardless of their actions or taunts."[31]

A few days later one of Queen's supporters, a man named W. H.

Orr, wrote from Juárez, extolling the virtues of the fugitive and condemning his enemies. Said Orr:

> I am in a position to know that Mr. Queen is a far superior man than those officers who are constantly trying to drive him to acts of violence. . . . Readers, place yourself in his position—hounded by a certain class of human wolves who are unscrupulous enough to deal him the same fate that Martin M'Rose fell a victim; living away from his native land, having left behind all that is dear to him and trying to make a start and then have the former of public opinion—the press—lend their aid to the officers to further crush a man who is endeavoring in every way to live the life of a gentleman and an honorable man."[32]

Beulah, who was now being referred to at times in the public print as Mrs. John Wesley Hardin, evidently had a surfeit of the sordid El Paso intrigue and on the fourteenth boarded a westbound train "to grow up with the country," said the *Times*. With a prescient sense of impending tragedy, she wired Hardin from Deming, New Mexico Territory: "I feel you are in trouble and I'm coming back." She returned briefly but left again later in the week.[33]

A new sensation temporarily freed Scarborough from the dangerous miasma of name calling and finger pointing in El Paso and Juárez and its potential for sudden violence. On August 16, two masked bandits held up the Keesey & Co. store at Valentine in Presidio County and got away with seven hundred dollars in cash, killing a local officer named Dick Ellsberry in an ensuing gun battle. Scarborough hopped a train to Valentine and joined Captain Hughes and a force of rangers in a search for the robbers.

The rumors and accusations swirling around El Paso extended all the way to the lawmen in the field more than a hundred miles away; word was received that one of the bandits they were tracking might be none other than Vic Queen. "People in El Paso believe that Victor Queen is one of the masked men who killed Ellsberry," said the *Times* on August 18. "Queen is not in Juarez and it is reported that he and M'rose had planned to start on just such an expedition the night M'rose was killed. Friends of Queen, in Juarez, say that he is in Chihuahua . . . but notwithstanding this testimony, officers in El

Paso believe that Queen could tell all about the robbery and murder at Valentine.[34]

The El Paso situation was a prime conversational topic for the officers as they combed the hills for the Valentine bandits. To his biographer, Captain Hughes related a discussion he had with another officer on August 19. "They say Wes Hardin is cutting capers in El Paso," this lawman remarked to Hughes. "What's going to happen, Captain?"

"Why, someone will kill him," replied Hughes.

"Who?"

"See that man in the blue britches over there?" said the ranger. "He might do it."

The man in the blue breeches was George Scarborough.

Early on the morning of Tuesday, August 20, Hughes and Scarborough left their posse and boarded a westbound train. The captain had business at his Ysleta headquarters, and Scarborough would continue on to El Paso. Both officers frequently rode this line and the conductor knew them well.

"Have you heard the news in El Paso?" he asked as he checked their passes.

"What news?"

"Why, Wes Hardin was killed."

"Who did it?" Scarborough asked.

"John Selman."

Scarborough nodded, unsurprised. "I'll bet he shot him in the back," he said.[35]

Scarborough was in town only a few hours before heading east again, but he was able to learn the details of the Hardin shooting and to confirm that his guess was correct. According to the story Selman was telling, Hardin's displeasure over the arrest of Beulah by John Selman, Jr., almost three weeks earlier was the cause of the shooting. "I met Wes Hardin about 7 o'clock last evening close to the Acme saloon," old John said in a statement before Justice W. D. Howe. "When we met, Hardin said, 'You've got a son that is a bastardly, cowardly son of a bitch.'

"I said: 'Which one?'

"Hardin said: 'John, the one that is on the police force. He pulled my woman when I was absent and robbed her of $50, which they would have not have done if I had been there.'

"I said: 'Hardin, there is no man on earth that can talk about my children like that without fighting, you cowardly son of a bitch.'

"Hardin said: 'I am unarmed.'

"I said: 'Go and get your gun. I am armed.'

"Then he said, 'I'll go and get a gun and when I meet you I'll meet you smoking and make you shit like a wolf around a block.' "

Hardin then went into the Acme and Selman remained outside, where he spoke with his son John and Frank Carr of the city police, informing them that he expected trouble with Hardin but wanted them to stay out of it. "It was," he said, a personal matter between Hardin and myself. Hardin had insulted me personally."

He was sitting on a beer keg outside the Acme when E. L. Shackelford came by about eleven o'clock and insisted that Selman go in and have a drink with him. Said Selman:

> Hardin and [Henry S.] Brown were shaking dice at the end of the bar next to the door. While we were drinking I noticed that Hardin watched me very closely as we went in. When he thought my eye was off him he made a break for his gun in his hip pocket and I immediately pulled my gun and began shooting. I shot him in the head first as I had been informed that he wore a steel breast plate. As I was about to shoot the second time some one ran against me and I think I missed him, but the other two shots were at his body and I think I hit him both times. . . . I am willing to stand any investigation over the matter. I am sorry I had to kill Hardin, but he had threatened mine and my son's life several times and I felt that it had come to the point where either I or he had to die.

Selman neglected to mention that he and Shackelford had left the saloon after taking their drink and then reentered. Testimony of witnesses Frank Patterson, E. L. Shackelford, and R. B. Stevens agreed on this point. Hardin, shaking dice at the bar, had his back to the doorway. Brown, who was closest to him, said, "When the shot was fired Mr. Hardin was against the bar, facing it, as near as I can say, and his back was towards the direction the shot came from."

After the shooting Captain Carr removed two .41-caliber Colt pistols from Hardin's body, one with a white handle and the other

Tools of the Mankillers. Top: Hardin was carrying this Smith & Wesson (SN 352) when he died. Bottom: Selman's Colt (SN 141,805) with which he dispatched Hardin. The notched handles obviously have been replaced. *Courtesy Jim Earle.*

with a black. The bullet that passed through Hardin's head struck the frame of a mirror and fell on the back bar. There were three bullet holes in a triangular pattern in the floor, showing where Selman had shot Hardin after he fell.

Doctors S. G. Sherard, W. N. Vilas, and Alward White examined the body and found that a bullet had entered the back of the head, coming out just over the left eye. There was another wound in the right breast, near the nipple, and another through the right arm. Their official report, signed by all three, certified "that the wound causing death was caused by a bullet; that the bullet entered near the base of the skull posteriorly and came out at the upper corner of the left eye."[36]

Justice Howe found "that on the 19th day of August, 1895, one John Selman of his malice aforethought . . . did shoot the deceased with a revolver, inflicting upon him, . . . about three inches behind the right ear, a gunshot wound, from the effects of which . . . deceased died."[37]

Hardin's body was taken to the Powell undertaking parlors for embalming. Powell reported that when he stripped the dead gunman, he found "his body covered with the scars of old wounds," including "two old gunshot wounds close together on the right side just above the hip bone; gunshot wound on inside of left thigh midway between the knee and groin, and a similar wound on inside of right thigh; gunshot wound on back of right elbow; large knife cut wound just below rib on left side; besides numerous small scars."[38]

Hundreds filed by the body to take a last look at a Texas legend before he was laid to rest in Concordia Cemetery, two graves removed from that of Martin Mroz. Two carriages and two buggies

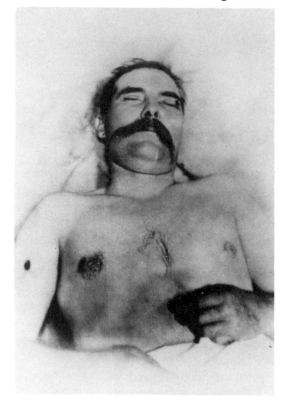

John Wesley Hardin after Selman finished with him. *Courtesy Western History Collections, University of Oklahoma Library.*

carrying friends followed the hearse to the cemetery, passing slowly by the quiet figure of John Selman, who stood on a street corner and watched the procession file by.[39]

"The people of El Paso breathed a sigh of relief" when they heard of Hardin's death, said the *Times*. "Some said it looked like murder, but all agreed that it was what they had been expecting." Most thought Selman "had done the proper thing in killing Hardin and taking no chances," while some admitted that Hardin's death was probably a good thing for El Paso but thought he should have been given a better chance. The paper had a one line editorial on the shooting: " 'Bad Men' have always found their equal."[40]

Selman was released on bond of one thousand dollars and caused a stir when he told reporters that to his "certain knowledge" Hardin and "a number of pals had planned to make a descent on the State National Bank with Winchesters and six-shooters and get out of the country with the plunder before the local authorities could attack them."[41] Oddly, the papers did not pursue Selman's charge that before his death Hardin was planning to turn to banditry, although it was commonly known that he had been meeting regularly with Vic Queen in Juárez and, as we have seen, the newsmen were quick to publish any rumor or allegation about Queen's felonious intentions.

A *Houston Post* article titled "Texas Bad Men," commenting on the passing of the notorious gunman and his brief history in El Paso, was later reprinted in the *Times:*

> With the passing of John Wesley Hardin Texas is left without a single "bad man" of National or even State wide reputation. The State has produced several of them, but the past few years have seen them exterminated. . . . It is true that there are quite a number of "killers" scattered over the State, but most of these have been content with a local reputation, based on one murder, and a few of them have risked the penitentiary by a second. A very few have reached three, but these are exceptional. . . . This sort of man generally dies with most of his clothes on.
>
> An El Paso man was in Dallas . . . and [said] the way John Wesley was carrying on, it would be a miracle if somebody did not put out his light within a month. This man said John Wesley had the town terrorized, did as he pleased, and was ready to shoot at the drop of a hat or anything else.

The people all wanted him killed, but every fellow was waiting for somebody else to do the killing. Nearly every barkeeper in town kept a sawed-off shotgun loaded with buckshot for John's benefit, but whenever John came in and swiped the glasses off the bar with his gun, the bartender would ask Colonel Hardin what was his pleasure.

John grew more reckless and overbearing the longer his liberty lasted. . . . Two weeks ago [he] publicly announced in El Paso his intention to go to Dallas during the fair next fall to take in the glove contest and to kill Jack Duncan.

The *Times* ran the article without refutative comment, so presumably the editors agreed with the views expressed.[42]

"The death of such a notorious character as Hardin will furnish a topic of conversation for some time to come," said the *Herald,* adding, with much prescience, that "some people are looking for another tragedy."[43]

When we first walked around there was the first time I suspicioned anything. He kept monkeying with his gun.

—GEORGE SCARBOROUGH, APRIL 5, 1896

-9-

"He Kept Monkeying with His Gun"

The citizenry of El Paso, partly repulsed but very excited about the deadly drama unfolding in their city, waited expectantly for another tragedy, but for the next few months the remaining actors in the El Paso melodrama provided rather mundane news.

Squabbling began over the few effects of the late Wes Hardin, particularly the almost completed manuscript of his life, which, with other property, had been turned over to Alderman J. L. Whitmore, husband of a Hardin second cousin.

Beulah, "widowed" twice in seven weeks, was in Phoenix, Arizona Territory, when Hardin was killed. She started back as soon as she got the news. According to the *Phoenix Republican,* while in Arizona she had represented herself as Hardin's wife: Mrs. John Wesley Hardin of El Paso, who had been in Phoenix several days visiting her parents, left last night for her home. She had not heard from her husband since her arrival and yesterday she telegraphed to him. She received a reply that her husband had died on Monday and was buried."[1]

Back in El Paso, Beulah said she wanted it understood that she sought no trouble and wanted only "to secure control of Hardin's manuscript to reimburse herself for money advanced."[2] Through her attorneys, Charlie Patterson and George E. Wallace, she filed suit in the district court for Hardin's autobiographical manuscript, his pocket watch, a revolver, and two rings. She estimated the total value of the property to be ten thousand dollars.[3] As proof of her claim she produced a paper that read: "El Paso, Texas, July 18, 1895. I, John Wesley Hardin, on this day take Mrs. Bula M'rose as

133

a full partner in my manuscript and all business also as a confidential correspondent clerk. (Signed) John W. Hardin. (Witness) Bula M'rose."

J. L. Whitmore had been appointed temporary administrator of Hardin's estate by Judge Hunter, and he kept possession of the property, saying he would turn it over to Hardin's son when he was located. On August 23, Chief of Police Fink had received a letter from Jefferson Davis Hardin, a brother of Wes who lived near Austin, inquiring about the dead man's property.[4] But apparently no family member came to El Paso until almost three months later, when another brother, Barnett Gipson Hardin, arrived to the accompaniment of war rumors in the Texas press. A Waco dispatch said:

> Young Gip Hardin, a brother of John Wesley Hardin, is en route to El Paso to secure the manuscript that Wesley Hardin wrote. . . . He says the manuscript rightly belongs to him and he will have it or have a fight.[5]

Commented the *San Antonio News:*

> Gip Hardin, younger brother of John Wesley Hardin, is going to El Paso to demand the manuscript left by the dead desperado or have a fight. Even money that he don't get the manuscript, ten to one he gets a fight if he seeks it, and twenty to one he loses the fight if he makes it.[6]

The *El Paso Times:*

> The thoughtless manner in which young Hardin fires off his lip would indicate a relationship to the late unlamented who, when he first came to El Paso, intimated that he was going to make the officers take to the brush. . . . If young Hardin is coming for a fight, it might be more healthy for him to keep 'er comin', but to never arrive. El Paso does not take kindly to fighters, unless they are built on the physical culture plan.[7]

However, Gip Hardin, when he arrived and stopped over with Alderman Whitmore, "emphatically denied" to a *Herald* reporter that he had come on anything but a peaceful mission, saying that the story that he had come to fight was a "fake." He had "no bloodthirsty inclinations whatever" and was in town "to secure through legal means the possession of the biographical ms. left by his brother."[8]

The following February, Beulah's suit for Hardin's effects was dismissed in district court and the woman who had been central to the entirely sanguinary intrigue disappeared from El Paso and the pages of history.[9]

The family took possession of the property and later that year the book was published by Smith and Moore, a small country press in the town of Seguin, Guadalupe County, Texas. Paperbound and printed on cheap paper, it sold for fifty cents, was peddled in train depots throughout the state, and did much to keep alive the Hardin legend.[10]

Little was heard of Vic Queen after the erroneous reports of his involvement in the Valentine robbery and murder in August. He still maintained residency in Mexico. Late in the year the *Herald* noted that he had gone to work for the Corralitos Company. "As far as can be ascertained," said the paper, "[he] is attending strictly to his own business."[11] A month later he got into a little altercation, however: "Vic Queen 'threw down' on a man over in Juarez the other day, but did not fire. It is said he was fined $15 for his little theatrical demonstration."[12]

Tired of life as a fugitive, Queen rode back to Eddy in January 1896. "Vic Queen . . . came in yesterday and offered to give up to the authorities," said the *Eddy Current* of January 30th. "Vic says he left Juarez . . . and rode across the country to Eddy for the purpose of forever silencing all charges against his character by giving up, standing trial and demonstrating his innocence. He says many of the loudmouthed officials around El Paso were very severe in their denunciations of him, and that now they can have an opportunity to prove their allegations."

Queen was ready to face the music but found that lawmen were not playing his song anymore. "Victor Queen, who went up to Eddy and surrendered to the sheriff, [learned] there was no warrant there for his arrest," noted the *El Paso Herald*. "[He] crossed the river below here, giving El Paso the go-by. There was no reason why he should do so as there was no Texas charge against him and no warrant here."[13] The following April an Eddy County grand jury failed to bring an indictment against him. "Vic, who is now free from all charges, will engage in business in the county and settle down," said the *Eddy Current* of April 16.

Queen engaged in various cattle-raising and mining occupations for the next eight years and appeared to have put his outlaw period behind him. Late in 1904 he was employed by the Burro Mountain Copper Company of Grant County, New Mexico Territory. At three o'clock on the morning of December 13 he was in the small mining town of Central, near Silver City, together with D. A. Turner, a company guard and former deputy sheriff. Turner, who previously had a disagreement with Central saloon owner James Wiley and his friend E. E. Freeman, had enlisted Queen's aid to resolve the matter. A gun battle erupted in which Turner suffered a minor wound, but Vic Queen was killed. Violent death thus claimed another of the participants in the El Paso drama.[14]

Sunday, September 1, 1895, was the occasion for a happy event in the home of George Scarborough. Frank McMahan and "Miss Alice Hunter of Fort Mason, a charming and most estimable young lady," were joined in marriage at the Scarborough residence on that day by the Reverend L. R. Millican, pastor of the First Baptist Church of El Paso. Only a few close friends and George's family attended. "The groom has an excellent reputation in this country where he is well known as a faithful and reliable officer," said the *Herald*, "and this young couple have the best wishes of a large number of friends."[15] McMahan and his bride set up housekeeping in Valentine, where he had been assigned to take over the duties of federal deputy marshal in the district that had once been the domain of Baz Outlaw.

When Jeff Milton left town to take a job as a Wells Fargo messenger on a rail run from Benson, Arizona Territory, to Guaymas, on the west coast of Mexico, the only principals remaining on the El Paso scene were George Scarborough and the John Selmans, father and son.

In September 1895, Scarborough had a run-in with Chief of Police Ed Fink that was reminiscent of his confrontation with Wes Hardin a month before. Fink had been making remarks around town about Scarborough that George found offensive and he braced Fink on the street and made "war talk . . . , throwing at him language that fairly scorched the atmosphere." Fink walked off, muttering something about having Scarborough arrested. George then hunted up Officer Chipman and requested arrest so he could square off again with Fink in court. In police court the next day, September 6, he entered a plea of not guilty to charges of disturbing the peace. Chief Fink failed to appear to press the charges, however, and Scarborough's case was dismissed.[16]

Justice inched forward, meanwhile, in the Selman-Hardin murder case. In September 1895, Selman was indicted in the district court. Bond was set at five thousand dollars, which Selman secured on October 15.[17] A venire of one hundred candidates was exhausted without selecting a jury in November, and Judge C. N. Buckler ordered a continuance until the next term of court.[18] On February 5, 1896, the case was called and the state presented its evidence. Substantially the same as that given before W. D. Howe at the coroner's hearing, it seemed to show beyond doubt that Hardin was shot in the back of the head by Selman. The defense attorneys, led by A. B. Fall, introduced testimony that indicated Hardin had sensed Selman behind him or seen his reflection in the bar mirror and reached for his pistol before Selman fired. Other testimony questioned the doctors' findings that the fatal bullet entered the back of Hardin's head and argued that the condition of the wound over the eye was consistent only with bullet entry and not exit. Fall further confused the jury by suggesting that even if the shot had been in the back of the head, it had resulted from Selman's meeting Hardin's eyes in the mirror and Hardin's quick move toward a hip pocket. Selman had drawn and shot instinctively and still stuck doggedly to his story that Hardin was facing him because he was looking him in the eye when he fired.[19] Sufficient doubt was raised that the jurors could not reach agreement, and on February 12 they reported that they were hopelessly deadlocked. Judge Buckler dismissed the jury and rescheduled the case for the next term of court.[20]

That winter, El Paso was swept up in a different kind of excitement that temporarily pushed the sanguinary saga of its pistoleers into the background. When promoter Dan Stuart announced plans for a heavyweight title fight between champion Gentleman Jim Corbett and Australian challenger Ruby Bob Fitzsimmons, El Paso businessmen invited him to use their city as a site. These town boosters envisioned the title bout as the center piece of what they billed as a "Great Fistic Carnival" that would include other prizefights, baseball and football games, shooting contests and a rodeo, with bullfights staged just across the river in Juárez.

The city's religious leaders, led by Baptist minister L. R. Millican, protested what they viewed as a barbarous exhibition and were successful in rushing through the Texas state legislature a hastily conceived measure banning prizefighting within Texas's borders.[21] Other states had passed similar prohibitions, and promoter Stuart's options were few. He favored El Paso because of its isolation from the rest of the state and its proximity to two jurisdictional entities over which the antiprizefight forces currently had no control: the Territory of New Mexico and the sovereign nation of Mexico. Commented the *Herald:*

> Of course we want that scrapping match . . . and we want it very badly, [not] for the scientific display of the manly art itself, but . . . we want the samolians [*sic*] that the boys will bring with them. . . . Did it ever strike you in the noggin that El Paso, although she has more capacity in that line than any city of the same size in the country, will be jammed, crammed and crowded, if say 20,000 people would come here? Or cut the number in twain and make it 10,000. Why the town would be filled and people would fairly slop over . . . 10,000 people is within a couple of thousands of El Paso's normal population and we would have to put up tents, build castles in the air, and utilize the storeboxes, etc., etc. But if Mr. Stuart will bring his physical culture show along, we will try and demonstrate that the town is built on the India rubber plan and can stretch like a stick of molasses candy in a hot sun.[22]

The promoters suffered a temporary setback when Jim Corbett retired in November to seek a career on the stage. But Stuart, undaunted and with more enthusiasm than logic, proclaimed a pugilist named Peter Maher to be the new heavyweight champion and in December announced that a fight between Fitzsimmons and Maher for the title would be held somewhere near El Paso on Valentine's Day, February 14, 1896, for a purse of ten thousand dollars. The fighters would train in El Paso and all the hoopla and festivities connected with the Great Fistic Carnival could go forward as planned.

Millican and other embattled religious leaders took their case to Congress, where in three days legislation was passed prohibiting prizefighting (and bullfighting) in any of the United States territories, with prison sentences of one to five years prescribed for violators.[23]

State and federal lawmen poured into El Paso to see that the laws were upheld and no fistic contest took place on soil from which it had been banned. Texas Adjutant General W. H. Mabry arrived with all four ranger captains and enlisted men numbering almost forty, virtually the entire ranger enrollment, to protect the state from this threat.[24] U.S. Marshal Edward Hall of New Mexico Territory showed up with thirteen deputies.[25]

Sporting men from all over America inundated El Paso. Former heavyweight champion John L. Sullivan appeared, as did W. B. ("Bat") Masterson, celebrated frontiersman, law officer, gambler, and gunman, who was attaining a national reputation as a boxing authority. Also arriving were the usual underworld characters who flocked to extravaganzas such as this. "Never has any town been host to a finer collection of pugs, thugs, and assorted camp followers and hangers-on than was El Paso," said Owen P. White. "I watched them arrive and was proud and happy that the town in which I had been born was being so honored."[26]

The month of February was crammed with excitement for the

Texas Rangers massed in El Paso to prevent the Fitzsimmons-Maher prize-fight. In the front row are, left to right: Adjutant General W. H. Mabry and Capts. John R. Hughes, J. A. Brooks, Bill McDonald, and J. H. Rogers. *Courtesy El Paso Public Library.*

folks of El Paso. On the first it was learned that longtime fugitive
Vic Queen had gone back to Eddy to face the charges against him.
Three days later came the report of the disappearance and presumed
murder of former El Paso resident and frequent visitor Albert J.
Fountain and his small son in the White Sands region of southern
New Mexico Territory, a mystery that would fascinate the people of
the Southwest for years to come.[27] That same day, Bat Masterson,
looking "suave" and "younger than ever," arrived with a large contingent of Denver sports and announced that he had made arrangements
for a special train, equipped with Pullman and chair cars, to leave
Denver on the morning of February 12 and arrive in El Paso on the
afternoon of the thirteenth. It would bring fight fans from Helena,
Butte, Salt Lake City, Cheyenne, Denver, Colorado Springs, Cripple
Creek, Leadville, Aspen, Pueblo, Trinidad, Silverton, and Du-
rango.[28]

Court was in session in February and on the eighth of the month
the trial of John Selman for the killing of Wes Hardin began, competing with the Great Fistic Carnival for attention until the jury deadlock
on the twelfth. Scarcely noticed was the dismissal of Beulah Mroz's
suit for Hardin's property the same week.

In addition to the Texas Rangers and deputy U.S. marshals on
hand to prevent the prizefight, a passel of feuding gunmen from
Dona Ana County, New Mexico Territory, wearing an assortment
of municipal, county, territorial, and federal badges, were assembled
in El Paso to attend a meeting called by New Mexico Gov. Poker
Bill Thornton and U.S. Marshal Edward Hall, a session intended to
cool partisan tempers inflamed by the Fountain case. The city's news
editors became edgy with all the heavily armed and stern-faced
gunmen stalking the streets. "Disarm them all," advised the *Herald*
on the eighteenth, warning that "an outbreak is feared" and "the
Rangers may have to look after the New Mexico parties." Noting
that even Albert Fall, who had been in town to defend John Selman,
was seen boarding a train to Las Cruces carrying a rifle, the paper
pointed out that "there are not a few men who secure appointment
as deputy sheriffs merely to get protection in wearing arms so that
they may terrorize other bad men."[29] The *Times* agreed, saying that
"all the sensational gun plays have been made by visiting officials."[30]
A few days later Marshal Hall responded to the criticism by revoking

the deputy commissions of Joe Morgan, Oliver Lee, Tom Tucker, and James Baird. These "decapitated officials" had become involved in the Dona Ana County feud, said the *Herald,* "and it is not safe to let them carry arms or exercise official authority."[31]

On February 16, policeman John Selman, Jr., was assaulted by three Mexicans and severely stabbed.[32] This was but one incident in a rash of street crimes that month brought on by the huge influx of footpads, pickpockets, and petty hoodlums attracted by the big fight festival. On one day, February 13, Sergeant Sullivan of the Texas Rangers assisted a city policeman and a river guard in arresting twenty-seven burglars and pickpockets.[33] Sullivan told a *Herald* reporter that even the redoubtable Bat Masterson, enlisted by Dan Stuart as master of arms and head of a force of Pinkerton guards hired to maintain order at the fight scene, fell victim to the criminals, losing nine hundred dollars to one of the slick-fingered pickpockets.[34]

Stuart had been forced to cancel the minor fistic bouts and postpone his big title fight once because of the pressure applied by the officers. As late as February 17 it looked as if the Fitzsimmons-Maher match might have to be called off also, but on that day he received a telegram from Judge Roy Bean at Langtry, Texas, 375 miles down the Rio Grande. "Invite you to hold fight in Langtry," Bean said, "I am law west of Pecos and guarantee protection."[35]

On the evening of February 20 a special Southern Pacific train of thirteen cars left El Paso with Stuart, the combatants, and an entourage of sporting men and state and federal officers. The next afternoon the long-awaited fight was held in a hastily constructed ring on a sandy island in the Rio Grande, just over the Mexican line and some two miles from Langtry. While the ticket-paying sports watched at ringside, the officers, having done their duty in preventing the event on American soil, observed from the riverbank. What they saw took about a minute. After a few feints by each fighter, Fitzsimmons landed one solid punch, Maher went down, and it was all over. Fighters, sports, and lawmen reboarded the train and returned to El Paso. The great title fight had been a flop, but February 1896 was a month to remember for the folks of El Paso. They would never see its like again.

While all this was going on, George Scarborough was carrying out his duties as deputy marshal, taking no part in the bizarre struggle by the competing forces in El Paso to present or prevent the prizefight spectacular. His expense records for the month of February show that the day of the fight he also headed southwest by train but rode the regularly scheduled run and got off at Alpine, where he conducted his business and returned the following day.

March was a quiet month for El Paso after the February ferment, but it was rather exciting for Scarborough, who, as related, was shot in the face while arresting Mexican revolutionary editor Lauro Aguirre.

Since the Hardin killing John Selman had been drinking heavily, seeking respite from the ghosts and fears that haunted his mind day and night. Following the indecisive trial he turned even more to the

Constable John Selman of El Paso with his cane and well-worn gun. *Courtesy Nita Stewart Haley Memorial Library, Midland, Texas.*

bottle and seemed always to be in some degree of intoxication. In addition to the hallucinatory apparitions beclouding his mind, there was the very real danger of a reputation-seeking gunman bracing the man who had put out the light of the most notorious gunfighting killer in the West. Selman appeared particularly wary of Mannie Clements, Jr., but he might well have feared other nearby Hardin kin, including M. Q. Hardin and particularly the homicidal Jim Miller. He continued to fulfill his duties as constable, but one of his two sons tried to stay near him out on the streets, day or night. Selman seemed obsessed with his reputation as a gunman. When carrying a full load of alcohol he would stop strangers on the street, drunkenly brag of his six-shooter prowess, and give demonstrations of his lightning draw. He cleaned and oiled the old six-gun daily and lined his holster with chamois to gain a fraction of a second on the draw.[36]

On April 1, 1896, all three of the remaining actors in the year long melodrama were recovering from injuries suffered on El Paso's violent streets. Old John used a cane, a visible reminder of the shootout with Baz Outlaw two years earlier. Young John's stab wounds inflicted by the three Mexicans six weeks previously still were not healed completely, and it had only been three weeks since Scarborough's gunshot wound in the face. Destiny brought these three scarred survivors together in the first week of April and the final act of the drama began.

On April Fools' Day, young Selman eloped with a fifteen-year-old girl, setting in motion a chain of events that culminated in the next tragedy the papers had been expecting since the previous August. Young John's beloved was the daughter of José María Ruiz, a former Mexican consular official and an important man in El Paso. He and his wife had vehemently opposed the liaison between their daughter and the son of El Paso's most notorious gunman. On April 1 the young couple pedaled bicycles across the bridge to Juárez and began a search for a civil official who could perform a marriage. Unsuccessful that day, they took a hotel room for the night. Ruiz was in Mexico City, but the mother was soon on the trail when her daughter failed to show up that night. She crossed to Juárez, alerted the mayor and the city police, and quickly located the lovers. Both were jailed that night. The following day, Señora Ruiz effected the

John Selman, Jr.'s romantic escapade led to his
father's final shooting affray. *Courtesy Nita
Stewart Haley Memorial Library, Midland,
Texas.*

release of her daughter and escorted her back home, but not before
filing kidnapping charges against John, Jr., who remained in the
Juárez lockup.

The El Paso papers treated the story lightly, finding it romantic
and rather amusing, but for young John this was serious business.
Not only had he apparently lost his prospective bride, but on April
2 he was discharged from the police force. It seemed preposterous,
but if Sra. Ruiz's charges held up—and the Juárez officials were
obviously currying favor with the influential family—he faced
twenty years in a Mexican prison.

This was the situation in the early hours of Easter Sunday, April 5,
when old John Selman and George Scarborough met in the Wigwam
Saloon. The previous afternoon, Selman had visited the Juárez jail
and told his son that he would return on Sunday and would bring
Scarborough with him.[37]

Scarborough had just arrived back in town from Fort Hancock,
where he had gone to fetch a prisoner, one Genaro Borrego.[38] Mollie

The Wigwam after it had been converted to a theater. Selman went down before Scarborough's gun in this alley. *Courtesy El Paso Public Library.*

was not at home; she had gone to Valentine to see her brother, Frank McMahan, who was seriously ill.[39] George walked down to the Wigwam.

"Last night, I don't remember what time, think between 12 and 1, I met Uncle John Selman in the Wigwam, down stairs," Scarborough told Justice Howe several hours later.[40]

> He told me he wanted to see me a minute and we walked outside. . . . He commenced talking as he had yesterday on several different occasions, about his son John being in jail on the other side. Two or three parties walked up to us while we were talking and he hunched me and said: "Come with me. I want to talk to you privately."
>
> We walked into the alley between the Santa Fe office and the Wigwam saloon. He said: "I want you to go over the river with me in the morning to see John." I asked him what time he wanted to go, and he said 11 or 12 o'clock.

Now in the dark of that alley Scarborough began to grow wary:

When we first walked around there was the first time I suspicioned anything. He kept monkeying with his gun—had his hand on his six-shooter.

He asked me where I would meet him. I told him at the corner of El Paso and San Antonio streets this morning between 10 and 11 o'clock and we'd go over the river.

He then said: "Let's go in and have a drink."

I told him I did not want anything to drink.

He threw his hand on his six-shooter and said: "You God damned son of a bitch, I'm going to kill you!"

We were standing face to face as he said this. I jerked my gun with my right hand and put it right at the left side of his head. Tried to shoot him through the head. Don't know whether I did or not.

He fell the first shot. He got up after the first shot and then I shot him three more times.

A policeman then came up and I surrendered to him and asked him to take me to the county jail.

John Graham, a resident of Dona Ana County, New Mexico Territory, testified that he had been present when Scarborough and Selman met in the Wigwam:

We all three stood there and talked awhile [and] Selman asked Scarborough to go outside as he wished to speak to him. . . . I followed. . . . Other parties came up and then Selman told Scarborough that he wished to speak to him privately. At that I turned and walked east on San Antonio street and Scarborough and Selman walked further down the alley.

I heard Selman say something to Scarborough about Bud. . . . Scarborough replied that he "had nothing to do with it." Shortly afterwards I heard a shot. . . . I then heard two or three more shots.
. . .
About the time of the first shot I heard a man say: "Don't kill me like that !" I do not know who uttered those words . . . made just before the first shot. I could not tell the man's voice, but think it was Scarborough's.[41]

Police Capt. Frank Carr, one of the first on the scene, saw Scarborough backing out of the alley with his smoking .45 in his hand. "George, do not shoot any more," he called. As Carr was examining Selman, who was conscious and in great pain, Jim Schoonmaker, "acting as an officer," in Carr's words, "came up and he and George began arguing. Schoonmaker was trying to get Scarborough to give him his gun." Scarborough evidently distrusted the Selman deputy, who had been thrown off the force for shaking down harlots, and refused to turn over his weapon to Schoonmaker.

Carr relieved the situation by sending Schoonmaker to telephone for Dr. White. Scarborough then submitted to arrest and was taken to the county jail by Officer Tyra and Jake Cathey.[42] There he slept for a few hours before being awakened at 10:00 A.M. to make a statement before justice of the Peace W. D. Howe, after which Howe released him on five hundred dollars bond.[43]

When Dr. White arrived in the alley beside the Wigwam, he had Selman removed to his home for examination. White found four gunshot wounds: a flesh wound through the left thigh just above the knee; another through the right hip bone from front to back, ranging slightly downward and backward; another flesh wound through the back of the neck, left to right; and another wound through the right ninth rib, penetrating the pleural cavity and lodging in the spinal column. The latter had resulted in total paralysis below the point where the bullet pressed against the spine.[44]

On Sunday, Selman's condition deteriorated. His abdomen distended with gas. Water had to be drawn from his paralyzed bladder. On Monday morning Dr. White turned him over to family physician Dr. Howard Thompson, who after consultation with Drs. S. T. Turner and J. J. Dooley, requested and received Selman's consent to an operation. The patient was moved to Sisters' Hospital, where the surgeons probed for the bullet lodged next to his spine but were unable to locate it. Selman's vitality gradually diminished and he died at 3:30 P.M. on April 6.[45]

Later that day Scarborough was charged with murder and released on two thousand dollars bond signed by Frank McMurray, T. M. Wilson, and himself. He was ordered to appear before Justice Howe's examining court on April 8.[46]

At the inquiry, the statements of George Scarborough and John Graham taken on Easter Sunday were accepted and put into the record without change. Called to testify were Dr. S. T. Turner, Frank Carr, C. A. Grinnell, John Reynolds, Charlie Christy, J. D. Ponder, Ott Smith, Tyrol Johceman, Frank Blum, and W. H. Wheat. Most of these were patrons of the Wigwam who had seen Selman and Scarborough together just before the shootings or officers who arrived at the scene immediately afterward. None could testify as to what transpired in the dark alley in those critical moments before the eruption of gunfire.[47] Justice Howe had heard only the testimony of Dr. Turner and Captain Carr when Deputy Sheriff Ten Eyck interrupted the proceedings to announce that the grand jury, then in session, had indicted Scarborough for the murder of Selman. Howe immediately adjourned the inquiry and Scarborough was taken before Judge C. N. Buckler of the district court. After examining the testimony taken at Howe's preliminary hearing, Buckler scheduled trial for the June court session. County Attorney Storms tried to convince Buckler that Scarborough should be held without bond, arguing that it was "high time this killing business was put a stop to," but the judge rejected his argument and set bond at four thousand dollars, which Scarborough raised the following day.[48]

One circumstance of the case immediately threw a veil of mystery over the entire affair and started tongues wagging throughout the town: John Selman had no weapon on him when he was found in the alley. Captain Carr, who, together with Schoonmaker, was the first to reach Selman, testified at the inquest that the old gunman "had his hand down towards his scabbard and was working his fingers." Said Carr: "I reached for Selman's gun to take it . . . but did not find any in the scabbard. So I commenced feeling all round there to see if there was any gun . . . but did not find any. . . . I said: 'John, where is your gun?' and he said: 'Somebody got it.' "[49]

In the first news account, Selman was reported as having said "that some one had taken his pistol from him while he was lying on the ground. He did not know who took the gun."[50] John Graham had testified at the initial hearing that Selman's gun was in its holster just before he, Selman, and Scarborough had walked outside. He said Selman had been telling of an encounter with a suspicious-appearing Mexican earlier in the evening and that when the man gave him "some slack," he had struck him over the head with his cane. "I then placed my hand on Selman's gun which was in a belt," Graham said, "and asked him why he did not use that. Selman said that he did not care to."[51]

The *Times* reported that Bud Selman, at his father's bedside on Sunday, had been told that it was Scarborough's suggestion to walk out into the alley and before Selman "had said a word or had any

intimation of what was coming a ball struck him in the neck. . . .
When he felt for his pistol it was gone, though he knew he had it
while standing in the saloon a few minutes before."[52] The other son,
John, Jr., later wrote that Bud was called to the scene of the shooting
while his father still lay in the alley and that old John had said, "Bud,
it is too bad this had to happen. I don't know what became of my
gun. If I had had my gun, things would have been different."[53]

The mysterious disappearance of Selman's gun "caused several
wild rumors to be set afloat,"[54] and "occasioned some very ugly talk
on the streets."[55] Selman's friends, said the *Times*, "charge that [the
gun] was taken from him in the alley before the shooting commenced" and that Scarborough's defenders assert "that some one of
Selman's friends captured the pistol to make it appear that he was
unarmed when killed. And so it goes."[56] There were early hints that
the officers knew who had the gun and it would "be produced at the
proper time and its disappearance accounted for,"[57] but by Friday,
April 10, almost a week after the shooting, that confidence had
dissipated. "The talk about John Selman's pistol being produced at
the trial was revived yesterday," said the *Times*, "but the officers do
not believe the pistol will ever be brought to light. All kinds of
theories are being advanced as to when and how Selman's gun was
taken from him."[58]

The riddle of the missing pistol did much to add to an air of
mystery that quickly surrounded Selman's killing and continues to
this day. The discovery of the weapon and the man who had it, three
weeks after the shooting, did little to dispel the "wild rumors" and
"ugly talk" that plagued the case from its beginning.

On April 27, Sheriff Frank Simmons of El Paso County received
a telegram from Deputy Sheriff John C. Chalk at Pecos: "Arrested
man with John Selmans pistol. Have him in jail. Answer."[59] At
Simmons's wired request, prisoner and pistol were brought to El
Paso by Reeves County Deputy Sheriff John Y. Leavell. There Bud
Selman positively identified the weapon as his father's regularly
worn sidearm. The man arrested was a young saloon hanger-on and
bouncer named Cole Belmont, who was known in El Paso as Kid
Clark.

The press was not given access to Belmont, but the *Times* reconstructed his story from information given by Belmont to Leavell,

Captain John Hughes, and others on the train from Pecos. Belmont
said he had been in the Wigwam on the night of the shooting,

> watching the antics of a drunken woman when he heard shots fired
> outside and ran out. . . . He reached the sidewalk in time to see the
> flash of the pistol as the last shot was fired. He went out in the alley;
> . . . his foot struck something lying at Selman's side, and, stooping
> down, he picked up the pistol, which was at full cock and loaded with
> six cartridges. . . . As the crowd gathered around the wounded man
> . . . he slipped the pistol into his pocket and returned to the front of
> the saloon.[60]

John Warren Hunter, who presumably got the story from his son-
in-law Frank McMahan, quoted Belmont in an article written in
1911:

> I was standing within a few feet of Sellman [sic] and Scarborough
> when the fatal shot was fired. It was intensely dark. I heard every
> word of their conversation and I saw the flash of a gun, heard a man
> hit the ground and heard footsteps of a man as he went away towards
> the saloon. I saw the gleam of his pistol as it lay by his side and I
> picked it up. I was aiming to leave El Paso that night. I reasoned that
> a dead man has no use for a pistol and I needed one in my business,
> so I took the pistol and got away before the crowd came out.[61]

Belmont was arrested after boasting in the Pecos saloons that he
had Selman's revolver. He did not explain why, with all the publicity
surrounding the missing weapon, he had not told the authorities
before, "but said he intended to come forward with the gun when
the case was called to trial."[62]

Funeral services for John Selman, bushwacker, rustler, horse
thief, and man with no soul, were held at the Myrtle Street Catholic
Church, after which a long procession, including a full contingent of
both Confederate and Union veterans, made its way to the cemetery.
Following the hearse was a visual tribute to a fallen soldier: Selman's
horse, an empty saddle on its back, a pair of empty boots tied to its
pommel. In the face of all odds, Selman had arrived at the end of
the trail respected and honored.[63] John Selman, Jr., was still locked
up in Juárez and Mexican officials, despite his pleadings, would not
release him to attend the funeral. The young man had taken his
father's death very hard and this was a double blow. Friends who
visited him at the jail said he "was grief stricken [and] his ravings

were pitiful and that he fainted from exhaustion several times."[64]
Young John himself would later write that his father's death coming
on top of his own troubles floored him. "For awhile I was pretty
sick," he recalled, "and for a few days did not know what was going
on."[65] Said the *Times:*

> It is being talked around on the streets that when young John Selman
> gets out of his trouble in Juarez he will avenge his father's sudden
> taking off. But the majority of young Selman's friends believe he will
> leave the matter with the courts and it is to be hoped that he will. El
> Paso has already had more killings than she can afford. The city is
> populated by civilized people whose patience has already been se-
> verely tested and it might refuse to stand any further strain. El Paso
> does not want to be known to the world as the home of "bad men"
> and killers, and her people are crying aloud for peace and good order.[66]

The next day young John was interviewed at the jail by a *Times*
reporter and confirmed that the war talk did not emanate from him:

> Some person has reported me as saying that as soon as I get out of
> this jail I intend to go after my father's slayer. I wish you to state
> through your columns of the *Times* that I have never said anything of
> the kind. I have been a peace officer for a number of years and know
> we have good laws in the U.S. If George Scarborough has committed
> willful murder with malice aforethought, the courts will punish him,
> and if he was justified in what he did, then the law will protect him.
> I have no idea of taking the law in my own hands, nor do I intend to
> make myself a murderer.[67]

Young John wrote later that he and his father had considered George
Scarborough to be their best friend in El Paso. They had discussed
bringing Scarborough into the Juárez jail problem, and Easter morning the young man was anxiously awaiting a visit from Scarborough
and Selman when a hack driver burst in with the news that his father
had been "shot all to pieces by George Scarborough."

"I was stunned," said John Selman, Jr. "I could not believe it.
. . . The one man father singled out . . . to help him get me out of
prison. Only a few days before I had ridden thirty miles into old
Mexico with Scarborough . . . after an escaped Federal prisoner.
Up to this time I have believed that Scarborough was our friend."[68]

On April 11, Scarborough resigned his position as deputy U.S.
marshal and was succeeded a few days later by George Majors, who

was transferred from Colorado City.[69] Scarborough's resignation was probably requested by Marshal Ware because of all the public censure of the deputy. It will be remembered that Ware has been criticized severely himself two years before over the actions of his deputy Baz Outlaw. Now he had another deputy who had two separate murder cases pending against him in a city which was fed up with all the gunplay.

There was vicious talk against Scarborough in the streets, but he did have his defenders. "I have known George Scarborough since he has been in El Paso," one man was quoted in the *Times*, "and I have never heard of his starting a quarrel. His is a genial, sunny disposition, and I'll gamble he did not start the trouble with John Selman."[70]

This brought a response in the *El Paso Evening Telegram*, headed "An Ugly Record," that spelled out many of the rumors about Scarborough being spread by Selman's friends:

> "The gentleman speaking through this morning's *Times* as having known George Scarborough since the latter has been in El Paso, and had never yet heard of him starting a quarrel, certainly knew nothing of current events," remarked an old timer last evening. "If he had known what was going on about town for the past year or so," continued the speaker, "he must have heard of Scarborough severely beating Si Ryan's cousin over the head with a 6-shooter in the Palace saloon; he must have heard of Scarborough drawing his gun on a railroad man at a Gem ball; he must have heard of Scarborough making a gun play at Dutch Charlie in the Bank saloon, when the latter disarmed him; he must have heard of Scarborough making a bluff at a well known ex-county officer in a gambling house, and when the latter knocked him down he arose with gun in hand and was disarmed by bystanders; he must have heard of Scarborough taking a poker pot away from John Selman while holding his 6-shooter in the old man's face, and, to say nothing of the decoying and killing of McRose and the killing of the disarmed constable. If the gentleman who wants to gamble he did not start the trouble with John Selman had inquired of any sport he would have learned that Scarborough has long been the terror of every gambling room in town."[71]

John Selman had been very popular with the sporting crowd in El Paso and Scarborough was obviously now a marked man. Without his deputy's commission, he could not openly carry a weapon. He needed another badge to pin on his vest, so he turned to his friend Capt. John R. Hughes and asked for appointment as a special ranger. Hughes had been close to Scarborough and his family for three years. He and George had ridden many a mile together after outlaws and, as Hughes told his biographer, he had often visited the Scarborough home as a dinner guest. "After the meal in the comfortable Scarborough home, the deputy marshal's daughters usually played hymns on the organ, and their father led the singing."[72]

This was an entirely different George Scarborough from the one described in the *Telegram* account, but Hughes had the newspaper story before him as he wrote his boss, Adjutant General William H. Mabry:

> Enclosed you will find a clipping from the El Paso *Evening Telegram* in regard to Mr. George A. Scarborough who has just resigned his commission as a Deputy U.S. Marshal and will be an applicant for a commission as Special Ranger.
>
> Mr. Scarborough is not as bad a man as this article would make it appear, but the fact that he resigned as deputy marshal on account of his troubles in El Paso, and that some of the newspapers are so bitter against him, it might be a drawback to the Ranger Service to have him become a member.
>
> Mr. Scarborough is a good friend to the Frontier Battalion and to me personally and I would like to see him prosper, and would endorse him anywhere except El Paso where he has had his trouble. Still I think it my duty as a member of the Frontier Battalion to try and post you as to his character. But if the best citizens of El Paso endorse him for the commission then I will be satisfied. I am only afraid the newspapers would use it against Governor Culberson or yourself.[73]

It is clear Hughes felt that it would have been politically unwise to saddle the rangers with the baggage Scarborough was carrying, and without the endorsement of the ranger captain it is not surprising that George Scarborough did not receive his special-ranger commission.

In June the Mroz and Selman cases were on the docket of the district court and as the time approached the names of Scarborough supporters began to show up in the social columns of the *Times:*

> G. W. and C. B. Scarborough, father and brother of Mr. George A. Scarborough, are in the city from Jones County. F. M. McMahan and wife of Valentine are also in the city visiting Mr. and Mrs. George

A. Scarborough. Capt. J. D. Milton, ex-chief of police of El Paso, is in the city from Nogales and Guaymas, and his friends are glad to see him.[74]

Of course the appearance of McMahan and Milton was not simply a social visit with old friends; both were also under indictment in the Mroz case. Only the appearance of Parson Scarborough and C. B. could be said to be strictly in support of George, but no doubt he welcomed all of them in his moment of greatest jeopardy.

The first case called in the Mroz affair was *State of Texas* v. *George A. Scarborough*, but on June 15 the prosecution chose to request another continuance, which was granted. The cases of Milton and McMahan were also continued.[75]

The Selman shooting case opened on June 17, District Attorney W. C. McGown and J. R. Harper conducting the prosecution, C. Q. Stanton and W. W. Turney representing Scarborough. The first two days were devoted to jury selection and then on the morning of the nineteenth the state began its case. Dr. S. T. Turner, who had introduced the medical testimony at the April inquest, was called to the stand to testify regarding Selman's mental condition before surgery. Dr. Turner said Selman acted like a man who knew he was going to die although he had been told he had a chance if the operation were successful. Dr. Howard Thompson testified that Selman could not have survived with the bullet pressing against his spine.[76]

The prosecution intended to show by the medical testimony that Selman believed he was on his deathbed and was presented as a foundation for the next witness, Jim Burns. A close friend of John Selman, Burns was also known as "the wickedest man in El Paso." He was the proprietor of the Red Light, a notorious low dive and brothel whose scarlet women had been described in the local press as "the most depraved and diseased in the Southwest."[77]

Burns testified that he had gone to see Selman the morning after the shooting and found him perfectly rational. "On entering the room," said Burns, "I told him to brace up as he was all right and would pull through. He said, 'No, Jim, I have been done up.' I then asked him how the whole thing happened."

Here the jury was removed while a legal point was argued with regard to whether Selman's remarks were to be considered a deathbed confession. Judge Buckler ruled for the prosecution, the jury returned, and Burns was permitted to continue. Burns quoted Selman in his testimony:

> "Jim and I were standing in the Wigwam when George Scarborough came down stairs and we spoke friendly together. He put his arm around my neck and said 'Uncle John, I want to see you,' and he led me out in the alley, and before I knew it he shot me in the neck and I fell. I said, 'My God, George, do you intend to kill me this way?' I reached for my pistol, but didn't have it, and felt around on the ground. It must have got away from me for I had it a short time before. If I had found it, I would have mixed things with him."

After sharp cross-examination failed to budge Burns, the prosecution rested its case. Curiously, no one was called to substantiate Burns's version of Selman's statements, including Bud Selman, whose quotations in the press had appeared prejudicial to Scarborough.

The defense presented testimony from Howard Bridges, Jim Schoonmaker, and John Graham, which added little to the version given by Graham before Justice Howe. Bridges said "Selman was talking about his son's troubles and led Scarborough into the alley." He thought he saw the flash of nickel plate on Selman's gun as they walked by. Schoonmaker said that in the alley he had looked for Selman's gun and Selman had said "it had got away from him." Graham repeated his story and said again that just prior to the first shot he heard someone exclaim, "For God's sake don't try to kill me that way!" He thought the voice was Scarborough's. No one else testified to having heard this.

The testimony of Cole Belmont, described in the *Times* as a "tough looking young fellow," was substantially the same as previously reported in the papers. He was subjected to rigorous cross-examination, but "all efforts to break down his testimony failed."

George Scarborough then went on the stand in his own defense. He told basically the same story he had told Justice Howe the morning after the shooting. He denied reports that he had told Selman, when asked to go with him to Juárez to help young John, that there must not be any "bad plays like the one Bud Selman made over the river a few evenings before," which remark reportedly infuriated the elder Selman and precipitated the shooting. He said that Selman cursed him and threatened to kill him "when he declined to take a drink and told Selman he (Selman) was already drunk." Scarborough admitted that some time earlier he and Selman had quarreled over a game of cards. He said that after that episode "he had been warned by Sheriff Simmons, Chief Fink and Captain J. D. Milton that Selman would kill him."[78]

After summations by prosecution and defense on June 20, Judge Buckler charged the jury, giving special emphasis to the disappearance of the Selman pistol and the testimony of Belmont. "With reference to the evidence of Cole Belmont," said Buckler,

> you are instructed . . . to consider . . . that he found the pistol of the deceased after he was shot, and to give his said statement such weight as you believe it is entitled to, but as to his connection with the pistol and his credibility as a witness [only]. The evidence wholly fails to show any connection between said witness and the defendant. You should not consider the connection of said witness with the deceased's pistol as any evidence or as even a circumstance against the defendant.[79]

The jury deliberated only a short time before bringing in a not-guilty verdict. According to the *Times,* "the verdict was expected by those who heard the testimony."[80]

Belmont, whose gun-swiping impulse had beclouded the entire affair from the beginning and was the source of the ongoing myth that Scarborough had shot down an unarmed man, was tried in county court in July, convicted, and given sixty days in jail.[81]

Scarborough still had to face trial for the Mroz killing, but the state repeatedly requested continuances and it was almost a year before the case finally came to court. Scarborough had long since departed from El Paso.

His last difficulty in El Paso reported in the El Paso press occurred a week after his acquittal. He and Mollie were enjoying some ice cream in the Edwards confectionery when three blacks, a man and two women, entered. The women sat down at the same table with Mollie, which action offended Scarborough's short-fused southern sensibilities. He immediately "offered to thrash the colored man and talked very plain" to Edwards, the manager, who, he said, should not have permitted such impudence. Jim Crow was alive and well in El Paso in 1896.[82]

*Professional gunmen were a cautious breed, and Selman
particularly so. Nobody could have "lifted" his gun from him
without his knowledge any more than he could have taken the
collar from round his neck.*

—WILLIAM MACLEOD RAINE, 1940

-10-

The Cautious Breed

George Scarborough was thirty-six years old in the summer of
1896. Mollie also had turned thirty-six on June 7. Their seven
children ranged in age from seventeen-year-old Edgar down through
the five daughters to little Ray, who would not be two until September. George was without employment in a city that suddenly seemed
hostile to him. He was an experienced professional lawman, but all
doors appeared to have closed for him in El Paso. Dick Ware had
accepted his resignation and replaced him. Appointment to the Texas
Rangers had not come from John Hughes. Sheriff Frank Simmons
did not appear eager to take him on as a county deputy. A job on the
city police force under Ed Fink was out of the question after their
bitter argument the year before.

George had many friends throughout the western part of the state,
however, folks he had come to know during the three years he had
crisscrossed the area as deputy U.S. marshal. Typical of them was
Mrs. Mary Pierson of Haymond, who, three-quarters of a century
later, remembered George Scarborough as "a most daring Federal
officer." She particularly recalled a time when he came into the
Pierson store in Haymond and asked her to stitch in a hatband for
him. "I remember," she said, "he was very chivalrous in manner."[1]
Walter S. Miller, a hotelman of Fort Davis, in 1927 also recalled
Scarborough well and favorably.[2]

The military post of Fort Davis, around which the town of the same
name had developed, was closed by the United States government in
July 1891, having outlived its usefulness as a base to protect white
settlement against Indian attack. The James family, which owned

157

the ground on which the fort had been built, offered the officers' quarters for rent as residences. Walter Miller and his family lived in one of the buildings; George Scarborough moved his large family into another.[3]

Scarborough took work with the ranchers of the region as a purchasing agent for cattle and horses. He was close to John Zack Means, a pioneer ranchman who had arrived in the area in 1884 and established headquarters near Valentine. Over a period of years Means acquired a spread that extended all the way from the Rio Grande to the Texas and Pacific Railroad, some one thousand square miles of territory.[4] Other important cattlemen of the area included Robert S. Sproul, who had arrived the year after Means and grazed cattle near Twin Mountains before acquiring strategic railroad and school sections north of Fort Davis; William L. Kingston, another 1885 arrival who established a ranch at the mouth of Madera Canyon; Philip H. Pruitt, who came to Fort Davis in 1880 and made his headquarters twenty-five miles north of Alpine in the Davis Mountains; George W. Evans, who began his operation eight miles west of Fort Davis near the head of Limpia Canyon and finally located his ranch home near Valentine; Jim P. Wilson, who ran a large store in Alpine in addition to his ranch holdings; and Joe D. Jackson, later president of the Cattle Raisers Association of Texas, who, with his partner, S. D. Harmon, had extensive cattle holdings in Brewster County.[5]

In August of 1896, Scarborough began a series of trips for these ranchers which over the next eight months took him as far west as California and deep into Mexico in search of stock.[6] He was back in El Paso in April 1897, together with Frank McMahan and Jeff Milton, to stand trial on the Mroz case, which had finally been called to court. Milton later claimed that District Attorney W. C. McGown, "catering to the rougher elements," had been requesting continuances for almost two years "just to chouse [us] around."[7]

The *Herald* took special note of Milton's appearance in town: "Ex-Chief of Police J. D. Milton arrived this afternoon from Nogales on a visit of a few days and is being warmly welcomed by many friends."[8] And two days later: "J. D. Milton's pretty phiz is once more seen on the streets. Milton's face is mild and pleasant to look upon, but his grasp of his friend's hand is of iron."[9] George

Scarborough must have noticed the contrast to the paper's terse announcement of his own return: "George Scarborough is up from Fort Davis."[10] Obviously he still was not popular in El Paso.

When John M. Dean of Fort Davis took over the district attorney's office, he announced he was ready for trial. W. H. Burges, who with C. Q. Stanton was representing the defendants, felt he had a strong case and had been ready for two years. He became particularly confident after a man named Charlie Newman called at his office. On June 29, 1895, Newman was employed at the Stanton Street bridge station, upriver from the railroad bridge Mroz and Scarborough had crossed. On that dark night he had been out on the dump and happened to be facing the Mexican Central bridge when the shooting began. He had seen the first flash, he told Burges, "which came from the side next to the river," or, evidently, from the gun of Martin Mroz.[11]

On April 27 jury selection was begun from a venire of more than seventy. Supremely confident, the defense lawyers challenged no one, taking "every juror who wanted to serve." Among the witnesses subpoenaed to appear in the Scarborough case were three Texas sheriffs, John Y. Leavell of Reeves County, Joseph R. Chadborn of Jeff Davis County, and S. S. Montgomery of Hall County.[12]

The cases were called in district court on April 28, 1897. After four witnesses had testified, District Attorney Dean announced to Judge Buckler "that he was not familiar with the case and did not know that the defendants were acting on a warrant [and] as he had no case . . . he was either willing to nolle prose [sic] the cases or accept the same evidence and require a verdict of not guilty against each of the defendants."[13] Judge Buckler so directed, and "the jury, without retiring and in their box, presented the verdict 'not guilty' " in all three actions.[14] The cases had been two years in coming to trial, a full day was expended in impaneling a jury, and the trial itself, according to the Herald, "only lasted thirty minutes from the time the first witness was heard until all the defendants were acquitted and walked out of court free men."[15]

"J. D. Milton . . . and George Scarborough are being warmly congratulated this afternoon by their many friends on the pleasant and successful outcome of the morning's experience in the district court," said the Herald, adding jocularly that William McCoy, the

El Paso Police Department in 1897. Seated, left to right: George Herold,
Capt. Tom Bendy, Chief Con Lockhart, Mannie Clements, Juan Franco.
Standing: George Cole, Pat Dwyer, Bob Ross, Joe Rogers, Frank Winkler,
John Denniston, Carl Schmidt. *Courtesy El Paso Public Library.*

jury foreman, seemed to have a better punch than Bob Fitzsimmons.
"It took Fitz two years to knock Corbett out, but McCoy knocked
the state out three times within half an hour."[16]

Gunsmoke had swirled around the head of George Scarborough
at the time of the Mroz and Selman shootings, smoke that only took
seconds to dissipate, and it had taken almost two years to remove
the legal cloud that had hung over his head after these killings. But
there was yet another cloud, which had begun building after that
night on the Mexican Central bridge and had become even more
dense after the Selman shooting, a cloud of mystery, fueled by loose
talk and rumor, that did not fade away after Scarborough's legal
exoneration but continued and is in evidence even to this day. Nature
abhors a vacuum; human nature abominates a conundrum. Where
mystery exists, speculation flourishes, and in the case of a series
of sudden deaths with mysterious overtones, the speculation tends
toward a direct linkage of the deaths, often with conspiratorial impli-

cations. Sufficient mystery surrounded the El Paso melodrama shootings to produce abundant speculation and imaginative conjecture. Some contended that the spate of shootings was simply a contest for supremacy between the veteran gunmen congregated in town. One who apparently subscribed to this theory was John Selman, Jr., who said: "When Wes Hardin came to town everybody believed Scarborough had him staked out as his especial prey. Gunfighters are jealous. Scarborough had reason to resent the fact that father dusted Hardin before he had a chance at him."[17]

Frank Collinson wrote that undoubtedly "Selman and Hardin were jealous of each other's reputations as killers. One of the other was sure to be killed. . . . Like all such fighters, they maneuvered for advantage. Selman got it and did the work. . . . Then here comes another killer to kill the man who had killed Texas' most notorious killer—and the good work went on."[18]

Later writers like Eugene Cunningham echoed this theme. "In my own mind," he wrote, "there is no doubt that Selman was perfectly willing to kill Hardin, given opportunity, if not actually 'laying for' him. There was much jealousy among the killer-type of gunmen. Each wanted to be cock of the walk. When one killed another, automatically he inherited the dead man's list of notches."[19]

Lingering, unresolved questions regarding the Mroz, Hardin, and Selman killings, mainly having to do with motive, produced individual theories which eventually coalesced to create a conspiratorial hypothesis linking all three. Mroz, Hardin, and Selman were all deliberately murdered, it is postulated, and the root cause of the killings was Mroz's money. The story goes like this: Hardin, in league with Selman, enlisted Scarborough to entice Mroz across the river where he could be killed and his money stolen. Scarborough brought Jeff Milton and Frank McMahan into the conspiracy. Hardin and Selman were present when Mroz was killed and Hardin got the money. When Selman did not receive his share of the loot from Hardin, he killed him, and when Selman grumbled around town that Hardin and Scarborough had split the Mroz money, Scarborough lured him into an alley and gunned him down.

Selman's biographer, Leon Metz, while not completely endorsing the accuracy of this scenario, makes a case for its strong possibility and cites the evidence favoring it. Central to the theory are the unpublished memoirs of George Look, described by Metz as "a saloon owner, an express guard, a wily politician, a man who corralled votes and delivered them for a price. Look either knew about or had his fingers in every bit of dishonest pie being cut in the community. For all these reasons he was the one person in a position to know the inside version. . . . He had no reason to lie."[20]

Writing in 1909, Look said that after Mroz's release from the Juárez jail Selman had approached him and sought permission to allow Mroz and Beulah to meet privately in the back room of Look's Gem Saloon. The meeting never came off, but Selman's request suggests an awareness of Scarborough's role as messenger between Mroz and his wife and the effort to bring them together. However, when Mroz was finally brought over the bridge by Scarborough, according to Look's account, "they met John Wesley Hardin, Milton and John Selman. Morose was killed by these men at the foot of the bridge. Then Hardin got to him first and took $3700 out of his pocket."

In a day or two, said Look, Hardin and Beulah were openly consorting, "riding around town in a hack. John Selman came to me and told me that Wesley Hardin had quite a roll—in fact, had Morose's roll." Hardin then went on a spree, said Look, that culminated in his holdups of the gambling games in the Acme and George Look's own Gem Saloon. This last act infuriated Selman, who went to Look and said, "George, you people may stand for it, but I won't. He has to come across or I'll kill him. . . . I believe he has cut with Scarborough, but he has not cut with any of the rest of us. What do you say—shall I get the son-of-a-bitch?" Look saw only two options for old John: to forget it or kill Hardin. Selman chose the latter, shooting Hardin to death "because he would not give him, Selman, hit cut of the Morose money."

After Hardin's death, Selman began to drink heavily and, according to George Look, was heard in the saloons muttering drunkenly about how Scarborough and Hardin had divided up the money of Martin Mroz. This was the reason, he said, that Scarborough called Selman into the alley behind the Wigwam and killed him.[21]

Support for the basic elements of this story are to be found in a few scattered sources. Frank Collinson contended that Hardin had been directly involved in the Mroz killing. In the Collinson version, Hardin, having stolen Mroz's woman, also coveted the reward money on the fugitive's head and eighteen hundred dollars that Mroz had deposited in an El Paso bank,

> so he concocted a plan to get . . . both. He had the woman write a note saying to McRose that if he would send her a check for the amount, she would meet him on the International Bridge and give him half. . . . On the appointed night Hardin and three or four more— two or three police among them—hid by the bridge. The woman went where McRose could see her. He came to the north end of the bridge [and] Hardin and his posse raised up and shot him dead. I saw the body next day at the Powers [sic] Undertaking Parlor. He was about the worst shot-up man I ever saw.

Scarborough, Milton, McMahan and Selman are not named by Collinson as parties to this assassination, although any of them could have been among the "two or three police" mentioned.

Collinson goes on to tell of the Hardin and Selman killings but makes no connection to the previous Mroz affair. He admits that he was not in El Paso when Selman shot Hardin but believed it resulted from gunman reputation jealousy and "several tilts" between the two, including the confrontation over young John's arrest of Beulah. Selman was shot, Collinson said, when he and Scarborough argued over getting young John out of the Juárez jail.[22]

Notes in the files of Southwest historian Robert N. Mullin indicate that at least two other El Paso residents, each with intimate knowledge of the city's treacherous undercurrents during this period, believed Hardin planned Mroz's death. Ed Bryant, a former city policeman, and Roy Barnum, owner of the Barnum Show Saloon, provided no details and failed to identify the source of their information, but both assured Mullin that they were convinced Hardin's was the guiding hand behind the elimination of Mroz.[23]

Hardin's alcoholic blusterings in the gin mills of the city that he had hired Scarborough and Milton to kill Mroz undoubtedly was the original basis for this story.

Vic Queen's letter, composed after Mroz was killed and telling of the two Mexican smugglers and what they supposedly saw transpire among the sunflowers, is introduced by Metz in an attempt to integrate it with the Look account and assign identities, including possibly Hardin and Selman, to the "fat man, tall man, thin man," etc., described by the smugglers.

Metz comes to no firm conclusions regarding the truth of the George Look conspiracy theory, putting it forward as a possible explanation of the El Paso shootings, especially Scarborough's shooting of Selman, which he seems convinced was deliberate and cold-blooded murder.

Another look at a conspiracy theory based on the theft of Martin Mroz's money and the resulting murders of Mroz, Hardin and Selman is in order. First of all, if Hardin wanted to lure Mroz across the river to kill and rob him, why would he bring John Selman into the scheme? He would need Scarborough because of the rapport the latter had developed with Mroz, but Hardin and Selman were not close. In fact, all evidence suggests the opposite. What did Selman have to contribute to such a scheme, his gun? Surely with Hardin, Scarborough, Milton, and McMahan already involved, there were sufficient guns. How many veteran gunfighters does it take to ambush one rustler? Unquestionably Scarborough, Milton, and McMahan were there. Within a very few minutes after the shooting they were joined by river-patrol guards Woody Bendy and Pat Dwyer and a short time later by Deputy Sheriff J. C. Jones. None of these other officers saw Selman or Hardin. Scarborough, Milton, and McMahan all admitted under oath that they had shot Mroz and were indicted for murder. During almost two years of waiting for trial and for the remainder of their lives, none ever suggested that anyone other than the three of them was present or was in any way responsible for Mroz's death.

Could it be possible that the conspiracy theory was only partly accurate, that Hardin and Selman had not been present at the bridge but had plotted the murder, and that it was Scarborough who lifted Mroz's bankroll, later splitting with Hardin but not Selman? This idea bumps into several imponderables as well. Without his actual participation in the crime, Selman's alleged right to a share of the loot becomes even less apparent. And why would Selman blame Hardin for not splitting the loot with him and kill him for it when Scarborough got the money and made the divvy?

Another glaring hole in the scenario is the presumption that Hardin planned the whole affair to get Mroz's money. What assurance had he that Martin would be carrying his wealth with him when he crossed the bridge? It seems much more plausible that the fugitive came over in an effort to *get* money, to salvage whatever portion of his funds Beulah still had, as suggested by Vic Queen and others.[24]

In the absence of any evidence placing Hardin or Selman at the scene of the Mroz killing or the existence of a bankroll on Mroz, the entire conspiracy theory falls apart. There are almost as many other holes in the George Look account as there were holes in the body of Mroz. According to Look, Hardin held up the Acme and Gem gambling games after the Mroz affair, thus provoking Selman to ask, "Shall I kill the son-of-a-bitch?" Hardin, however, pulled the holdups in the first days of May, two months *before* the Mroz shooting.

The Charles Perry visit to El Paso also occurred in May. If any credence is to be given to the *Times* story that Selman sicked Perry on Hardin and then hid on the stairs with a gun in his hand, then it is clear Uncle John was maneuvering to eliminate Wes Hardin long before the Mroz affair.

Look also said that after Selman spread it around town that Hardin and Scarborough had shared Mroz's money, Scarborough called him into an alley and killed him. However the only testimony at the trial indicating Scarborough initiated the move into the alley came secondhand from the disreputable Jim Burns; John Graham, Howard Bridges, and Scarborough all swore that it was Selman's idea to go into the alley. There was no hint in the Burns account of Selman's purported deathbed statement of the Mroz money's being a motive for his shooting by Scarborough.

With the advantage of time and perspective, we can today see yet another powerful argument why a murder and robbery conspiracy involving Hardin, Selman, Scarborough, Milton, and McMahan appears highly improbable. Knowing the further history of career lawmen Scarborough, Milton, and McMahan, we can see convicted murderer and former convict Wes Hardin and the "man with no soul," John Selman, were just not the type of men with whom they would conspire.

It has been shown that Milton detested Selman. As for the Scarborough-Selman relationship, there is no evidence that the two were close, despite young John's assertion that his father and Scarborough were the best of friends. On the contrary, the two gunmen had tangled on at least one occasion prior to that Easter morning and there was obviously bad blood between them. The newspaper story of "Scarborough taking a poker pot away from John Selman while holding his 6-shooter in the old man's face" had basis in fact, as evidenced by Scarborough's testimony at his trial, where he told of "a previous quarrel he had with Selman over a game of cards," and the subsequent warning by Simmons, Fink, and Milton that Selman would kill him. Jeff Milton alluded to this incident in his interviews with J. Evetts Haley, saying he had intervened at the time to prevent a shooting. "George was playing cards once [with Selman] and I walked into the saloon and I seen that they were getting ready to murder George and I said, 'You let this fellow alone.' "[25] According to Milton, this episode took place in the Acme and Wes Hardin was there:

> Selman would have killed Scarborough in the same place where he [later] killed Hardin. They were in [there] together and were just about to have [at] it and I walked in there and . . . I sort of smoothed it over and I says, "You boys don't be getting angry. You are both friends of mine." I never did know what the trouble was, but there was somebody wanting to hurt somebody.[26]

It is clear that Selman approached Scarborough to help get John, Jr., out of jail because George had influence with the Mexican authorities, not because there was any bond of friendship between them. McMahan's attitude toward Hardin and Selman doubtless mirrored that of his brother-in-law, the older and more experienced Scarborough, whom he emulated.

The original basis for the entire conspiracy theory appears to have been Wes Hardin's drunken boasts in El Paso's gin mills that he had hired Scarborough and Milton to kill Mroz. Apparently the gunfighter, who had obviously benefited from Mroz's taking off, having acquired sole "rights" to his woman and access to whatever Mroz capital she held, could not abide the public perception that such good fortune had not been of his own making and spread the tale that he had been behind it all. The officers' immediate angry reaction, forcing humiliating recantations by Hardin, did not erase the widely held suspicion that there must have been some truth to the tale.

But if there was no conspiracy, what was the reason for the string of killings? The "gunman's reputation jealousy" may have been an element in the Hardin shooting, but certainly it played no part in the Mroz affair and seems not to have been a factor in Selman's death. George Scarborough's reputation as a gunfighter was enhanced by the Selman killing, but there is no evidence that he ever took pride in it. The reputation, too, always was tarnished by the unarmed-Selman myth and the suspicion that, for whatever reason, Scarborough had murdered Uncle John in cold blood. Like Hardin's retractions of his Mroz killing lies, Cole Belmont's testimony accounting for the disappearance of the Selman gun did not eradicate the persistent notion that somehow John Selman had been unarmed and defenseless when Scarborough gunned him down.

Frank Collinson was still propounding it in 1935 when he wrote that Selman was shot when Scarborough *refused* Selman's request to help his son get out of the Juárez jail. "Selman got abusive and . . . reached for his gun. It was not there. . . . Someone who saw what was coming had slipped it out of his scabbard. . . . After the shooting someone [threw] it into the alley [where Belmont] promptly picked it up." Knowing a good deal about old John's bloodstained history, Collinson found it impossible to believe that if he were armed, "Selman could have been too drunk to shoot at least one shot, even if he'd been shot through the heart," and concluded that he "never had even the slightest chance to defend himself."[27]

In a publication that same year, John Selman, Jr., perpetuated the myth, saying that Belmont had stolen the old man's gun in the saloon only moments before Selman and Scarborough went into the alley. "To my certain knowledge," said young John, "Scarborough would not have stood a chance in a gun battle with father. The real reason my father was killed will never be known [but] at any rate George Scarborough killed an unarmed man."[28]

An El Paso old-timer named Uncle Jimmy Watts contributed to the disarmed-Selman tale in 1951, saying, "Scarborough saw Selman sitting in the Wigwam saloon asleep. He paid a Negro $20 to steal Selman's gun out of his holster. Then he sent someone in to tell Selman he wanted to see him outside," where he shot him.[29]

Owen White wrote that within hours of the shooting in the alley behind the Wigwam, "two versions of what happened were current on the street." The "picturesque" version was the one that he, "as a kid of sixteen, chose to accept." Selman and Scarborough" quarreled and, in order to settle their difficulties permanently, agreed to fight a duel." Back to back in the alley, they began walking "away from each other and at the count of ten they wheeled, drew and fired." But

> when old John Selman dropped his hand to his hip, it fell on an empty scabbard. . . . Scarborough, not knowing he was shooting an unarmed man, fired four bullets into his adversary's body. To this day nobody knows what became of Selman's gun. Some bystander in the barroom must have lifted it before the old man went into the alley, but Scarborough certainly had nothing to do with it. He was a clean fighter, with a fine reputation as a man. . . . As I remember it, he was not even tried for the killing.[30]

White did not bother to relate the other version being prattled on the streets. He called the story he gave "picturesque," but a better adjective would be "ridiculous."

Perhaps as ridiculous is the notion that John Selman, one of the West's most notorious gunmen, a man who had carried a pistol on his hip every day of his adult life and who owed his advanced age to that weapon and his skill in its use, could have that pistol taken from him and not know it.

William MacLeod Raine, western writer and student of gun-fighting days and ways, scoffed at the whole idea, saying that "professional gunmen were a cautious breed, and Selman particularly so. Nobody could have 'lifted' his gun from him without his knowledge any more than he could have taken the collar from round his neck. And nothing can be more sure than that before he left the [Wigwam] he knew the butt of a sixshooter was close to his hovering fingers. He was not a callow amateur, to take chances on such a vital matter."[31]

In his biography of Selman, Leon Metz does not dispute the Cole Belmont story and apparently accepts the fact that Selman was armed when he stepped into that alley, but he argues that at the trial "justice was not only blind—but bound and gagged." Other than Jim Burns, he writes, "no one stepped forward during the trial to hint that George

Scarborough might actually have been guilty of murder. . . . There was plenty of evidence if anyone had wanted to present it."

Metz cites as the most damning piece of evidence the location of the wound inflicted by what all agreed was the first shot, the left-to-right slash across the back of Selman's neck:

> The only way John could have received that first bullet was to have had his back to Scarborough or turned sideways to him with more of his back exposed than the front. The first shot, grazing the rear of his neck, could not possibly have been fired while John was facing the marshal. And if the two men were not facing each other, this was certainly a peculiar position for an old experienced gunfighter like Selman to be caught in, especially when he was allegedly threatening to kill a man.

Metz finds part of John Graham's testimony also damaging to the Scarborough defense. Graham testified at the initial Justice Howe hearing and again at the trial that he had heard someone call out, "Don't try to kill me like that!" Metz asserts that "Selman afterward claimed to have said words to this effect and no one ever disputed him. It seems likely that a man saying these words would be the victim and not the killer." His conclusion, while admitting that the whole truth will never be known, is "that George Scarborough deliberately murdered John Selman."[32]

Careful consideration of these questions, however, does not necessarily lead to the conclusion Metz has drawn but can be shown to be consistent with Scarborough's story. Metz's second major point, Graham's testimony about the cry he heard, can be disposed of most easily. It will be remembered that Graham thought it was Scarborough's voice he heard, not Selman's. Given the situation as Scarborough described it, Selman with his left arm around George's neck, his right hand "monkeying with his sixshooter," Scarborough suspicious, his senses razor sharp to a false move by this deadly killer, he could well have blurted out, "Don't try to kill me like that!" even as he went for his own gun.

The only source for this possibly being Selman's outcry was the testimony of Jim Burns, who seems to have taken several elements of Scarborough's story as it appeared in the press and turned them around to show Selman as the victim. Scarborough had said that Selman had initiated their discussion; Burns quoted Selman:

"[George] said, 'Uncle John, I want to see you.' " Scarborough testified that Selman draped his arm around him and took him into the alley; Burns quoted Selman as saying: "[George] put his arm around my neck and . . . led me out in the alley." Graham thought it was Scarborough's voice he heard crying out in alarm; Burns quoted Selman: "I said, 'My God, George, do you intend to kill me this way?' " The essentials of Scarborough's testimony were buttressed by Graham and Bridges; no testimony was introduced substantiating Burns's story.

Scarborough elaborated somewhat on the details of those critical few moments when he told Jeff Milton about it later. "Selman . . . went up and put his arm around Scarborough, around his neck," Milton related, "and it didn't look good. . . . Yes, put his arm around him. That is what George told me." Milton said Selman "went to get his gun out and so Scarborough just pulled his gun and shot the old stud. . . . Old John said, 'you so-and-so, I will fix you,' and reached for his sixshooter. . . . George had his ready and he just reached around and shot old Selman in the neck. . . . George [said] to me: 'He got me out there to murder me.' "[33]

The question Metz raises regarding the neck wound can also be answered in a scenario consistent with Scarborough's version of the event. Assume a tableau, the two gunmen standing very close together, partly side by side, with Selman's left arm still around Scarborough's neck. Scarborough stiffens as Selman snarls, "I'll fix you!" and drops his right hand to his six-shooter. Scarborough cries out in alarm while making two simultaneous motions: he pushes Selman away with his left hand as he jerks his pistol with his right. Selman, already unsteady on a bullet-shattered leg that necessitates his constant use of a cane and at this moment very drunk, starts a twisting collapse to his right. His right hand, holding his drawn six-gun, instinctively swings outward to break his fall. Scarborough, still encumbered by Selman's left arm, "just reaches around" and fires at the falling man's head. The bullet strikes Selman's turned and falling body in the left side of the neck. The pistol in Selman's hand is jarred loose and skitters away as he hits the alley on his right side. Stunned, he gropes for the weapon and struggles to rise. Scarborough, unaware in the darkness of the alley that Old John has not found the six-shooter, pumps three more rounds into his body, including the one that will kill him.

This is the way it could have happened. As Leon Metz admits, the whole truth will never be known, but a judge, a district attorney, and twelve jurymen found no difficulty in clearing Scarborough, and in the absence of any new information that casts doubt on their decision, history should do the same.

-11-

Afraid of No Man

When Jeff Milton returned to El Paso in April 1897 to stand trial with Scarborough and McMahan in the Mroz affair, he suggested to Scarborough that they join forces to go after the bandits then plaguing southern New Mexico and Arizona territories. Milton was employed by Wells, Fargo as a special express agent guarding shipments on the Benson-to-Guaymas run. With an outbreak of train robberies in the territories, the company asked him to take to the saddle and hunt down the bandits.

The mountain passes of New Mexico became attractive locations for train holdups during this period; in the years 1896 through 1899 there would be ten train robberies in the territory.[1] As early as 1887 the territorial assembly recognized the seriousness of the problem and its adverse effect on hopes for statehood and passed legislation making train robbery an offense punishable by death.[2]

Chief among the outlaw bands threatening the railroads in 1897 wa a gang called the High Fives, after a popular card game, led by a fugitive from Indian Territory justice named William T. Christian, who, because of his dark coloring, had picked up the nom de guerre Black Jack. Riding with him were his brother Bob, also wanted by Indian Territory authorities, and George Musgrave, Code Young, and Bob Hayes, Texas cowboys who had worked on Arizona and New Mexico ranches and knew the country well.

The gang formed early in the summer of 1896 and during the balance of that year were charged with an Atlantic and Pacific train holdup at Rio Puerco, New Mexico, a bank robbery at Nogales, Arizona, and a number of post office and stagecoach holdups in the sister territories. During a gun battle triggered by the Rio Puerco train robbery, Code Young was shot and killed by Deputy U.S. Marshal Will Loomis. By November the United States Post Office Department had posted a reward of one thousand dollars for each of the bandits.

That same month at a remote Diamond A horse camp managed by Walter Birchfield and located south of Deming in the Las Animas Mountains, lawmen found the remaining four members of the gang. Deputy Marshals Les Dow, Charles Ballard, and Fred Higgins and Grant County officers Baylor Shannon, Frank McGlinchy, and Steve Birchfield, brother of Walter, made up a posse that surprised the outlaws and in the ensuing gunfight Bob Hayes was killed.

In January 1897 the Post Office Department doubled the rewards for the remaining three gang members. Additionally, a one thousand dollar bounty was on Musgrave's head for the murder of George Parker, a Diamond A cowboy, the previous October. The gang, reinforced by new recruits Sid Moore and Theodore James, holed up at Cole Creek, New Mexico, a favorite outlaw haunt. On April 28, 1897, the very day that the Mroz killing case was opening in El Paso, lawmen sprang a trap at Cole Creek. Aided by information from an outlaw turncoat named Jim Shaw, Deputy Marshal Fred Higgins and two Graham County, Arizona, deputy sheriffs, Ben Clark and William ("Crook Neck") Johnson, waylaid the gang and killed Black Jack Christian.[3]

The original Black Jack was gone, but his range was still alive with outlaws and soon a new leader, Tom Ketchum, surfaced to assume the mantle and name of Black Jack. Milton, already in the hunt for the southwestern desperadoes, urged Scarborough to take a hand in the game as well.[4] He did not have to be very persuasive. Scarborough, out of the law-enforcement profession for a year, sorely missed the excitement of the chase. Closing out his affairs at Fort Davis, he moved his family to Deming, Grant County, New Mexico Territory, a town of about fifteen hundred residents and the next major community west of El Paso on the Southern Pacific line.

Milton held a deputy's appointment under U.S. Marshal William M. Griffith, named to the marshalship of Arizona in July 1897 by the new Republican president, William McKinley. Milton used his influence with his new boss and officials of the Southern Pacific

Railroad and Wells, Fargo to get a similar appointment for Scarborough in New Mexico Territory. Creighton Foraker, a Grant County rancher, had been named marshal for the territory at the same time Griffith was appointed. Although Scarborough was a Democrat, Marshal Foraker, faced with a serious outlaw problem and needing all the experienced help he could muster, welcomed the recommendation and conferred Scarborough with federal deputy authority.

At Milton's suggestion, Scarborough, who was not known in Arizona, went under cover to get information concerning the movements and plans of the Black Jack gang. In Cochise County he took a job as a cowhand with the San Simon Cattle Company, owned by Claiborne Merchant and James H. Parramore of Abilene, Texas, whom George had known since his days as Jones County sheriff. His arrival at the San Simon headquarters was recalled half a century later by Holmes Maddox, one of the ranch hands:

> A bunch of San Simon Cattle Co. cowboys, including W. O. Shugart, Young Bell, Oscar Cochran, and myself . . . , were shoeing up the San Simon remuda under the cottonwood trees at the old Cienega headquarters ranch in San Simon Valley, when a clean cut fellow, with blond hair and mustache, riding a good horse, came in, dismounted, and inquired for the foreman, Jess Henley. He introduced himself as George Scarborough, which at that time meant nothing to any of us. . . . [He] went to work . . . as a common cowboy [and] he did his full share of all the ranch work and was sent by the foreman, Jess Henley, on outside roundup as any of the other cowboys working there.[5]

In September 1897 the new Black Jack gang, Tom and Sam Ketchum, Dave Atkins, and Will Carver, held up a Gulf, Colorado and Santa Fe train near Folsom in the northeast corner of New Mexico, getting away with about three thousand dollars in cash. Two months later the remnants of the old Black Jack gang, Bob Christian, George Musgrave, and Theodore James, struck the Atlantic and Pacific at Grants in central New Mexico and hit a ninety-thousand-dollar bonanza, one of the most lucrative hauls in the history of western banditry.[6]

Although these crimes were committed far to the north of the area Scarborough was working, he was vitally interested, because the pattern for the Black Jack gangs had been to head for hideouts in the southern counties after a robbery. The identity of the gang members was not known to the officers at the time, but Scarborough suspected that some of them had recently worked for the Erie Cattle Company in Arizona's Sulphur Springs Valley. In time he would become convinced that the Erie, a ranch under absentee Pennsylvania Dutch ownership, harbored a nest of outlaw cowboys who worked cattle for their employers by day and hatched schemes to rob by night. He was particularly suspicious of the Erie foreman, Bob Johnson.

Whether because of the deliberate policy of Johnson or mere coincidence, the Erie did employ an inordinate number of hard cases and long riders. The Christian brothers had worked for the Erie after their flight from the Indian Nations, Bob under the road name Tom Anderson and Will as Ed Williams. When they began their string of train and post-office raids, they often used the familiar Erie ranges for hideout locations. The Utah bandit Robert Leroy Parker, better known by his alias, Butch Cassidy, rode into Arizona Territory and took work on the Erie spread when lawmen made things too hot for him in his northern haunts. In Arizona and New Mexico territories, Cassidy was known as Jim Lowe. With him came another member of the Hole-in-the-Wall gang, William Ellsworth ("Elzy") Lay, who used the alias Will McGinnis in the southern territories. Another Erie hand who rode with both the Cassidy Hole-in-the-Wall bunch and Tom Ketchum's Black Jack gang and was a primary link between these northern and southern freebooter bands was Will Carver, alias George W. Franks. Other Erie hands included Tom Capehart, Henry Marshall, Ed Cullen, Jim James, Andy Darnell, Frank Johnson, Irwin Bradshaw, Emery Cooper, and Perry Tucker, several of whom, perhaps through their association on the ranch with hardened criminals like the Ketchum brothers, Cassidy, Lay, and Carver, later drifted into outlawry.

Joseph ("Mack") Axford was sixteen years old when he broke broncs with Capehart and Marshall at an Erie horse camp in the winter of 1895. "Tom Capehart," he said, "was a noted bronco stomper; he had ridden the celebrated outlaw Glencoe of the San Simon outfit, even after he had unhorsed all of their top hands. Glencoe was still mentioned years later as one of Arizona's worst buckers. Henry Marshall . . . was a fair to middling cowhand, more noted for his pleasant disposition and for being a steady and hard worker."[7]

Capehart later rode for the Diamond A in New Mexico and Henry Brock, ranch manager, also attested to the cowboy's skill with broncos.

> He was a jolly sort of fellow, Capehart. . . . . Sometimes he'd get on a horse, a pitchin' horse, in the morning and it would start apitchin' off in big, high jumps, and he'd be all over, just makin' all kinds of motions with his head and like-a-that. . . . He didn't pay no attention to the horse, you know. The horse would be doing his best, but Capehart he was way back and way forward and goin' this way like a fella that can't ride, you know. That's puttin' up an awful job of it, you know.[8]

Deputy marshals Scarborough and Milton would arrest Capehart and Marshall, together with several others, after a Southern Pacific train was held up at Steins Pass, a small station near the New Mexico–Arizona border, on December 9, 1897. At the time, Scarborough was still fuming over a rumor reported in the *El Paso Herald* two weeks before that he and Frank McMahan had robbed the train at Grants on November 6.[9] The story was picked up and repeated in other papers, including the *Eddy Argus*, which added, with fine understatement, "George Scarborough's feelings are miffed."[10]

In early December, undercover agent Scarborough got word to U.S. Marshals Griffith and Foraker that within ten days a holdup of a Southern Pacific train was planned somewhere near the line separating the territories. Express-car security on the runs was augmented and on December 7 lawmen began assembling at an encampment near Bowie Station, thirty-five miles west of Steins Pass. Scarborough joined the group of some twenty officers, which included Foraker and Griffith; the noted Wells, Fargo detective Jonathan Thacker; Cochise County Sheriff Scott White; Sam F. Webb, collector of customs at Nogales, Arizona; Cipriano Baca, city marshal of Clifton, Arizona; and Jeff Milton.

On the night of December 9 the officers at Bowie were notified by wire of the holdup at Steins Pass. They split into two groups. One seven-man posse set out across the San Simon Valley for Skeleton Canyon, where it was believed the outlaws were headed.

The rest of the officers, including Scarborough and Milton, loaded their horses on a special train and sped to Steins, arriving on the scene two hours after the holdup. There they found the body of one of the bandits, later identified as Ed Cullen, the top of his head blown away by a shotgun blast. During a half-hour gun battle with the robbers, the express car had been defended well by messenger Charles Adair and guards C. H. Jennings and Eugene Thacker, son of Jonathan Thacker. In addition to killing Cullen, the Wells, Fargo men believed they had punctured the hide of at least one other bandit before the survivors rode off, empty handed except for a Winchester rifle and $11.20 taken from the station agent.

Griffith and Foraker went on to Lordsburg with Cullen's body, leaving the arduous mounted pursuit to their more saddle-tough deputies. At first light as the possemen prepared to take the trail of the bandits, they watched with fascination as a raven feasted greedily on a lob of Cullen's brain that had spilled out on a railroad tie.[11]

The trail of four horsemen led southwest toward the Ciénega Ranch of the San Simon Cattle Company. Before the ranch was reached, one of the outlaws left the others and turned westward alone. The following posse let him go and stayed on the trail of the remaining three, which led directly to the San Simon headquarters, where it seemed to end. Jess Henley, Oscar Cochran, and Holmes Maddox were the only men at the headquarters and some of the officers wanted to arrest them as the robbers, but Scarborough vouched for the three and said there had to be a trail heading out. It required some searching, but the officers finally picked up the trail of the fugitives, still heading south.[12]

The paths of the two posses converged near the southeastern edges of the Chiricahua Mountains and the combined force of lawmen continued on across Shake Flat. On the morning of December 12 they followed the trail up Tex Canyon to a known outlaw rendezvous, 120 miles from Steins.

The site has been described by an Arizona rancher named Jesse James Benton, who had stumbled onto it not long before and, marveling at its wild beauty, coveted it for his own:

> One day I rode up lonesome Tex Canyon in the Chiricahua Mountains looking for cattle to buy, and I run onto a ranch in a wild and beautiful locality at the south end of the range, a wooded region with a pretty

spring, and a chinked log house in a clearing. . . . When I saw that
place my heart skipped a beat. That ranch I wanted for myself. . . .
"Smoke [was] coming out of the house, so I rode up to it. I were
surprised to find eight outlaws there in a bunch. . . . They was all
wanted men and tough hombres. Some of them [later] took part in the
famous Stein's Pass train robbery. . . .
    A man named Cush was the owner. I bought a few cattle off him,
and then I said, "You want to sell this place?"
    "Not for sale," he said.
    I knew why. It was an ideal outlaw hideaway."[13]

John Cush, alias Vinadge, was a man of unsavory reputation who
had once owned the notorious Bucket of Blood Saloon in the mining
camp of Pearce. He was not on hand when the posse arrived, but
Leonard Alverson, Bill Warderman, and Walter Hovey were. Alverson was a former Erie rider who told the officers that he and his
partners, Warderman and Cush, were running a small herd of cattle
drifted over from Mexico. The lawmen suspected, however, that
most of the herd had been rustled from the large ranches of the San
Simon Valley.

Hovey, who also went by the names Walter Hoffman or Huffman
and Fatty Ryan, was flat on his back in the house with a fresh
bullet wound in his leg. This, of course, interested the lawmen
immediately. Scarborough produced a pair of overalls he had found
along the trail and showed that a hole through one leg matched the
location of Hovey's wound. Milton had picked up a handkerchief
bearing the initials "T. K." at the robbery scene. When former Erie
cowhands Tom Capehart and Henry Marshall rode up to the camp
a few hours later, someone suggested that maybe the initials stood
for "Tom Kephart."

All five cowboys at the cabin were placed under arrest and charged
with complicity in the holdup. Alverson and Hovey later claimed
that the prisoners suffered severe abuse under interrogation by the
officers. "The only man of that posse I can speak a good word for
is Jeff Milton," Alverson said. "He acted like a man all the way
through. . . . I have heard he did some big talking afterwards but I
didn't pay any attention to it. I knew he was not that kind of a man
and I told them if Jeff Milton had anything to say bad about me he
would say it to my face."[14]

Leonard Alverson had few good words to say about the arresting officers. *Courtesy Kansas State Historical Society.*

Hovey said the officers confiscated all weapons and ammunition at the camp and then "would walk one of us at a time down the canyon to hold a court of inquiry. They would yell and fire their six-shooters at our heads, vilifying and insulting us. They struck Tom Capehart in the face and over the head with a gun and jabbed him in the stomach with a cocked .45." Strangely, Hovey singled out Cipriano Baca, not Milton, for approbation. "There was never any doubt but that for one member of the posse, Cipriano Baca, we would have lost our lives then and there. 'If any of these men are murdered I will kill the officer who fired the shot,' he declared."

Walter Hovey's bullet wound matched the holes
in the overalls Scarborough found. *Courtesy
Kansas State Historical Society.*

Because of his condition, Hovey was not taken out for questioning
but was grilled where he lay, particularly regarding how he got the
wound in his leg.[15]

The stories told by the prisoners were implausible and conflicting
in details. "We were working cattle along the border," Alverson
said. "I chanced to run across a smuggler with ten gallons of mescal
and I held him up and took it away from him. Guess I hadn't ought
to have done it, but I did. . . . Then Hoffman and I got drunk. . . .
I stumbled over some brush and fell. I had my pistol in my hand and
as I hit the ground it went off, the ball ranging up through the calf
of Walter's leg."[16]

Hovey said they were working the Silver Creek country to round up strays to keep them out of Mexico. . . . We made a late camp and shortly thereafter we saw three riders driving four pack animals before them. . . . They were Mexican smugglers heading for the mining camp of Bisbee. . . . We learned that they were carrying . . . contraband, including mescal, whiskey, and opium. Later in the evening, with most of us more or less intoxicated, we decided to highjack them. . . . In the fight that followed I was shot and the Mexicans took their leave.[17]

With the trail having led directly to the camp in Tex Canyon, Hovey's fresh gunshot wound, the torn overalls, the handkerchief, and the suspicious, inconsistent stories, the officers felt they had a

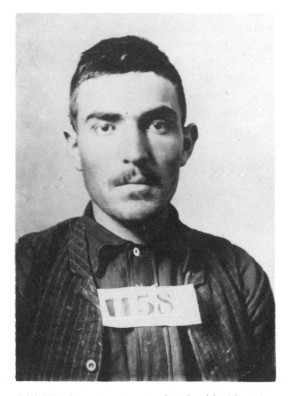

Bill Warderman was convicted with Alverson and Hovey. *Courtesy Kansas State Historical Society.*

good case. But Alverson, who always maintained his innocence, later said that "in order not to have any witnesses for the defense [the lawmen] had to implicate all of us. . . . They were as desperate as the outlaws. There had been innumerable holdups and robberies and no one had been caught, so they had to make an example of some one."[18]

A guard detail under Sam Findlay conveyed Alverson, Hovey, Warderman, Capehart, and Marshall by wagon to San Simon Station. There they were placed on a train and taken to jail in Tucson. Scarborough, Milton, and the rest of the posse remained to continue the pursuit of John Cush, Tom Ketchum, and Dave Atkins, who were believed to be still in the area. After several days most of the possemen wearied of the chase and cut a trail for home. Milton later said their leave-taking was prompted by discovery of an outlaw hideout. As Milton prepared to storm the redoubt, possemen suddenly recalled family responsibilities and begged off. Disgusted, George Scarborough said, "Milt, you know I'm married and got a wife and a lot of children, and damned if they can't take care of themselves. Let's you and me go."[19]

So only Milton and Scarborough stayed on. They closed in on the outlaw camp, but their quarry had flown. High in the crotch of a pine the bandits had hidden a cache, "molds for counterfeiting, Indian blankets, potatoes, and cans of honey, wrapped up in a big bed tarp. But a bear had found it, torn it up, hammered the cans of honey to pieces on the rocks, and scattered the supplies all over the flat."[20]

Sign indicated that Ketchum and Atkins had ridden out of the Chiricahuas but Cush had doubled back toward his ranch. Milton later reported an exchange between Scarborough and himself as they approached the cabin in Tex Canyon:

"Wells Fargo won't mind," mused Scarborough, "so let's just kill old Cush."

"We can't kill him in cold blood," objected Milton.

"We'd get rid of a good nuisance," Scarborough growled, with a logic Milton could not counter.

But when Cush was finally taken, it was Milton and not Scarborough who froze him in fear. He was not at the house when the officers arrived, so Scarborough remained on watch while Milton scouted the area. Meeting Cush and another rider on the trail, Milton threw up his rifle and centered Cush in his sights. "Milton came there to kill me," Cush said at his trial. "I could see it in his eyes. I never saw such eyes."[21] But John Cush was not gunned down, either by Milton then or Scarborough later. They released his companion and took Cush back to join his pals in jail.

Although the crime with which they were charged had been committed in New Mexico Territory, the suspects initially had been taken to the jail in Tucson, which was considered safer. Later they were moved to Silver City, New Mexico. For a time the young cowboys treated the whole affair as a lark.

Said Alverson: "I remember Walter asked as they took us from the jail in Tucson, 'What do you suppose they are going to do with us?'

"And I said, 'Hang us, I guess.'

" 'Well,' he answered, 'I hope they leave my legs untied because I would like to kick the block off one or two of them.' Guess we laughed too soon."[22]

On February 19, 1898, indictments were brought against the six prisoners by a grand jury of New Mexico's Third Judicial District for conspiracy to rob a train and the attempt to do so. Other indictments against Alverson, Warderman (under the name Watterman), and Hovey (Huffman) were returned for the robbery of the Steins postmaster, and Capehart, Marshall, and Cush (Vinadge) were indicted as accessories after the fact in this crime. Bond was set at ten thousand dollars per man, which none was able to raise.

Trial before Judge Frank W. Parker began at once. W. B. Childers, U.S. district attorney, first called the train engineer, T. W. North, who positively identified Hovey and Alverson as two of the robbers. Other crew members thought they recognized these two and Warderman as the men who had attacked the train. Possemen testified how the bandits' trail had led directly to the cabin in Tex Canyon, where they had found "dynamite, fuses, ammunition, and other articles such as would naturally be used in outlawry of the kind tried." Testimony was introduced linking the dead bandit Cullen with the defendants. Summing up, Childers argued that a strong case had been made for conviction of at least five of the six defendants.

Frank Cox, attorney for the Southern Pacific who had assisted Childers, "made one of the greatest speeches for the prosecution ever heard in New Mexico," according to the *Silver City Enterprise*.[23]

Defense counsel James S. Fielder came in for a share of praise from the paper, having "fought the case on behalf of the defendants with dogged perseverance and marked legal ability." He produced some alibi witnesses and a horde of character witnesses—Hovey said forty-two came from Arizona to testify on behalf of the defendants. Fielder brought out the improbable story explaining Hovey's leg wound. Acknowledging that the suspicious materials cached at the ranch belonged to outlaws, but Fielder maintained that they had been put there by the Black Jack gang and the innocent cowboys in the dock "dared not offend these outlaws and were of necessity aware of what was going on but could only remain quiet."[24]

On March 8, after sixteen days of testimony and argument, the case was turned over to the jury. The *Enterprise* reported that it "was the general opinion of those who attended the trial throughout, that the evidence against some of the accused was absolutely convincing as to their guilt." But after deliberating less than half an hour, the jury returned with a verdict of not guilty.[25] A furious Judge Parker called the jury's decision the "worst disgrace in a courtroom" he had ever seen and vowed that he would never again hold court in Silver City.[26] "Never before or since," said Walter Hovey, "have I witnessed such utter dejection [as] in that courtroom by the posse who had made this gigantic capture of train robbers. They had counted on the $5,000 reward for each of us."[27]

The officers' dejection and the defendants' elation were short lived, however, Childers filed federal charges against all six for the robbery of the post office at Steins. He later dropped the charges against Capehart, Marshall, and Cush, but the other three were moved to Las Cruces, in Dona Ana County, to stand trial at the fall term of federal court.

The Las Cruces jail, said Walter Hovey, was "a huge adobe dungeon with but one door and no windows, complete with "all the known vermin and filth . . . , bedbugs, lice and mosquitoes. . . . The only ray of light came through the steel-barred door. The heat was intense, yet the pieces of filthy blanket lying on the floor were damp to the touch. . . . The sheriff who was the manager of this torture chamber was . . . the notorious Pat Garrett."[28]

The prisoners spent more than six months in this jailhouse before coming to trial in September. Alverson said Garrett "had the jury packed with some of his professional jurymen. They were the most damnable looking kind of Mexicans. . . . Two were not even citizens. . . . The whole thing was a farce. . . . Of course we were found guilty and sentenced to ten years each. It was hell."[29]

Leonard Alverson, Walter Hovey (under the name Huffman), and Bill Warderman (under the name Watterman) were delivered to the territorial penitentiary at Santa Fe on September 28, 1898, to serve their time as federal convicts. John Cush and Henry Marshall disappeared from history's pages, but Tom Capehart, whether guilty or innocent of complicity in the Steins Pass robbery, turned to outlawry after this episode. A day was to come when he would figure prominently in the destiny of George Scarborough.

The core of the Black Jack gang, Tom and Sam Ketchum, Will Carver, and Dave Atkins, were still on the loose. They were called the Snaky Four by cowboys of the region because "they were like a snake—if they got riled up they would not run from anybody but would strike and strike hard."[30] But in the spring of 1899, Tom Ketchum's inherently quarrelsome nature became too much for the others and brought on a breakup of the gang. Dave Atkins cut loose and drifted up into Montana, and Sam Ketchum and Will Carver rode off, leaving Black Jack to go his way alone.

In July 1899, Sam Ketchum and Carver, with new gang member Elzy Lay, struck at Folsom, holding up a train and escaping with a haul estimated at seventy thousand dollars. A pursuing posse located the gang in Turkey Creek Canyon near Cimarron, and in a bloody gun battle two lawmen were killed and another posseman, Sam Ketchum, and Lay severely wounded. Ketchum was captured, but Lay, with Carver's help, managed to escape. Ketchum was taken to the territorial prison at Santa Fe. He developed blood poisoning from a gunshot wound in his arm but refused permission to amputate and died on July 24.[31]

In August, Elzy Lay was captured in Eddy County, New Mexico Territory, by Sheriff Cicero Stewart and subsequently tried and

convicted of the murder of Sheriff Edward J. Farr of Huerfano
County, Colorado, in the Turkey Creek Canyon fight. Sentenced to
life imprisonment, he served a little more than six years before being
released in December 1905. He is said to have dug up the balance
of the loot from the Folsom robbery, amounting to about $58,000,
settled in California, and lived comfortably until his death on November 10, 1934.[32]

After the gang's dissolution in the spring of 1899, Tom Ketchum,
like an old wolf banished from the pack, made his stealthy, solitary
way through the backcountry trails of New Mexico. When he learned
of the rich haul taken by his former pals at Folsom, he became driven
by jealousy and foolhardy bravado and attempted a single-handed
holdup of the same train at the same location only a month later.

Conductor Frank Harrington of the Colorado and Southern, had
been held up twice before and, tiring of the game, now kept a shotgun
within easy reach. During Black Jack's holdup, Harrington saw an
opportunity and blasted away at the lone bandit. Ketchum fell and
staggered off into the darkness. Searchers found him, weak and
bloody, along the track the next morning. He was arrested and taken
to Trinidad, Colorado, and later Santa Fe. Ketchum's arm had been
mangled by Harrington's shotgun blast. Like his brother Sam, he at
first refused to allow the doctors to cut it off, but later, as mortification
set in, he changed his mind and on September 3 his arm was amputated. A year later he was tried on a charge of felonious assault on
a railroad train, a capital crime in New Mexico Territory. Found
guilty, he was sentenced to death by hanging and the execution was
carried out at Clayton on April 26, 1901.[33]

Two hours before his execution Ketchum told his lawyer, John R.
Guyer, that he wanted to make a statement about the Steins Pass
train robbery. This took the form of a letter, couched in the language
of the attorney, and directed to the president of the United States,
William McKinley:

> Being now at the town of Clayton, New Mexico, awaiting my
> execution which is set for this day. . . . I desire to communicate with
> you by this letter some facts. . . . There are three men in the Santa
> Fe Prison serving sentences for the robbery of the United States mail
> at Steins Pass, New Mexico, in 1897. They are Leonard Albertson,
> Walter Hoffman and Bill Waterman. They are as innocent of the crime

as an unborn baby. The names of the men who did commit the crime are David Adkins, Ed Cullen, Will Carver, Sam Ketchum, Bronco Bill and myself.

I have given to my attorney in Clayton means by which articles taken in said robbery may be found, where we hid them. And also the names of the witnesses who live in that vicinity. . . . The fact that these men are suffering impels me to make this confession to prove their innocence. . . .

I wish to do this much in the interests of these innocent men, who as far as I know never committed a crime in their lives. I make this statement fully realizing that my end is fast approaching and that I must very soon meet my maker.[34]

McKinley agreed to look into the matter, but four months later was struck down by an assassin's bullet at Buffalo, New York. Two and a half years passed before, on March 29, 1904, President Theodore Roosevelt signed pardons for the three and Alverson, Hovey, and Warderman were released.[35]

The convicted men had always maintained their innocence and the Ketchum brothers, before their deaths, each made official statements exculpating them. Most historians have accepted the claims of the trio's innocence of involvement in the Steins Pass holdup, including Jeff Burton, an English scholar who has delved deepest into the confusing story of the various Black Jack gangs:

> It is plain that the three men were accessory both before and after the fact. . . . Whether they were in treaty with the bandits through inclination or as a matter of prudence is of small account, for they were . . . convicted not as accessories but as robbers. . . . It would be unfair to assert that all of those responsible for the ultimate conviction of these men knew them to be innocent of the principal charges, or that some were not acting—however misguidedly—in pursuit of some notion of rough justice. The conclusion, however, . . . is that the conviction of Alverson, Hoffman and Warderman was callously engineered by men who, in the main, neither knew nor cared whether the three were innocent or guilty and had no regard for the letter of the law, for justice as an abstract, or indeed anything except their own political future and personal well-being.

Burton names Jeff Milton, "[who] did not permit the finer mesh-work of the law to interfere with his understanding of justice," and George Scarborough, "[whose] efficiency as a stock detective made him the hobgoblin of rustlers [while] his methods and his manner were such that he was loathed by nearly everyone," as "the chief authors of the prelude to a judicial travesty," the arrest and conviction of Alverson and company. This came about, he says, "through their strategy of making the law work for them in thinning out the crop of thieves, smugglers, and abettors of outlawry."[36]

Implicit in this argument is the conclusion that a policy pursued by two of the arresting officers, Deputy Marshals Milton and Scarborough, was followed by the other fourteen members of the posse; their superiors, U.S. Marshals Griffith and Foraker; and the entire legal establishment, including District Attorney Childers and Judge Parker. It will be remembered that the judge was apparently so convinced by the evidence of the defendants' guilt that he exploded when a verdict of not guilty was returned at the first trial.

Justice may have miscarried in the conviction of Alverson, Hovey, and Warderman, but there was clearly sufficient evidence to bring them to trial and convince one jury, at least, of their guilt. George Scarborough's views on the case have not been recorded, but certainly Jeff Milton still was convinced of the guilt of the three young cowboys forty years later.[37]

Old Scarbrow was a mean old overbearing son of a bitch.

—J. E. HOWARD, JULY 24, 1945

-12-

Old Scarbrow

Scarborough's usefulness as an undercover agent ended when he tipped off the marshals about the Steins Pass robbery plan and came out in the open to help pursue the gang. He now returned to his home in Deming and took work as a cattle detective for the Grant County Cattlemen's Association. With the help of this organization, which worked in concert with similar ranchers' associations in New Mexico and Arizona territories, he eventually was issued deputy-sheriff papers for Grant, Sierra, Dona Ana, and Socorro counties in New Mexico and Cochise County in Arizona[1] Although these commissions carried no compensation, they enabled him to make arrests over a wide sweep of territory ranging from the Organ Mountains east of Las Cruces to the Whetstones and Huachucas west of Tombstone, an area more than two hundred miles north to south and almost three hundred miles east to west.

Within this vast range he would roam for the next twenty-seven months and his name would be cursed by lawbreakers and their apologists. Many brave and highly respected law officers fought the battle against outlaws in this region during the waning years of the century, men of the caliber of Jeff Milton, John Slaughter, Scott White, Cipriano Baca, Les Dow, Fred Higgins, Charlie Ballard, and Pat Garrett, but none of them inspired fear and hatred among the outlaw element as did George Scarborough.

Some of this undoubtedly could be attributed to the man's total devotion to his profession; unlike some of the others, who ranched or invested in other enterprises while holding positions of law enforcement, Scarborough had no other financial interests, and his

189

determination and tenacity as a manhunter remained undiluted. Deep religious beliefs, instilling within him clear-cut convictions of right and wrong, played a part, as did his sense of responsibility as head of a large family. His lack of ranching investment put him at odds with the small ranchers of the area, who perceived him as a tool of the large cattle companies, many of them controlled by absentee owners.

But the major reason Scarborough was so disliked was due to a change in personality after the El Paso episode. Because he was embittered by the lies that had been spread about him, his entire attitude changed and he vented his pent-up anger on lawbreakers and people who befriended them. "Nobody liked him very much—I didn't like George Scarborough," said Henry Brock, who bossed the Diamond A during this period. His view was probably typical of ranch managers who excused outlaws on the basis of personal friendship as long as they did not prey on their herds. "The officers used to think that I ought to do something about [the outlaws]," Brock admitted. "I told them . . . they were friends of mine and I had nothing to do with [their crimes]."

John Cox, who worked on the Diamond A, said: "Scarborough was a killer and men like Brock and Walter Birchfield and Joe Taylor . . . that managed the outfit didn't approve of that [the killing] but the owners apparently did approve of havin' a gunman on the range." Jeff Milton, added Cox, "was a killer too." Brock said "the stock companies down there wanted to hire [Milton but] I wouldn't stand for it. . . . I didn't want Scarborough as far as that's concerned, but I had to put up with it."[2]

During the years that the Black Jack and other gangs depredated through the southwestern territories, the work of the lawmen hunting them was made more difficult by this attitude, which was shared by the small ranchers, who viewed the officers as minions of the large financial interests, the railroads, the banks, and the absentee owners of the large spreads. The activities of the outlaws, most of them cowboys who often worked for the small ranchers, were viewed as not threatening and perhaps even admirable.

"The country was full of outlaws," Leonard Alverson said.

> If anyone tells you they bothered the ranchers they are wrong. They came and went freely at all of the ranches and we fed and bedded

them as we would any other white man, and asked no questions. Mrs. Hunsaker used to say she had a darn sight rather feed an outlaw gang than a posse and felt safer with outlaws; they were gentlemen, they left their guns outside, they appreciated what was given them and always helped with the chores, even sometimes washing the dishes. But the bar room rounders who usually formed part of the posse would stomp in with their spurs and hats on and spit tobacco juice all over her floor."[3]

Walter Hovey agreed, saying, "These posses were usually composed of around a half-dozen Americans and fifteen to twenty Mexicans and Indians. These [posses] were far more dangerous at your camp than the outlaws themselves."[4]

A Sierra County rancher named Ben Kemp related to his biographer an incident that illustrates the prevailing attitude of small ranchers toward outlaws and lawmen at the time. Kemp, who believed Wells, Fargo had helped Scarborough receive his federal appointment with the understanding that he would hunt down and kill or capture the members of the Black Jack gang, was stopped one day by Scarborough and "another tough-looking character."

"Mr. Kemp," Scarborough said, "I understand you let Tom Ketchum and his gang stop at your ranch."

"Scarborough," Kemp answered, "I am a rancher, and it is an established custom in this country that when a man rides up to your house in late afternoon and asks to stay overnight, you ask him in. I never make it a point to ask a man who he is, what he has done, or where he is going. I treat everyone alike. If you or anyone else comes to my ranch, he will be welcome if he acts like a gentleman. Under the circumstances, what would you do?"

Kemp said Scarborough considered this reasoning a moment, then nodded. "Well, I guess that is about all you could do," he said, and rode off without another word.[5]

The officers also had difficulty recruiting cowhands to join their posses. Jim McCauley, an Erie hand, was at a line camp in Mud Springs Canyon one winter day when a bunch of heavily armed possemen rode up looking for two bandits who had stopped briefly at the camp in their flight. "George Scarbrough [sic], the head of the posse, tried to get me to go with him," McCauley said. "I told him they would know me and I was not hunting outlaws, that I was working for the Erie Cattle Company and I wanted to still work for them, and probably if I went off with him after them train robbers, my time would soon be up working for any cow outfit."[6]

Some of the cowpunchers who knew and worked with the outlaws may have harbored resentment against Scarborough for spying on them while working undercover, but that feeling was not universal. Holmes Maddox of the San Simon described Scarborough as "one of the bravest, most fearless and cleanest peace officers in all the Southwest."[7]

Jeff Milton, aware of the change in his friend, said that after El Paso "sometimes George would want to do something a little bit rash." As an example of this rashness he cited Scarborough's suggestion regarding Bob Johnson, range boss at the Erie spread, whom George believed knowingly hid out outlaws at remote Erie camps. Johnson "was a tough hombre [with] the reputation of starting a row with everybody," Milton said. Scarborough was all for settling his hash. "I will go down there and let him start a row with me," Milton quoted Scarborough as saying, "and we'll see who is the best man." After ten minutes trying to talk his friend out of this idea, Milton finally exclaimed, "Damn it, George, I won't stand for it!" He and Scarborough then "went over the law of the work together." Of course Milton had the highest regard for his friend and fellow officer:

> Me and Scarborough was together intimately for a great many years and we never had a cross word once. . . . I didn't have to look around to see whether Scarborough was there or not. That was one reason we got along so well together; we had confidence in each other. We knew if we went together that the other fellow would be there all the time. . . . Scarborough wasn't afraid of no man.[8]

After the arrest of the suspects in the Steins Pass train holdup, Scarborough turned his attention to a desperado who would top his personal most-wanted list in 1898. William ("Broncho Bill") Walters, aka Broncho Bill Williams, Walter Brown, William Raper, Billy Swingle, and Kid Swingle, had been a general hell-raiser and troublemaker for southwestern peace officers off and on for most of the decade. Scarborough probably knew him in Baylor County, Texas, back in 1890 when George was a stock inspector and Broncho Bill, going by the Williams handle, was a young cowboy racing horses and enjoying the sporting life around Seymour with Fred Higgins and Bob Beverly. Later that year, Broncho turned up in Grant County, New Mexico Territory, at Separ, went on a drunken tear, and got himself arrested by Sheriff Harvey Whitehall.[9]

New Mexico cattleman John Cox said Broncho Bill was a top hand, the "outworkin'est" man he ever knew, "always in a good humor, but bad to drink. . . . Bronco would do anything for devilment." The trouble at Separ came about over a woman, one Alice Brewer, the station agent there, said Cox. Broncho, who always had an eye for the ladies, took a shine to Alice, but she snubbed him because he was a cowboy and she favored railroad men. Brooding over the rebuff and full of alcohol, Broncho watched Alice walking to the depot and bet someone a drink he could cut her skirts with a bullet. Alice ran screaming to the station office with Broncho's bullets kicking up dust around her.[10]

Walters and a cohort named Mike McGinnis were slapped into the Grant County Jail by Sheriff Harvey Whitehall, where they remained four months. On the night of February 15, 1891, they suddenly confronted the jailer with a cocked revolver and made their escape. "There are strong suspicions," said the *Silver City Enterprise*, "that members of a very respectable Silver City family are implicated in the rescue of the criminals." John Cox said an admirer of Broncho, rancher Henry Holgate, arranged the escape.[11]

Walters made tracks across the border to Palomas, Mexico. Deputy Sheriff Cipriano Baca followed and, appealing to Broncho Bill's well-known weakness for the ladies, enticed him back over the line on the pretense of engaging a fiddler for a dance. Once across the border, Baca arrested his man and returned him to Silver City for trial. In May 1891, Walters was convicted of unlawful discharge of a deadly weapon and sentenced to a year at hard labor.[12] After his release, Walt Birchfield signed him on as a hand at the Diamond A. "He was a tough one," Birchfield recalled, "a dead-hard hombre [who] had been an outlaw all his life." Soft-spoken, dark-eyed and dark-complected, with a "kind of a set iron jaw," Broncho Bill weighed only 135 pounds but was a good, hard worker, "a real ranch hand [who would] wrangle horses, cook, clean out mudholes, punch cows, anything," said Birchfield.

One of the reasons the lawmen had difficulty getting the cooperation of the ranchers in ferreting out the outlaws was the loyalty and trustworthiness shown by the outlaws toward their employers. "You could trust any of those cowpuncher outlaws if they was working for you," Birchfield said. "They'd do anything for you. They'd even risk their lives for you." Broncho Bill was no exception.[13]

Walters stayed out of trouble while working for Birchfield but later drifted up into the Mogollon country, where he was arrested for stealing a horse and jailed at Socorro. On February 26, 1896, he and about ten other prisoners tunneled their way out and escaped.[14]

A month later Walters appeared in Deming and had a gun battle with local officers. The *Silver City Enterprise* related the story in a humorous vein, saying the gunfire that awakened the Deming citizenry at one o'clock in the morning was occasioned by "a jubilee in honor of the arrival of Bronco Bill, a criminal who escaped from the Socorro county jail a few weeks ago." Deputy Sheriffs Frank Peters and John Phillips had been looking for "Wild William," as the paper dubbed Bill, and located him in an open lot near the Cabinet Saloon. The officers, each employing "rapid fire, poor-aim pistols" and their forces augmented by the night watchman, "armed with a Wells Fargo sawed-off scattergun," engaged Walters in combat at a distance of fifteen feet. "Wild William, being short on field pieces, was compelled to retreat after fifteen shots had been fired." No casualties were suffered, and "an hour later the contending forces again engaged in battle without fatal results. Six shots were fired during the second engagement." The paper was shocked at this shameful exhibition of close-range marksmanship:

> Our desperadoes are degenerating to the level of French or Italian duelists. While there may be some excuse for the bad aim of the officials, there can be no excuse for . . . a bad man who carries such a suggestive sobriquet as "Bronco Bill." His nerve in standing off the three officers was all right, but his pistol practice, missing all three of them, makes us weary. "The old west ain't what it used to be." Such shooting makes us feel sad and forlorn.[15]

On May 27, Walters was quietly having a beer in El Paso's Senate Saloon when he was recognized by police officer Mannie Clements. The *El Paso Times* said Clements hunted up Deputy Sheriff Ed Ten Eyke, who secured a fugitive warrant for Walter's arrest, and the two officers returned to the Senate and took Broncho into custody.

Walters was coatless with no weapon in sight but when searched was found to have "two big pistols concealed in his shirt."[16]

It was John Cox's recollection that George Scarborough assisted Clements in the arrest of Walters and conveyed him back to Sorocco.[17] Scarborough was still in El Paso in May 1896, awaiting the action of the district court in both the Mroz and Selman shooting cases, but this was the period when he held no regular law-enforcement position and was, at least to Juan Hart of the *Times*, persona non grata in El Paso. He probably took no part in the arrest, but his friend Sheriff Simmons may have deputized him for the specific assignment of delivering Broncho Bill to Socorro County authorities. If Scarborough and Walters did make the trip together to Socorro, they necessarily became well acquainted, a significant fact in the light of later events.

In December, Broncho Bill was convicted of petty theft and sentenced to thirty days in jail and two dollars in costs. In June 1897 he stood trial at Roswell for attempted murder in the Deming shootout and was released on his promise to quit the territory.[18]

But instead of leaving New Mexico, Broncho Bill threw in with Tom Ketchum's gang and moved into the criminal big leagues. It is not known whether he participated in the gang's first Folsom train robbery in September 1897, but both Tom and Sam Ketchum named him as one of the gang that struck the Southern Pacific at Steins Pass in December of that year.

After the Black Jacks split up following the Steins Pass job, Broncho Bill recruited some of the unattached outlaws with which the surrounding ranches seemed well supplied and formed his own gang. A story swept through the country in early January that Broncho Bill was bringing this gang to Silver City to liberate Alverson, Hovey, and Warderman. Newspapers carried the report, and the *Silver City Enterprise* even traced Broncho Bill's movements, saying he had come up from the south and crossed the railroad between Separ and Lordsburg. "The officials here were notified and had a warm welcome awaiting the gang," said the paper. "They scented the danger and shied off into the Burro Mountains."[19] Whether Walters ever planned a rescue attempt for the Steins Pass accused is not known, but his notoriety soon had George Scarborough and Jeff Milton on his trail.

After the arrests in Tex Canyon, Milton loaded his horse on a train and headed for Old Mexico to meet Colonel Emilio Kosterlitzky of the *Gendarmería Fiscal*, the Sonora mounted police, and help him investigate a report that Black Jack gang members were holed up at a mountain rendezvous. Along the line the train was flagged down by a young man who had a message for Deputy Marshal Milton. It was George Scarborough's son, Ed, turned out to follow in his father's profession. Scarborough had begun to assemble a crew of riders to help him cover the vast rangeland in the cattlemen's interests, and eighteen-year-old George Edgar, known to all as Ed, was his first recruit. Walt Birchfield, Frank McMahan, Dan Hathaway, and others joined him later.

Ed's message was that George was detained on other business but had sent his boy to side Milton wherever the trip took him. "He was just a kid," Milton recalled, "[but] I took him with me and got him a horse."[20] They went south to San Bernardino in Mexico to meet Kosterlitzky, the Russian Cossack *comandante* of the *rurales*, heading a troop of twenty disciplined Mexican fighting men, well mounted and supplied. This action was one of many in which Kosterlitzky cooperated with American lawmen to control the outlaws from both countries operating back and forth across the border.

The officers found the outlaw rendezvous but the birds had flown, leaving splintered pine trees all around the campsite where the gang members had practiced their marksmanship. About this time the posse was joined by George Scarborough, who, said Milton, "just fell on our trail and come right on to find us and caught us at Chuhuichupa. . . . We was way up at the top of them mountains on this strip."[21]

Coming down out of the Sierra Madre, they struck the Mexican Central Railroad at Casas Grandes, where a Wells, Fargo telegram awaited them. The reports that Broncho Bill was maneuvering his gang in an attempt to spring the Steins Pass prisoners at Silver City had reached the company and Milton was directed to get after him. Milton and the Scarboroughs, father and son, took the train back by way of El Paso.

Dropping Ed off in Deming, the two veteran officers continued on into Arizona Territory, where they formed a posse with Sheriff

Scott White, Sam Webb, and Orville Cooper. Cutting Broncho's trail, they dogged him and his gang for two hundred miles through the Burro Mountains and by Frisco and Eagle creeks to the Black River. Unable to shake their pursuers in the mountain fastnesses, the outlaws then swung southward, setting their faces toward the Mexican border. The posse was close on their heels when they struck the railroad at Steins Pass.[22] Milton said later that the lawmen were confident they could have taken Bill and his cohorts right then if Jeff had not ridden into Steins from his camp one night and learned that the authorities at Silver City had been telegraphing to every station for them. The trial of Alverson and company was in progress and the testimony of the officers was urgently required, so the manhunters went from trail to trial. They entrained for Silver City, leaving Broncho Bill to his own devices.[23]

Walters wasted little time in making those devices apparent. On March 29, only three weeks after the trials in Silver City, an attempt was made to rob the westbound Santa Fe Pacific at Grants Station, ninety miles west of Albuquerque. Named as participants in this holdup were Broncho Bill Walters, Bill ("Kid") Johnson, Jim Burnett, Dan M. ("Red") Pipkin, and Ed Colter, alias Jim Hightower, said to be a convicted murderer and prison escapee. Messengers C. C. Lord and C. H. Fowler resisted the gang's attempt to break into the express car, and in the gun battle the train's fireman was wounded. The robbers withdrew with only the loot they had extracted from the pockets of the crew and a few passengers. They were pursued by a posse led by Fred Fornoff, city marshal at Albuquerque. Jonathan Thacker and Jeff Milton organized another posse at Geronimo, Arizona Territory, to scour the American Valley in search of the bandits. Fornoff's party had a firefight with the fugitives on Eagle Creek and Colter was left to die along the trail, but the other train robbers made their escape.[24]

Two months later, on May 24, the gang struck again, stopping a southbound Santa Fe train at Belen, some thirty miles below Albuquerque. Broncho Bill, Kid Johnson, Red Pipkin, probably Jim Burnett, and others never identified participated in a robbery that was more successful, with a reported haul of twenty-five thousand dollars.[25] It was said that when the safe was dynamited, "Bronco

Jonathan N. Thacker, noted Wells Fargo detective, rode on manhunts with Scarborough. *Courtesy John Boessenecker.*

Bill grabbed a thousand dollar bill, and was heard to yell out: 'Oh, you long green, come let me kiss you, honey, for I've been a-hunting you a long time!' "[26]

Valencia County Sheriff Francisco Vigil and his chief deputy, Daniel Bustamante, quickly organized a posse of Pueblo Indians and started in pursuit. They overtook the gang at Alamosa Creek and one of the West's deadliest fights between outlaws and officers ensued. Broncho Bill's men poured heavy and accurate fire on the posse from the rimrock, killing Vigil, Bustamante, and one of the Indian trailers.

Walters took a bullet through the left thigh, Johnson was hit in the neck, and one or more of their cohorts were killed. After their leaders fell, the Indian possemen withdrew, taking the dead officers with them. The surviving outlaws had lost their horses but escaped on foot, leaving their dead. For years afterward hikers in the area found human bones, believed to be the remains of the slain outlaws.[27] Other posses were mounted and scoured the mountains south and west of Belen in search of the surviving gang members, but Broncho Bill and his pals had vanished. Commented the *Silver City Enterprise*:

> Broncho Bill has just made his latest bow to the public in the holdup at Belen and . . . has sought safety in haunts at Black River. He is stealing some of Black Jack's prestige as the boss bandit of the Southwest and if an intense rivalry for the reputation of the worst bad man could be promoted between these two ruffians, they might be induced to kill each other off.[28]

Shortly after the Belen holdup, Scarborough and Milton decided to go after the bandits. They intended to operate strictly as bounty hunters without the support of Wells, Fargo or the railroad companies, their only aim to collect the five hundred-dollar reward offered for each of the robbers. Milton took leave from Wells, Fargo and Scarborough turned his cattle-detective chores over to subordinates. As they prepared for a long scout into the mountains, Colonel Epes Randolph, division manager of the Southern Pacific Railroad at Tucson, heard of their plans and sent word that he would provide a special railroad car for the conveyance of themselves and their horses and pack animals, as well as papers authorizing passage on any rail line in Arizona or New Mexico territories.

The manhunters outfitted in Nogales, Arizona, hooked their car onto an eastbound train, and went to Deming, where they enlisted two more expedition members, Eugene Thacker and a Diamond A cowboy named Martin. Young Thacker, son of the celebrated Wells, Fargo detective, had distinguished himself as an express guard during the Steins Pass holdup the previous year. Martin was recommended by Diamond A boss Walt Birchfield, who assured Scarborough that, unlike many of his ranch hands, the young fellow had no ties to the outlaws. "A long, slim fellow [with] a fine layout," Martin showed up wearing a fancy pair of chaps. "Fellow," Milton said, "better not

Eugene Thacker, son of the well-known detective, was enlisted by Scarborough and Milton to assist in the hunt for Broncho Bill. *Courtesy John Boessenecker.*

take those up in that country where we are going. Somebody's liable to kill you for them."[29]

On a tip that Broncho Bill was planning a holdup at Holbrook, Arizona Territory, the four-man posse hitched onto an Atichison, Topeka and Santa Fe train and rode it north to the junction with the Santa Fe Pacific above Los Lunas and from there went west to Holbrook. They camped out of town and rode the express cars back and forth through Holbrook waiting for the gang to strike.

During these tiresome train rides and at night in camp after long scouting trips in the mountains, Scarborough laboriously recorded the day's activities in a journal. "Scarborough was a peculiar fellow. He kept a diary every day . . . every night he wrote it down," said

Milton, who remembered holding matches so that his partner could see to make his journal entries.[30]

After several weeks of wearisome vigil in the Holbrook area, the manhunters received a telegram that Walters and Kid Johnson had shown up 120 miles south in Geronimo. They had gone on a buying spree, spending three hundred dollars on five suits of clothes and other articles, including every cartridge in town that fit their guns. Then they had appeared at a Fourth of July dance being held at a nearby schoolhouse. While Johnson stood guard at the doorway, Broncho Bill, with his well-known penchant for disporting with the ladies, went down the line of women present, demanding a dance with each. When a redhead named Tillie Windsor declined, pleading fatigue, Broncho (or Johnson in some versions of this tale) shouted, "Damned if I don't see that you do!" and started pumping bullets around her feet. The room cleared in seconds. Tillie, whose escort at the dance was a local law officer, said later she could not remember who went through the window first, the lawman or herself.[31]

No railroad lines extended south through the White Mountains, so the officers had to retrace the circuitous route they had taken to Holbrook, hitching rides for their special car over the lines of the Santa Fe Pacific, the Atchison, Topeka and Santa Fe, the Southern Pacific, and the Gila Valley, Globe and Northern through New Mexico and Arizona.

On the night of July 13 they unloaded horses, saddles, pack animals, and supplies at Buttermilk Point, fifteen miles from Geronimo, made camp, and then rode into town to interview those who had attended the dance and pick up any information regarding the gang's later movements. On their return, they set out for the San Carlos military reservation.

"There we commenced a ride, the like of which I have not made in many, many days," Scarborough told a reporter three weeks later. "Skirting the Gila River that night, we made our way to San Carlos." The trip was made over the mountains in a heavy downpour and violent electrical storm. They camped outside San Carlos and went into the post the next morning to talk to the officer in charge, for whom they had a letter explaining their mission. He offered the services of his Apache scouts as guides and they took along two but soon became displeased with the Indians and sent them back. "From there we struck across the mountains for Fort Apache, seventy miles distant," Scarborough said. "We didn't travel any trails either, just kept to the hills all the way. After two days hard riding we reached Fort Apache and from there struck out towards Black River and knew we were then within the rendezvous of the outlaws."[32]

For days they searched the rough White Mountains terrain for a sign of the outlaws. Once they followed a faint trail leading up to the crest of a peak called Old Baldy and found a stone cairn containing a tin can scratched with the brand of the Diamond A, the New Mexico ranch far to the east. Broncho Bill, they knew, had cowboyed for the Diamond A. "Bill's work, or I'll eat my hat!" exclaimed Martin. It was the first real clue they had that the outlaw might be close, and they pushed on with new enthusiasm.[33] Said Scarborough:

> After several days scouting, taking great care that we showed ourselves to no one, on the morning of July 29th we made our way into Hampson's horse camp on Black River. We had heard nothing of the outlaws, but had made up our minds to raid some of the adjacent cow camps Saturday night and see what we could find. At the horse camp we found the horse-wrangler and did not allow him to leave there that day. Saturday morning we had gathered in six cowboys who had rode in there and was holding them while we made preparations for the raid that night.[34]

The horse camp belonged to Joe Hampson of the Double Circle Ranch. Held with George Felshaw, the wrangler, were Double Circle riders John Gibson, Tom Bennett, Henry Banty, J. E. Howard, and Rufus Nephews, called Climax Jim because he favored Climax plug chewing tobacco.[35] An old bear hunter who happened to have stopped at the camp also was detained because the officers wanted to be absolutely certain that no one tipped off the outlaws. Everyone in the camp was relieved of all weapons and ammunition.

Of course these high-handed actions brought on much complaining by the detainees, the most vocal of whom was the bear hunter, who felt that he was not a part of the whole affair. All were incensed, however, and one of the cowboys, J. E. Howard, was still angry, especially at Scarborough, thirty-seven years later. "I will say," he wrote Jeff Milton, "that you, [Jeff], was the only officer in the bunch that had a hart [sic]. Old Scarbrow [sic] was a mean old overbearing son of a bitch after he had us disarmed and we had no guns, but you was kind to all of us."[36]

On the morning of Saturday, July 30, Scarborough and Thacker were at the camp guarding the cowboys while Martin went up on the mesa looking for horses. Milton had taken some fishing line and hooks out of his gear and, with Tom Bennett, one of the cowboys, had gone downriver a hundred yards after trout. Said Scarborough:

> About nine o'clock Saturday morning, I saw three men come riding down the hill about three or four hundred yards away. While I was looking at them, two stopped and commenced shooting at a rattlesnake that was under a large rock. The third man, who was in the lead, rode on down towards the camp. . . . Up to this time I had no idea who the man was, but as we had been holding every man who came in, I intended to hold him, whoever he might be. He rode up to within thirty feet of where I stood and got off his horse.

Scarborough eyed the stranger closely. "Who is that man?" he asked one of the cowpunchers.

"That's Hinton," the man answered.

But the bearded, dust-covered rider was Broncho Bill Walters. Scarborough did not know him at once, but Broncho recognized Scarborough's voice and immediately swung back up in the saddle. "Hold on there, Cap. I want to talk to you," Scarborough said in a normal tone.

Seeing Scarborough at this remote camp, Walters was aware at once he had ridden into a trap. "In a second Bill had his sixshooter spitting fire," Scarborough said. "As soon as I could bring my Winchester into play I opened up." Milton, who had hurried back from his fishing hole when he heard the first pistol shots, arrived in time to get in on the action. Both he and Thacker "took a hand in the little game," said Scarborough. "At the fourth shot Bill tumbled to the ground. . . . About this time we were conscious that somebody else was in the fight. A bullet sung by my ear and tore up the earth a short distance behind me."

The two riders who had stopped to shoot at the rattlesnake were Kid Johnson and Red Pipkin. When the firing began at the camp, they both dismounted, took cover behind a large boulder, and opened up at long range with their rifles. "I could just see their hat brims," said Scarborough. "They were about four hundred yards from us at

the time. We commenced a bombardment of the rock and made it
so hot for them that they ran."

Seeing that the outlaws were going for their horses, the lawmen
shot and killed both animals. Then, said Scarborough,

> Johnson took refuge behind a large Juniper tree close by and returned
> the fire. All I could see was his hips. I took a dead rest and fired and
> Johnson fell over and commenced to yell like a panther. I knew that
> he was bad hit. Pipkin fled over the hill and we never saw him again.
> We went up to Johnson and found he was shot through the hips and
> was suffering great agony. We carried him down to camp and laid
> him beside Broncho Bill, who had just regained consciousness.
>
> The fight was over. We had expected to stay in that country for
> three months if necessary, but in less than three weeks, we had
> captured our men.[37]

Milton had gone over to Broncho Bill as he lay unconscious on
the ground with "a 40-70 Winchester bullet lodged under his left
shoulder and [a] shattered right upper arm and shoulder."[38] The
outlaw was not breathing and Jeff thought he was dead. Grasping
him by the heels, Milton started to haul him toward the tent. When
he did, blood poured out of Broncho's mouth and he gasped for air.
Doctors later told Milton he had saved the man's life by dislodging
the blood that was choking off his lungs.[39]

Milton cut the bullet out of Walters's shoulder, but little could be
done for Johnson. His hip had been splintered by the bullet, which
had coursed up into his abdomen. Johnson was in terrible pain and
it was obvious that he would not survive. Milton scrawled a message
on a scrap of paper and dispatched Climax Jim to Fort Apache,
twenty-five miles away, to wire the Graham County sheriff at Solomonville. The telegram's brevity was typically Milton: "Send a
coffin and a doctor."[40] Another rider was sent to Clifton, and by
Sunday night Deputy Sheriffs Simpson of Geronimo and Clark of
Clifton were at the site. Also arriving was a detachment of soldiers
from Fort Apache with a post surgeon, who did little for the wounded
men but left some morphine to ease their pain.

Kid Johnson's cries before he died could be heard for two miles,
Scarborough said. George thought it strange that, although Walters
and Johnson lay side by side on the same cot for more than a day,
they spoke only a few words to each other. When Johnson was asked

if he wanted to leave a message for his father, a rancher living only forty miles away on Blue River, he said, "Tell Father not to grieve after me. I brought it all on myself. Tell him to hold no one responsible for my death. Just tell him, boys, that Bill said 'Good bye.' "[41]

Johnson died Sunday night. Before they wrapped his body in a blanket for burial, Scarborough reached over and pulled off the new pants that Johnson had bought in Geronimo only a few weeks before. "Reckon I need these worse than he does now," he said, putting them on in place of his own tattered trousers, which had almost been reduced to rags by the spined and daggered vegetation of the region.[42] They buried Johnson along the river, but according to J. E. Howard, "in a few days the bears dug him up and et him."[43]

"Monday morning the start was made for Geronimo with Broncho Bill," Scarborough said.

> An improvised bed was arranged on a pack horse and he was laid on it as gently as possible. . . . Broncho Bill stood the pain as long as possible and then . . . he said: "Boys, just throw this pack outfit over the hill and saddle me a horse, and I'll lead the way into town." This was done and Bill led the procession, and what nerve! Although suffering great pain every step, he laughed and joked with the posse, telling of numerous little scrapes in which he had played the leading part. Whistling and laughing, and shot through and through, he went to meet his fate as if it was a picnic excursion.[44]

When it arrived at Geronimo, the posse found the town in a state of excitement. Reporters representing papers from as far away as Los Angeles were on hand, and the depot was thronged with people who had come to the remote end-of-track town to see the celebrated outlaw Broncho Bill and the intrepid officers who had effected his capture. Milton and Scarborough made Walters as comfortable as possible on a spring cot in a passenger car of the waiting train while Thacker and Martin were detailed to the loading of the horses and equipment onto the officers' special boxcar for the journey to Santa Fe.

A full account of the search, gun battle, and capture, based primarily on a long interview with Scarborough conducted during the trip, was written by a reporter for the *Arizona Bulletin*. He described Broncho Bill as looking "pale and haggard with his right arm in a sling." He was surprised at the appearance of the outlaw. "Instead

of the big, bully, wild and ferocious looking desperado I had expected," he wrote,

> before me lay a boy with features like a girl; his once clear, blue eyes
> had been dulled by pain, but no complaint was uttered by those thin
> lips that remained shut tight, as if in death. I stepped back and the
> eager crowd of spectators shoved forward. They gathered around his
> body as if some strange animal had been caged. . . . Bill was tired
> and . . . just a little disgusted at the curiosity manifested by his
> visitors.

Milton and Scarborough were "tired and dirty" with broad belts
encircling their waists, "filled with the latest Winchester cartridges
and the trusty rifles [were] close at hand." Scarborough, "after some
coaxing and with admonitions not to use his name in the paper,"
agreed to relate the story of the hunt and capture, which the reporter
took down and later published, ignoring Scarborough's request to
omit his name. "During the ride to Bowie [Broncho Bill] made
frequent calls for "the bottle' but never entered into any conversation.
He ate peaches and smoked a cigar."[45]

A large crowd was waiting at the depot in Solomonville to get a
glimpse of the badman. When the mob converged around the open
window of the coach, Milton leaned over and whispered, "Bill, do
you suppose if I raised up your head, you could say 'boo' at those
fellows?"

"I will try to say it to the sons-a-bitches," Broncho answered.

Milton lifted him up and Broncho shouted "Boo!"

The crowd stampeded in sudden panic, those nearest the window
knocking others down in their hasty retreat, some getting pushed off
the platform onto the tracks. Broncho Bill laughed so hard "it liked
to have killed him," Milton said.[46]

At Bowie, where the party transferred to a Southern Pacific train,
the officers quickly conducted Walters through another depot crowd
and into a hotel. After eating he sat in bed, flanked by his captors,
and finally submitted to being interviewed by the newsmen who had
tried unsuccessfully to get him to talk during the journey. He said
his true name was William Walters and that he would be twenty-
nine years old in October. He related some details of his adventures
during the previous twelve years in Arizona and New Mexico territories, Texas, and Old Mexico. "I have had some pretty scary times in

Broncho Bill Walters's prison photo after he was captured by Scarborough and Milton. *Courtesy Kansas State Historical Society.*

those twelve years," he said, but he insisted that he had never murdered anybody. "When I rode into that horse camp last Saturday morning I knew the game had come to a showdown," he said. "I knew there was no escape left for me but I thought if I made the fight the other boys might be able to drag it. I opened the ball, boys, and you know the rest."[47]

Walters was delivered safely to the penitentiary at Santa Fe, where he was held until the December term of the district court at Socorro, when the grand jury brought three indictments for murder against him. His counsel for a time as he battled these cases in the courts was the celebrated New Mexico lawman Elfego Baca, but later Baca withdrew and when Walters finally came to trial in November 1899, he was defended by another lawyer. Convicted of second-degree murder, Walters was sentenced to life imprisonment.

By 1909 he was trying to obtain a parole, basing his plea, at least in part, on a claim that the officers who tracked him down, Scarborough and Milton, intended to kill him. In a letter to Henry Brock in September 1909, Broncho Bill wrote:

Dan ("Red") Pipkin eluded the officers at the
Double Circle horse camp but was captured later
in Utah. *Courtesy Yuma Territorial Prison State
Historical Park.*

Dear Old Friend. My friends are going to try to get me out of this
and I don't know but you can help me too. You will remember that
the talk was made by the officers before my arrest that they would kill
me and make the arrest after they were shure [*sic*] that I was dead.
And if you know such to be the case you can do me all the good in
the world by writing Mr. J. W. Raynolds, the superintendent [of the
New Mexico Territorial Penitentiary]. What we are trying to do is to
show that the men who were after me had no intention of arresting
me but to shoot me down wherever found. My friend[s] are going to
take my case to the board of peril [*sic*] October 9 and there is not
much time to spare. The official[s] here are doing all they can for me
but they advise me to write someone that knew the case and have him
write the super and I learned your address and thought it possible that
you had herd [*sic*] this talk and write the people for me. Yours in
haste, W. Walters.

Brock said that although many believed the officers had agreed to shoot Walters on sight, he could not personally confirm this from his own observation.[48]

Broncho Bill finally secured a pardon in April 1917, and returned to work on the Diamond A. Four years later, on June 16, 1921, he was killed when he fell from a windmill.[49]

Dan ("Red") Pipkin, who had made his escape on foot from the shootout at the Double Circle horse camp, was credited in some newspaper accounts with being the leader of a new gang that held up the westbound Santa Fe at Grants on August 14, 1898, but Pipkin was still afoot and hiding out in the mountains at that time. In September he appeared at Joe Hampson's ranch on Eagle Creek and "helped himself to three horses, at the same time threatening the lives of Joe Terrel and E. A. Von Arnim." Scarborough hounded his trail and Pipkin fled the country. In March of 1899 he was arrested near Moab, Utah, taken to Winnemucca, Nevada, held as a suspect in a train robbery attempt at Humboldt, and finally brought back to Los Lunas, New Mexico, by Eugene Thacker. He was indicted for the March 1898 robbery, but before his case came to trial, the Arizona courts in October 1900 tried, convicted, and sentenced him to ten years in the Yuma prison for the theft of the Double Circle horses. Released in April 1907, he lived out his remaining years in New Mexico, serving for a time as a deputy under Henry Brock when Brock was undersheriff of McKinley County. On July 6, 1938, at Gamerco, a village near Gallup, Dan Pipkin shot and killed himself.[50]

I will go to A. T. . . . after some cow thieves. . . . We are
having lots of fun out here at present.

—GEORGE SCARBOROUGH, APRIL 2, 1900

-13-

Gone to A. T.

With the breakup of the Broncho Bill gang, Jeff Milton returned to his messenger's assignment with Wells, Fargo and George Scarborough went back to patrolling the ranges of southern New Mexico and Arizona territories for the cattle companies. Scarborough was now using his son much more in this effort. Adept with gun and rope and knowledgeable about horses and cattle, Ed seemed well suited to follow in his father's chosen career of range detective. On December 13, 1898, Ed married sixteen-year-old Ruby Angelina Fuqua in Deming. The following September, Ruby gave birth to a daughter, named Corrine, and George Scarborough became a grandfather.[1]

Frank McMahan moved to El Paso in 1899 and worked on the city police force but often was able to get away to help his brother-in-law when called upon. George was in El Paso frequently, either on business or to visit his in-laws, but never was he at ease there after his rancorous experience following the Mroz and Selman affairs.

J. Marvin Hunter, newspaperman and Texas historian, related a story illustrating Scarborough's edginess when in the city. Hunter, whose sister had married McMahan, assisted the McMahans in the relocation to El Paso. On the day of that move, Scarborough wired that he would arrive in town on the evening train from Deming. McMahan was on night police duty and asked Hunter to meet Scarborough at the depot and take him to the new house. Hunter arrived a few minutes late and spent some time looking around the station for his man. It was dark, but he finally spotted Scarborough walking down San Antonio Street away from the depot. Running after him, Hunter shouted, "I've finally caught up with you!"

Instantly Scarborough whirled around, his six-shooter in his hand. "Who are you?" he snapped.

Hunter skidded to an abrupt stop and talked fast: "I'm Marvin Hunter, McMahan's brother-in-law. You know me."

"Boy," Scarborough said, holstering his gun, "don't ever come up behind me and say you've caught me."

Later Hunter admitted being badly frightened. "I was scared, all right. If he had two pistols on, one may have barked, leaving the other to ask questions."[2]

Another upon whom Scarborough could call for help in his cattle-detective duties was Walt Birchfield, Diamond A ranch foreman. A cattleman all his life, Birchfield was born in Uvalde, Texas, in 1870, the son of a rancher who drove herds to the Kansas railheads every year from 1873 to 1880. At the age of nine, Walt had gone up the trail with his father.[3] He had smelled gunsmoke, too. He was eighteen, cowboying for the Chiricahua Cattle Company in Arizona Territory when he was involved in a shootout with Mexican sheepherders on Bonita Creek in which three sheepmen were killed and he suffered a leg wound that left him with a stiff knee for the remainder of his life. Charges were brought against Birchfield and two other Chiricahua cowboys, but in April 1889 a Graham County grand jury refused to indict them.[4]

Other Grant County cowboys and sometime lawmen whose services were enlisted by Scarborough to assist in the constant war against horse thieves and cattle rustlers included Dan Hathaway, Walter Weatherwax, Roscoe Gill, W. D. ("Keechi") Johnson and Miles Marshall. Their work received little attention in the press. Since El Paso, Scarborough had distrusted newspapermen and felt that he and his men could do their job more effectively without publicity. This was apparent in his insistence that his name not be used when he was interviewed at length after the Broncho Bill capture. The fact that the reporter chose to break his promise hardly softened Scarborough's already jaundiced view of newsmen in general. Usually Scarborough or his men turned suspects over to local authorities and let them take credit for the arrests. Although he held county and federal commissions, Scarborough's remuneration came from his cattlemen employers. Unencumbered with the necessity of running for office or seeking appointment, he felt no need for public

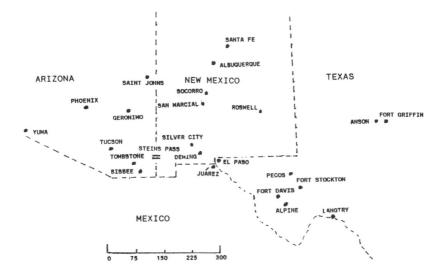

Outlaw Country. The Range of George Scarborough, Lawman.

approval to please an electorate or political boss. As long as his employers knew that he was on the job, he was satisfied.

Occasionally a brief news item appeared, however, such as this April 7, 1899, piece in the *Socorro Chieftain:* "George Scarborough captured Clay Hunter and Frank Wilson, who had a bunch of stolen horses in their possession at Kiehne's ranch 35 miles west of Patterson this week. Hunter and Wilson were lodged in jail yesterday. The horses were left at Kiehne's pasture. Mr. Scarborough went west again this morning."

Even an event as dramatic as a gunfight he had with an outlaw named John Williams on Black River received almost no mention in the press because Scarborough wanted it that way. Although wounded in the exchange, Williams got away. His escape was to lead to another confrontation in Geronimo. The fight on Black River had taken place on November 26, 1898. Early in January 1899, Williams showed up in Geronimo, where John Selman, Jr., had just taken a job as deputy under Graham County Sheriff Ben Clark.

After he escaped from the Juárez jail, young Selman had gone to Brown County, Texas, where he worked as a deputy sheriff. At Brownwood he fatally shot a man named Tom Turner and thus joined the mankilling fraternity of which his father had been such a prominent member. Although legally cleared in the shooting, Selman knew that Turner had friends and believed it prudent to seek other scenes. He went west to Arizona and landed in Geronimo, then in its heyday as an end-of-track town. Like all western boom towns, Geronimo was full of hardcase drifters and fugitives from the law. Old-timers used to say that on hot nights in Geronimo when folks slept on rooftops to escape the heat, you could tell which rooftops had outlaws because their ladders were always drawn up.[5]

Ben Clark gave Selman a deputy's badge and the local merchants agreed to pay him the munificent sum of $150 a month to keep the peace. He had been there only a week or two when Clark wired instructions to arrest and hold Williams for the sheriff's arrival by train the next day. Selman found the wanted man laid up in bed, still suffering from a six-week-old gunshot wound. The holding of prisoners presented a problem for the young deputy. "There was no jail in Geronimo," he said, "but I had a big pile of piñon logs in the yard and I chained their legs to the logs." Williams was in such bad condition, however, that Selman hesitated to chain him out in the open in the dead of winter:

> I told him that I had orders to arrest him on a wire from the sheriff, but I would leave him at home under guard. I found a fellow who was pretty trustworthy and deputized him to guard Williams through the night. . . . The next morning . . . the deputy reported to me that while he had stepped out of the house for a short time, some of Williams' friends had taken him away in a wagon. . . .
>
> It put me in a very embarrassing position. The sheriff was due in a few hours on the train. . . . I never felt so humiliated in my life as I did when I met him and had to tell him what had happened.[6]

In addition to his humiliation, John Selman, Jr., was in for a shock, for stepping off the train with Sheriff Clark was George Scarborough, a shotgun in his hand and blood in his eye. George did not know yet that his bird had flown, but according to a story in the *Santa Fe New Mexican*, he had been advised before getting off the train that friends of Williams "and other bad men whom he had made the country too warm for, had been laying in wait with Winchesters and sixshooters to take his life when he appeared."

Scarborough was undaunted, said this highly colored and melodramatic newspaper yarn. He

> took the situation in, but never flinched, and told the conductor to send his body back to Deming where his wife would give it a decent burial. The railroad men urged him to take refuge in the depot or stay on the train, but the detective knew no fear and walked out in the open with his repeating shotgun in his hand.
>
> Four of the gang who had been especially detailed by their comrades in crime to do the killing were standing some distance off with their guns, and everybody in sight expected murderous work to begin at once. But George was ready with his repeater, his eagle optic was peeled for business, and, had any one of those men drawn a bead on him, at least two would have gone down with him. But a criminal is always a coward and . . . the detective kept an unflinching lookout and not one of those wretches in that outfit dared to fire.[7]

Selman recorded none of this, saying the tension that developed upon Scarborough's arrival was strictly between the two of them and was due entirely to the fact that this was the first time he had set eyes on Scarborough since the death of his father almost three years before. Said young Selman:

> I went to the train to meet [Sheriff Clark], and received the surprise of my life. Who should step off the train with him but George Scarborough! George started toward me and I reached for my gun. Ben Clark jumped between us and said, "For God's sake, John! Don't have any trouble here."
>
> He was right. I was his deputy and it would have been a bad mess. He took Scarborough across the street to a hotel and remained there with him until train time and left with him. I learned later that it was Scarborough who wanted Williams and that it was Scarborough's bullet that Williams was packing. I never saw Scarborough again.[8]

The story was picked up in other southwestern papers and treated as a rather dramatic meeting between the well-known gunfighter Scarborough and the son of his most notorious victim. According to the *Arizona Republican*, for instance, young Selman confronted Scarborough with "some angry and ugly words" about the death of his father and only the intervention of Sheriff Clark prevented serious trouble.[9]

Much of the hyperbole in the *New Mexican* story was undoubtedly the work of the writer, but it is clear that the essentials came from George himself and were intended as a sort of advertisement in which his portrayal as the bold, fearless, quintessential frontier lawman, nemesis of badmen, was done for a definite purpose. For several years the territorial legislatures of New Mexico and Arizona had been lobbied by various cattlemen's associations to establish a company of mounted state policemen, patterned on the Texas Rangers, to combat increasing outlawry, especially in the southern counties. Some newspapers supported the campaign, as is shown by this 1898 editorial in the *Phoenix Gazette*: "When such conditions exist, a company of paid 'Rangers' are required to stamp out and destroy the characters that bring about such a state of affairs. Let us have a Territorial Ranger Service."[10]

When Scarborough was interviewed in Santa Fe in January 1899,

Scarborough's Rangers ready to take the trail. From left to right: Dan Hathaway, Edgar Scarborough, George Scarborough, and Frank McMahan. *Courtesy Kansas State Historical Society.*

he was in the state capital "on legislative business," according to the news account. That business was to make a pitch for himself to be named captain of a New Mexico ranger company then under consideration by the legislature. "Mr. Scarborough," said the *New Mexican*, "has many friends who are morally certain that if he is made captain of the proposed troop of New Mexico rangers, he will clean out the foul roosts that have caused so much trouble in the southwestern part of the territory."[11]

The New Mexico legislature rejected the ranger proposal at the 1899 session. Neither territorial legislature was yet ready to expend the funds required to form and maintain a ranger force. It would be two years before the Arizona Rangers were established and six years before New Mexico would organize its Territorial Mounted Police.[12] Scarborough's Santa Fe visit did achieve a measure of success, however. Gov. M. A. Otero authorized a force of six rangers under Scarborough's command. Commission as special officers of New Mexico Territory were issued to Scarborough and his designated appointees by order of the governor. The territory would assume no financial responsibility, however, and it was understood that the New Mexico Cattlemen's Association would pay the men seventy-five dollars per month. This was intended only as a temporary arrangement, the forerunner of an official ranger company that would be established when the legislature finally appropriated the necessary funds.[13]

In June 1899, Scarborough was called from his duties; his father was dying. Family members were assembling at Cameron, in Milam County, central Texas, where the parson had settled in his final years. George took an eastbound train, hoping to reach his father and to speak with him one more time, but north of Cameron the train stopped. Severe storms bearing torrential rains had lashed central Texas, and the Brazos was in flood. The tracks were under water and a bridge across the river was awash. The conductor notified the passengers that the train would have to wait until the water subsided. Scarborough went forward and talked to the engineer, telling him how important it was that he get through. The engineer said he could not risk the safety of the passengers by taking them across the flood. The passengers need not be jeopardized, Scarborough argued. The locomotive could be unhitched and driven across without the cars. He was very persuasive.

Family tradition has it that the combination of George's persuasive powers and the flash of a one-hundred-dollar bill convinced the engineer to unhitch the engine and plow on through, but one hundred dollars was a lot of money for George Scarborough in 1899 and he may have flashed instead one of his badges and shown the engineer the business end of his .45. At any rate, the locomotive crossed the bridge and Scarborough got to Cameron in time to see his father before the parson died.[14]

George W. Scarborough died June 27, 1899, at the age of sixty-eight, an honored pioneer leader of the Baptist Church to which he had devoted his life. In twenty-five years he had helped found Baptist churches in many Texas towns, including Anson, Abilene, Stamford, Haskell, Big Spring, Colorado City, Snyder and Sweetwater.[15]

Parson Scarborough and his wife, Martha, had moved to Cameron to spend their declining years in the home of their youngest son, Lee, who had followed his father's calling and become a Baptist preacher. All the children of George W. and Martha Scarborough had been encouraged to pursue higher education. C. B. had attended a military and agricultural college at Baton Rouge, Louisiana, and Ada had gone to a Baptist school at Sherman, Texas, and completed one year at Judson College in Alabama. But it was Lee who chose an academic and religious career. He received an A.B. degree from Baylor University in Waco in 1892 and was a Phi Beta Kappa student at Yale, from which he graduated with another A.B. degree in 1896. After leaving Yale he returned to his parents' home, which was then in Abilene. He applied for and received a license to preach and delivered his first sermon at Abilene in June 1896. Later he preached at his father's old church in Anson and at the church of the eminent theologian B. H. Carroll in Waco. In October 1896 he became the pastor of the Baptist Church of Cameron. He was still unmarried when his father died.[16]

C. B. still ranched in Jones County, where he remarried after the death of his first wife. The two marriages produced seven children.

Sister Ada married C. C. McCargo of Anson and was the mother of three boys and three girls.

Lee Rutland Scarborough followed his father in
a religious career. *Courtesy Mrs. Evelyn
Linebery.*

Will married Kara Wiman and moved to Midland, where he
acquired extensive rangeland in western Texas and eastern New
Mexico and became successful first in cattle and later in the oil
business. He and his wife became the parents of five daughters and
a son.[17]

On the long train ride back to Deming after the burial of his father,
George must have reflected on the turnover of generations; in a few
months Ed's wife Ruby would have a baby, he would become a
grandfather, and a new Scarborough would replace the one passed
on.

On September, 10, 1899, train robbers hit again in Scarborough's
country. At 1:30 in the morning bandits held up the crew of the
westbound Southern Pacific at Cochise Station, twelve miles southwest of Willcox, Arizona Territory, blew the express car open with
giant powder, and escaped with booty variously estimated at between

Cicero Battle Scarborough. *Courtesy Moliere Scarborough, Jr.*

five thousand and thirty thousand dollars.[18] Local officers, including Willcox policemen Burt Alvord and Bill Downing, and Billy Stiles, constable at Pearce, were soon in the saddle, pounding over the mountain trails and checking out known outlaw hideouts. Sheriff Scott White mounted two posses to search the hills. Veteran man-hunters Jonathan Thacker and George Scarborough joined him as soon as they could reach Cochise County by rail after news of the holdup hit the wires. For four weeks the lawmen combed the region for signs of the robbers but turned up nothing.

Scarborough had been back in Deming only a few days when he nabbed a well-publicized bandit, albeit one of undeserved notoriety. The previous May, an unlikely pair of highwaymen had stopped a stagecoach near Globe and robbed the passengers of some four

Ada Scarborough McCargo, sister of George.
Courtesy Mrs. Evelyn Linebery.

hundred dollars. Quickly captured, the two turned out to be a minor criminal named Joe Boot and his female accomplice, a former diner cook named Pearl Hart. The novelty of a feminine road agent piqued the public interest and the newspapers gave Pearl a lot of ink, especially after she escaped from the Tucson jail with one Ed Sherwood, another small-time crook.

At Deming in late October, Scarborough recognized Pearl from a picture he had seen in *Cosmopolitan* magazine and traced her and her companion to a seedy hotel he described as an outlaw hangout. Barging into their room, he found the pair in a state of undress. As he put them under arrest, Pearl profanely protested that she couldn't possibly go with him as all her clothes were at a Chinese laundry. Scarborough directed her to dress herself in the clothes of her companion, and it was in male attire that Pearl Hart was conveyed back

As sheriff of Cochise County, Scott White rode on many manhunts with George Scarborough. When this photo was taken in 1928, he was warden of the Arizona State Prison and still had rewards out for Scarborough's son. *Courtesy Arizona Historical Society Library.*

to the Tucson hoosegow. Scarborough later described Pearl as one of the most foul-mouthed persons he ever had heard.[19]

In the early hours of February 15, 1900, train robbers struck again in Cochise County, holding up the New Mexico and Arizona train at Fairbanks, a station a few miles west of Tombstone. But this train was guarded by Wells, Fargo messenger Jeff Milton, who put up a stubborn fight and prevented looting of the mail and express car. During the battle, Milton blasted one bandit with his sawed-off shotgun before he himself went down, his left arm shattered by a rifle bullet. As blood spurted from a severed artery, Milton slammed the express-car door shut and threw the way-safe keys into a far corner. With rifle bullets ripping through the car, he managed to apply a tourniquet to his arm before fainting from loss of blood.[20]

Milton came close to death but survived. It was thought that his arm would have to be amputated, but the tough old fighting man refused to allow it and the arm was ultimately saved, although he got little use from it during the remaining forty-seven years of his life. The bandit he had shot, one Three-Fingered Jack Dunlap, was deserted by the gang at Buckshot Springs, where he was found and arrested by trailing officers. Dying from his wounds and embittered by the treachery of his cohorts, Dunlap named Bravo Juan Yoes, Bob Brown, and the Owens brothers, Louis and George, as accomplices in the foiled robbery attempt. Scarborough, who had once again rushed to Cochise County, joined Sheriff White in a sweep through the Sulphur Springs Valley, which netted them Brown and the Owens brothers. Yoes was captured later in Mexico.

The prisoners talked and named as planners of both the Cochise and Fairbanks holdups the Pearce and Willcox officers Stiles, Alvord, and Downing, aided by a pal named Matt Burts. Sheriff White and Scarborough descended on Willcox and took all four into custody.[21]

A month later, on Monday, April 2, 1900, George Scarborough received a telegram in Deming from Walt Birchfield, who was then managing the Triangle Ranch in the San Simon Valley of Arizona. Birchfield had come across a slaughtered beef at a campsite on the ranch and wanted George to join him in a search for the culprits. Scarborough was preparing to go to Las Cruces to attend a session of federal court but quickly made a change in plans. At the Deming station, waiting for the westbound train, he dashed off a card to his brother Will, now living in Matador, Texas:

Deming 4-2-1900
Dear Bro. & F.
Your card at hand. Glad Mother is better. I am sorry that our meeting has been changed but I will try & get there. This leaves all well except Mollie. She is in very bad health. I am at the depot now waiting for a train to go west. Will go to A. T. to freight after some cow thieves.

Edgar & my other man left this morning after some more. We are having lots of fun out here at present. Love to all. Write often.

Your bro G. A. S.[22]

It was the last thing he ever wrote.

Riding over the line he had traversed so often, past the familiar stations—Tunis, Gage, Separ, Lisbon, Lordsburg, Summit—he may have mused over a laudatory editorial that had appeared in the *Lordsburg Liberal* a few days before and wondered whether it might help get those politicians up in Santa Fe finally moving toward creation of a force of rangers with himself at the head:

> The cattlemen of Dona Ana County are profiting by the experience of their brothers in the Southern part of Grant County and are going to put a man in the field to look after their interests and to round up the festive cow thieves in their county. Since the cowmen of Southern Grant County put George Scarborough in the field, he has nearly wiped out the rustlers in this section of the country. Having him in the field is the cheapest and best insurance against losing cattle by thieves that the cattlemen ever invested in. One consequence of his riding the range is that the thieves are more plentiful than ever on the adjoining ranges. They have been driven from this section and it looks as though some of them had moved lower to Dona Ana County. Ultimately the cattlemen of both territories will have to adopt such methods to rid themselves of the rustlers.[23]

At San Simon Station, Birchfield was waiting with a mount for Scarborough. The property of Birchfield's employer, Mrs. A. E. Rook, it was a good horse named Old Smokey. Birchfield led the way to the point where the slaughtered Triangle cow was found, some eighteen miles to the northwest. There they camped for the night and early on the morning of April 3 took the trail of what they believed were Mexican smugglers operating between the border and the mines at Morenci.[24] The trail led south toward the Chiricahua Mountains. "We thought it was Mexicans at first," Birchfield said later. "Then we saw one of the horses had number one shoes on and found some Winchester shells and knew they weren't Mexican smugglers. . . . If I had known that outlaws had killed the beef . . . I wouldn't have sent for [Scarborough], as I wouldn't have tackled them just for the beef."[25]

When interviewed after the capture of Broncho Bill almost two years earlier, Scarborough had made a point of explaining the vulnerability of lawmen when trailing desperate outlaws. "Let me tell you something, right here," he said. "Don't you ever go trailing along behind an outfit like that; they can lay behind a rock and pick you off too easy."[26] He had been chasing outlaws for almost twenty years now and had trailed some of the toughest and wiliest desperadoes the Southwest ever produced. He did not know who the men were that he now followed, but he started from the basic assumption that if cornered they would prove to be armed, dangerous, and ready to fight. As the trail led higher and deeper into the mountains, he and Birchfield became increasingly wary. Shortly after noon they came to a place known at the time as Triangle Canyon but later called Outlaw Canyon, some eighteen or twenty miles southwest of San Simon. Here the men they were following had stopped for lunch. A lard pail used as a coffee pot was on the coals of a fire and, since the coffee was still hot, the officers helped themselves.[27] Continuing on up the canyon, at about two o'clock that afternoon, near a dry creekbed known as Triangle Springs, they encountered their quarry and, in Walt Birchfield's words, "matched the fight."

The story of that fight was widely reported in the press and has been written many times since. Almost invariably the battle is described as an outlaw ambush into which the officers blundered. Of the participants in the battle, only Birchfield has left recorded accounts, the first in a letter to Will Scarborough written eighteen days after the fight and the second in a 1939 interview with historian J. Evetts Haley. The stories contain discrepancies, as might be expected with a thirty-nine-year interval between them, but basically they are consistent, very graphic, and at odds with the popularly accepted version of what transpired at Triangle Springs.

Birchfield said they were not surprised by the outlaws but saw them first. "When we matched the fight the outlaws were in camp," he said. "We dismounted . . . and Scarborough said there was no use to call on them to surrender. They hadn't discovered us—at least we didn't think so—and they were about seventy-five yards off. Scarborough fired three or four shots and I fired once. They took to the rocks and then we couldn't see anything to shoot at. I don't think any of them were hit."[28]

In the letter he wrote less than three weeks after the incident, Birchfield guessed the range at this first engagement at two hundred yards: "George shot at a man's head that showed from behind a rock. It disappeared. He shot twice more at the place he saw this head. I never shot. I saw nothing to shoot at. We lay there about one half of an hour. Nothing showed up." Unable to tell whether the outlaws had pulled out or were just watching and waiting, Scarborough said, "Let's get up and put our guns in the scabbard and ride down the canyon. We have no showing here."[29] Birchfield said Scarborough had no intention of withdrawing but wanted to improve their location:

> Before we started to move position, I saw we didn't have any chance and I asked him if they opened up on us what he wanted to do, fight or pull out. 'Fight 'em.' he said. So that was our agreement. . . . We got back on our horses then and circled for another position.[30]
> When we got about three hundred and fifty yards from them they opened fire on us. They shot George the first shot. He was never able to pull his gun.[31]
> He was behind me and I heard him holler and heard the bullet hit him. It popped like it had hit a rock, and he fell off his horse.[32]

A .30-40 high-powered rifle bullet had struck Scarborough in the right thigh a few inches above the knee. It had smashed the bone, passed out of his leg, penetrated his saddle blanket, and lodged just under the skin of his horse.[33] Old Smokey reared, throwing Scarborough to the ground, but did not run away.

Meanwhile, Birchfield was having difficulty with his own mount:

> I jumped from my horse to pull my gun. The bullets were hitting so close and scared my horse until I couldn't handle him. He knocked me down and run over me and got loose with my gun.[34]
> He was a nervous sort of high-strung horse [and] he jerked me down. They were hitting gravel all around us in the creek bed. When my horse got loose and ran off with my Winchester, I went to Scarborough. . . . He was unconscious on the ground and I thought he was dead.[35]
> I run to his horse and jerked his gun from the scabbard.[36] I got his .30-.40 Winchester and took off his belt, as I had a .30-.30, and got rid of my belt and got behind a sycamore tree. The outlaws . . . were throwing lead all around us. The lead would hit the rocks and bust, and would sound almost as loud as when shot out of a gun. The splattering lead cut my head and arms.[37]

One of the ricochets tore through the meaty part of Birchfield's left shoulder, causing a painful if not serious wound.

> Scarborough came to then and called me. He tried to crawl to me, but he couldn't make it, so I crawled to him.[38] He [said], "I am dying. I am no more." [But] he got better directly and crawled in behind a tree with me. Bullets were hitting close and thick about that time.[39] . . He said that they had our range and we'd better back up.[40]
>
> They were a pile of rocks about thirty steps behind us. George says, "If we were there we would be all right." I says, "You lay here and I will go and build us a fort." I got the fort built and George crawled part of the way and I packed and drug him the other part of the way.[41]
>
> We . . . laid up the rest of the day. They called down to us to surrender and I told them, "nothing doing," as I knew they'd kill us both.[42]
>
> We lay there until dark and then I covered George up with his coat and overcoat and saddle blanket and then I went for help.[43] I got George's horse and struck out for the San Simon headquarters. It was . . . stormy and cold, and my horse fell with me and turned regular wildcat. I lost my gun in the dark, but held on the reins, and I'll bet I was fifteen minutes feeling around on the ground for my gun before I found it.[44]

The nearest place he might get help was the San Simon Ciénega Ranch headquarters, but when he arrived he found the place deserted.[45] He pushed on through rain, sleet, and snow seventeen more miles to the railroad station at San Simon. Reaching there at three o'clock in the morning, he found Holmes Maddox and two other cowboys playing poker. News of the fight was wired to Deming with a request for a doctor. Birchfield and the cowboys immediately started back with a buckboard to get Scarborough.

They took the wagon as far as they could and then proceeded by horseback, reaching Scarborough about daybreak on the morning of April 4. The outlaws had long since disappeared. They found Scarborough very weak but conscious, still lying behind a small blackjack oak and the rude rock fortification Birchfield had constructed. The base of the tree had been splintered and torn by high-velocity rifle fire, and great chunks had been chipped from the stones.[46]

Scarborough's first request was for water. He said he had suffered badly from thirst and during that long night would gladly have given one thousand dollars if he had it for a single drink of water.[47] A litter was improvised to carry the wounded man down the mountain to the buckboard. Then began the long, rough ride to the station at San Simon.

George's son Ed and Dr. Samuel D. Swope were waiting at the station when they arrived, having come from Deming in response to the telegraphic message. Dr. Swope found Scarborough's condition serious, as he was suffering from shock, exposure, and loss of blood. The arduous journey back had brought on renewed bleeding from his wound, and he was in extreme pain. Dr. Swope dressed his mangled leg and gave him morphine to relieve the pain while they waited for the eastbound train. Also at the station were Sheriff Edward Beeler and two deputies, who were on the trail of outlaws who had murdered two possemen near Saint Johns in Apache County on March 27. Beeler and his men had been following the gang for a week on a trail moving south through Graham County into the Chiracahua Mountains of Cochise County. It appeared that this gang of killers was the same bunch that Scarborough and Birchfield had battled. The similarity of the Apache County events and the Scarborough and Birchfield experience was striking. The outlaw band had been trailed after discovery of a slaughtered beef. They had turned on the trackers and gunned down two with remarkably accurate rifle fire.

After receiving medical attention for his arm wound, Walt Birchfield snatched some badly needed rest and then insisted on joining Beeler's posse, which, augmented by officers arriving from Deming, was taking to the field again. When the eastbound train arrived, Dr. Swope and Ed put Scarborough in the baggage car and the train started for Deming. At Separ they found the station in an uproar over outlaw excitement of still another kind. Six prisoners had escaped from the Silver City jail on March 28. Two of the six had been jailed for minor offenses, so little effort was made to apprehend them. Two others had been quickly captured at Cow Springs by one of Scarborough's men. The most dangerous, George Stevenson and Jim Brooks, under murder indictments, were still at large and had been seen crossing the tracks at Separ only an hour before. Weakened

George Scarborough's gravestone in Deming,
New Mexico. *Courtesy Phillip G. Nickell.*

as he was, George Scarborough was still the nemesis of outlaws.
Unable himself to take this hot trail, he directed his son to go. Ed
reluctantly left the train and joined the chase.

At three o'clock in the afternoon the train reached Deming, where
a large crowd, including several newspapermen, had gathered at the
station. Although she was ill, Mollie was there. During twenty-two
years of marriage to George Scarborough, Mollie had mentally
prepared herself for situations like this and appeared calm and composed. "How is he?" she inquired of the doctor. Assured that her
husband would be all right, she said, "Very well. Everything is ready
at home. Do you need anything I can get you?"

As George was being lifted out of the car, she said, "George, you're all right. We'll have you out in a few days." "I'm out now," he answered with a smile.[48] At the Scarborough home, Dr. Swope, assisted by a Dr. Broadneck, prepared the patient for surgery. It was doubtful that the damaged leg could be saved, but Dr. Swope wanted to try. Shattered pieces of bone, some six inches long, had to be removed. That evening, chloroform was administered and an operation performed to remove the bone splinters.[49] But when the operation had been concluded, it soon became apparent that in his weakened condition Scarborough was not coming out of the anesthetic properly. He did not respond to stimuli, and his vitality gradually diminished. By two o'clock on the morning of April 5, he was dead.[50]

Dr. Swope later told Jeff Milton that Scarborough had a heart condition that prevented his recovery. "I asked the doctor about [George's death]," Milton said. "I says, 'Didn't you kill him with chloroform?' He says, 'This is exactly what happened. We didn't know he had a weak heart. But he laid out all night and he had lost a little blood and his heart was weak and they didn't know it and he never came out from under the chloroform.' That was what the doctor told me."[51]

Funeral services for George Scarborough were conducted at 2:00 P.M. Friday, April 6, at the Odd Fellows Hall in Deming under the direction of the Reverend Strong of the Baptist Church. Scarborough had been an active member of Lodge No. 6, Independent Order of Odd Fellows, and, of course, of the Baptist Church. According to the *Silver City Enterprise*, the funeral procession from the hall to the Deming cemetery was "the largest ever seen in Deming."[52]

The Odd Fellows later erected an impressive monument marking Scarborough's grave. It bore the following inscription:

Geo. A. Scarborough
Was Born
Oct. 2nd 1859
Died
April 5, 1900
Gone but not forgotten[53]

The identity of the outlaws is thought to be known.

—SILVER CITY INDEPENDENT, APRIL 17, 1900

-14-

Outlaw Identity

Tributes to George Scarborough appeared in newspapers all over the Southwest. He was described, accurately, as "the well-known brave and fearless detective"[1] and "a man of highest personal courage and integrity of character."[2] And he was also characterized, extravagantly, as "the best-known officer in west Texas, beyond a doubt, [who] had perhaps arrested more bad men in the past fifteen years than any officer in the history of the state."[3]

The El Paso papers that had failed to defend him during his difficulties there, now competed in panegyric. "The man who knew not fear, the terror of outlaws in New Mexico and Arizona . . . will fight no more," said the *Herald*. "[His death] removes one of the best known characters in this section. . . . He was brave as a lion. . . . That is the universal testimony of all who knew him."[4] The *Times* story was picked up on the Associated Press wire and reprinted in Phoenix, Los Angeles, and other western cities. "Scarborough," it said, "was considered absolutely fearless and has done valiant service in breaking up numerous outlaw bands that have ventured into Arizona and New Mexico to plunder. Since becoming an officer he has sent several members of the various gangs that he has gone to arrest to the happy hunting grounds, thereby saving the Territories many dollars in court fees."[5]

Of course the Scarborough family was devastated by the death of the husband, father, and sole breadwinner. George had been only forty years old, and six of his seven children were still in school. Edgar, the eldest, was twenty but was himself a husband and father now and had his own family to support.

230

Help for Mollie Scarborough's immediate financial burden came from Walter Birchfield's father, Uncle Steve, a resident of Deming and a director of the New Mexico Cattlemen's Association. Interviewed in El Paso a few days after George's funeral, Birchfield said Scarborough had renewed his contract with the association on January 1 for the year and that he would introduce a resolution at the next meeting honoring that agreement and committing the association to payment of Scarborough's salary for the entire year.[6] This proposal was agreed to at the meeting and Mollie was so notified. "Cattlemen as a rule are big hearted and generous," said the *Holbrook* (Arizona) *Argus* in reporting the arrangement.[7]

Daughters Martha, eighteen, and Georgie, sixteen, were old enough to find productive work to help Mollie support the other three girls and little five-year-old Ray. Although in 1900 job opportunities for women were limited, the Scarborough girls, as might be expected, were capable and enterprising, with a great deal of their father's determination. J. Marvin Hunter lived in Deming in 1900 and worked at the local paper, the *Headlight*. He recalled that Georgie, "a pretty little blue-eyed girl, quiet and modest, but always energetic," worked as a typesetter for the paper that year.[8] She later taught school at San Simon, where one of her pupils was A. F. Nolan, who lived on the ranch where Scarborough had fought his last battle.[9]

In 1899, George's brother Lee had begun a two-year course of study at Southern Baptist Theological Seminary in Louisville, Kentucky. He was about to take the final examinations when word of George's death reached him. He never took those tests, but immediately closed his books and took a train to Deming to console the family and offer his support in their crisis.[10] "Rev. L. R. Scarborough, brother of the late George Scarborough and pastor of the Baptist church at Cameron, Texas, is visiting his relatives in Deming and took part in the services at the Baptist church Sunday," noted the *Silver City Enterprise* of April 20.

Mollie's health was poor and the blow of her husband's death had not improved her condition. One of her younger daughters was also not well. Thinking a change of scenery might help her in her grief, she took the three youngest children and went to Santa Monica, California, in July to visit relatives. She stayed two months, returning early in September in time for the children's new school year.[11]

Shortly after Scarborough's funeral, Frank McMahan, who had been serving on the city police force at El Paso, was appointed by the New Mexico cattlemen to replace his brother-in-law as head of the association's rangers and moved to Deming with his wife and baby daughter. "Mr. McMahan has been in the detective work on the frontier for a number of years and comes highly recommended," said the *Silver City Independent*. "He will be assisted by Edward [*sic*] Scarborough, who was his father's trusted assistant while serving the cattlemen of this district."[12]

However miffed he may have been by inaccurate name identification in the papers and, because of his youth and inexperience, being passed over to replace his father as head of the group, Edgar was nonetheless vigorously in the hunt for the killers. It was a particularly hectic period for lawmen of the sister territories. There were at least three posses in the field searching for the men who had given George his death wound: Sheriff Beeler's Apache County party, still on the trail of the killers of possemen Gibbons and LeSueur; Grant County Sheriff Jim Blair, with possemen from Silver City and Deming; and a group of lawmen led by John Slaughter, former sheriff of Cochise County, who were searching known outlaw hideouts along the border. The officers thought the outlaws who shot Scarborough were the same ones who had killed Gibbons and LeSueur but were not certain, for a number of other dangerous criminals were loose in the area. The escapees from the Silver City jail, George Stevenson and James Brooks, had eluded Ed Scarborough and other pursuers and were now believed to have crossed the border into Mexico. Some thought members of the notorious Bill Smith rustler gang had drifted down from their usual haunts in the Black River country and fought Scarborough and Birchfield at Triangle Springs. Unidentified bandits who had held up the George D. Bowman & Son bank at Las Cruces at February 12 and escaped toward the Mogollons and the Arizona line were still at large.

Two days after Scarborough's funeral came a new sensation and further headaches for the officers. Billy Stiles, one of the accomplices in the Cochise and Fairbanks train robberies, had been freed on a promise to testify as a prosecution witness. On April 8, Stiles entered the Tombstone jail, shot the jailer, and broke out two of his pals,

Burt Alvord and Bravo Juan Yoes. Now another posse, led by Cochise County Sheriff Scott White, took to the field after the three. Reported sightings of the various groups of fugitives kept the lawmen racing across the vast stretches of the southern counties, and the confusion of the officers was reflected in the southwestern press. On April 13 the *Silver City Enterprise* reported that

> during the past week the air hereabouts has been heavy with rumors of fights and killings in the neighborhood of the Chiricahuas. . . . It is said that at least three posses are hunting for the trail of the outlaws who murdered Scarborough. . . . All ears are open and eager for news, and the disappointment will be bitter if something stirring is not heard soon.

How wild these rumors were and how distorted the news coverage became is shown by one story that appeared in Texas papers datelined April 10:

> A report from Lordsburg, N. M. this afternoon says that a Sheriff's posse encountered the fugitive murderers, Burt Alvard, Bravo John, and Billy Stiles in the mountains southwest of that point late yesterday afternoon and that Stiles was killed in the fight that followed. Al Ward, Bravo John and Stiles broke jail at Silver City, N. M., a week ago and afterward ambushed and murdered Officer George Scarborough and wounded Officer Birchfield, who were in pursuit.[13]

Beyond the relatively minor difficulty with the names of Burt Alvord and Bravo Juan Yoes, this report obviously confuses the escapees from the Cochise County, Arizona, jail with Stevenson and Brooks, who had broken out of the Grant County, New Mexico, jail almost two weeks earlier. Scarborough and Birchfield had not been in pursuit of these fugitives either. But the most serious error in a story replete with errors is the attribution of Scarborough's shooting to the Tombstone fugitives. That jailbreak took place five days after Scarborough's outlaw battle, and Stiles, Alvord, and Yoes could not possibly have been involved in his shooting. There was no gun battle with Stiles and company in the Chiricahuas as reported, and Stiles was not killed. The whole report was a confusion of errors, but it and similarly inaccurate stories emerging after the shootout at Triangle Springs have compounded a mystery associated with the affair that exists to this day.

Immediately after the Scarborough shooting the press reported that his killers were the Apache County murderers and identified them as John Hunter, alias Dick Smith; Bob Johnson; one Wilson, alias Smith; Tod (or Kid) Carver; and one other unknown.[14] Two weeks later the posses of Sheriffs Blair and Beeler had combined forces in Arizona and were combing the Chiricahuas for this gang, which they believed was holed up there. Sheriff Blair had returned to Silver City on April 15 and stopped briefly on his way to Belton, Texas, where he was scheduled to get married. He told reporters that riding in the combined Arizona and New Mexico posse were Deputies Hart, Lewis, Gould and Wilson from Apache County; Ed Scarborough, W. D. ("Keechi") Johnson, and Miles Marshall from Grant County; and Texas Ranger J. W. Matthews.[15] Others who had previously been members of the posse but who had by now apparently dropped out to pursue their normal activities included Walt Birchfield, Walter Weatherwax, and Roscoe Gill.[16]

Sheriff Blair appeared confident that the posse would soon trap and do battle with the Apache County outlaws, but as time passed and no confrontation developed, there seemed to be less certainty that this was the bunch with whom Scarborough had tangled. Later in the month when Deputies Johnson and Marshall got on the trail of the escaped jailbirds Stevenson and Brooks, tracked them for more than one hundred miles, and finally nabbed them in Sonora, Mexico, some papers tried to pin the Scarborough killing on them. "Caught at Last. Scarborough's Alleged Assassins Are Now In The Toils," headlined the *El Paso Herald*, which went on to say that the officers were holding their prisoners awaiting extradition papers.[17] But two months later when the officers returned and deposited the escapees once again in the Silver City jail, no charges were lodged against them for the affair at Triangle Springs because it was obvious that they had not been involved.[18]

On May 26, Sheriff Jesse Tyler of Grand County, Utah, and a deputy named Sam Jenkins were shot and killed by outlaws near Thompson, Utah. After seeing descriptions of the murderers, Sheriff Edward Beeler went to Utah and conferred with Sheriff William Preece of Uintah County. The descriptions of these lawman killers, according to Beeler, matched the Apache County fugitives he was seeking "in every particular" down to the brands on their horses. He

For a time, James Brooks, escapee from the Silver City jail, was believed to have been one of George Scarborough's killers. *Courtesy New Mexico Penitentiary Record No. 1362, State Records Center and Archives.*

said there were five in the band, which always traveled in two units, with the second party of one or two members bringing up supplies. These bandits were responsible for six murders, he said, and Arizona was offering a reward of five thousand dollars for their capture.[19]

Interviewed by a reporter for the *Salt Lake Herald*, Beeler characterized the gang as "one of the most accomplished and systematic aggregations of bad men in the West." He said he had been following them since March and had logged thirteen hundred miles in Arizona and New Mexico territories, Old Mexico, Utah, and Wyoming. He had lost the trail before but always managed to pick it up again. If necessary, he said, he would "follow them to hell." The *Herald* correspondent said the outlaws had been given no rest by "this

George Stevenson, fugitive accomplice of Brooks, was later shot to death by the warden of the New Mexico Territorial Prison. *Courtesy New Mexico Penitentiary Record No. 1402, State Records Center and Archives.*

determined man" and had shot Sheriff Tyler believing him to be Beeler. "My turn will come," said Beeler.

> The boys [LeSueur and Gibbons] that these cowardly villains shot to pieces in the south were my friends and sacrificed their lives to assist me, and I will even up the score. These fellows may as well fight me [in] one place as another, as the time we meet is bound to come. I know them all, and [am] as positive of their identity as though they were behind the bars. All this talk of Cassidy, Joe Rose, and others being the slayers of the Grand county officers is moonshine. They are the same men that I have been trailing. I am positive of that.[20]

But the months slid by and neither Sheriff Beeler nor any other officer was able to corner the mysterious gang. No one was ever arrested and charged with the Scarborough shooting, and the confusion evident in the contemporary papers concerning the outlaws responsible has been carried on and compounded by western historians ever since. Some of these writers have identified the outlaws involved with assurance and positivity, but with little evidence or corroboration.

Charlie Siringo, Texas cowboy, Pinkerton detective, and recurrent autobiographer, was an early contributor to the confusion when he wrote in 1919: "Kid Curry . . . had been a cowboy along the line of New Mexico and Arizona, under the name of Tom Capehart. . . . Several years previous, Capehart had shot and killed George Scarborough, the man who did a noble deed when he killed John Selman." As an undercover Pinkerton detective Siringo would become intimately acquainted with some members of the Utah-based Wild Bunch, or Hole-in-the-Wall gang, a crew of well-publicized brigands that included Harvey Logan, alias Kid Curry; Robert LeRoy Parker, better known as Butch Cassidy; and Harry Longabaugh, the Sundance Kid. But it was a year after the Scarborough killing that Siringo's investigation of the gang led him to New Mexico, where Logan, Parker, and Elzy Lay, another gang member, had worked on and off as cowboys on the WS Ranch near Alma. His knowledge of the Scarborough shooting was therefore not firsthand, but anecdotal.[21]

The criminal successes of the Wild Bunch had brought them national notoriety: large rewards had been posted for their capture, and many public and private manhunters had joined the search. Cowboying on the remote WS Ranch became a good way for the outlaws to drop out when things became too hot. Parker, who was even better known by his alias, Butch Cassidy, adopted the name of a minor member of the gang, Jim Lowe, while working on the WS. Elzy Lay was known as William McGinnis, and it was under that name that he drifted off to join the Black Jack gang and got himself shot, captured, and imprisoned. Harvey Logan, whose nom de guerre Kid Curry was also widely known, needed another, and he took the name of a popular New Mexico cowpuncher and bronchobuster named Tom Capehart. The use of aliases, especially the borrowing of the names of others by these criminals, was intended to confuse manhunters, but newspapermen of the period and later writers also

have had much difficulty in sorting out events and participants because of the identity entanglements deliberately created by the
outlaws.

Tom Capehart was a cowboy who had been well known in the
southwestern territories for at least five years. In Arizona he had
worked for the CA Bar on the Gila River and the Erie Cattle Company
and in New Mexico on the Diamond A. Wherever he worked he was
highly regarded by cattlemen for his skill as a bronchobuster. He
had been acquitted in the first Steins Pass train robbery trial in 1897.
"After he was turned loose," Leonard Alverson said, "he joined an
outlaw gang and I do not know what finally became of him."[22]

Although Siringo was probably intentionally ambiguous about
whether the Tom Capehart of the Scarborough shooting was the New
Mexico cowboy or the Utah outlaw using that name, later writers
have been less cautious. In 1926, Owen P. White named Scarborough's killer "Tom Capehart, alias Kid Curry."[23] In 1968, Brown
Waller, biographer of Harvey Logan, described the Triangle Springs
fight in detail, crediting Logan for participation but identifying none
of his companions.[24] And in 1970, Jeff Burton confidently named
Capehart, clearly meaning Logan, as a gang member.[25]

The available evidence strongly supports the argument for the
presence of Tom Capehart at the Triangle Springs fight—but Tom
Capehart, bronc buster and Steins Pass robbery suspect, and not
Harvey Logan, alias Kid Curry, alias Tom Capehart. When Sheriff
Jim Blair came back to Silver City in mid-April 1900 on his way to
be married, he had been in the field for more than a week with Sheriff
Beeler and his deputies and had had an opportunity to talk at length about
the suspects in the Apache County killings and go over their physical
descriptions and mannerisms. After comparing notes with his fellow
officers, Blair was sure he knew one of the men they sought.

"The identity of the outlaws is thought to be known, or at least
four of them," said the *Silver City Independent* after an interview
with Blair.

> One of them is said to be Tom Capehart, who was for a long time
> confined in the jail here, awaiting trial on the charge of being impli-
> cated in the Southern Pacific train hold-up near San Simon [and] was
> acquitted of this charge in the United States court at Las Cruces. The
> others were said to be Tod Carter, Jeff Black, "Franks," and one

whose name was unknown but was described as a "tall, well-proportioned man and a hard fighter."[26]

This unknown man was later identified as Bob Johnson, alias Mack Steen.

The *Enterprise*, the other Silver City paper, provided additional information about Capehart several days later:

> The trial and acquittal of Capehart is still fresh in the memories of the people of this county. After being acquitted Capehart went to work for an Arizona cattle company. . . . The evidence in Capehart's trial developed the fact that he was exceedingly anxious to rob or hold up a train. It is believed that he organized the band of outlaws who slew Scarborough . . . to hold up trains, but in killing a beef at St. Johns, Ariz., the band got into trouble earlier than was expected.[27]

Blair had undoubtedly recognized Capehart from a description of one of the outlaws first identified as "Wilson, alias Smith." According to the reward notices being posted for the Apache County killers, this man had worked for the Wabash Cattle Company in Apache County a year earlier:

> He is about 5 ft. 10 in. high, weighs about 175 lbs. [He] has slightly dark complexion, dark hair and mustache, had short black beard when last seen, is stoop shouldered but quite well appearing, has blue eyes, and is of very pleasing address, but not over-talkative, has a peculiar way of ducking his head from side to side when he talks and he usually smiles a great deal when talking. He is an expert bronch trainer.[28]

Tom Capehart's description as filed in an 1899 Cochise County sheriff's report matches the above almost perfectly:

> Height, 5 ft. 10 in.; 170 lbs.; dark complexion; black hair inclined to baldness at front; dark blue eyes; black mustache, not heavy; not very talkative. When he laughs it is very loud. Heavy drinker and he is very fond of dancing.[29]

Neither Scarborough nor Birchfield got a good look at the outlaws, but Birchfield did recognize one of them—by voice, as he later explained to Henry Brock. "All at once there was a big yell after they'd shot Scarborough and he'd fell off the horse," he said. "There was a big yell and it was old Capehart. I would have knowed

him anywhere." Birchfield could be so sure because he knew Tom
Capehart well, having been his boss on the Diamond A.[30]

After he had conferred with the New Mexico officers, Sheriff
Beeler's reward notices substituted Tom Capehart for Wilson, the
name Capehart apparently was using on the Arizona ranches. Bob
Johnson was also listed under the name Mack Steen. Tod Carver,
Jeff (or Jess) Black, and Franks were still wanted.[31]

Will Carver, who had been an active member of both the Black
Jack Ketchum and Hole-in-the-Wall gangs, was known to use the
alias George W. Franks and has frequently been mentioned as one of
the Triangle Springs outlaws. In 1928, two accounts were published
naming Will Carver as a participant in the fight, one by Michael
Williams, who claimed to have interviewed an informant "who was
a great friend of the gang," and the other by Lorenzo Walters, a
former railroad special agent and Tucson police officer who presum-

The Hole-in-the-Wall gang got dressed up for this portrait taken in Fort
Worth in December 1900, nine months after George Scarborough's death.
Standing, left to right: Will Carver and Harvey Logan; sitting: Harry
Longabaugh, Ben Kilpatrick, and Butch Cassidy. *Courtesy Western History
Collections, University of Oklahoma Library.*

ably had access to official files and the opportunity to talk to other officers who had been active during the turn of the century.[32] Walters even credited Will Carver with firing the shot that finished Scarborough: "Bill Franks, alias Bill Carver . . . fired the shot which struck Scarborough in the leg. . . . Thus passed one of the bravest officers which the Southwest has ever known." Curiously, Walters added that "while Harvey Logan is also credited with having fired the shot which caused the death of Scarborough, it is generally believed, and so stated in Arizona and New Mexico, that Franks, alias Carver, actually fired the shot; Scarborough made this statement before he died."[33] Nowhere else is there any indication that Scarborough was able to identify the outlaws or made any such statement.

Will Carver's biographer, while acknowledging that his subject "was given credit for the shot and for the death of one of the finest and most popular lawmen of that day," questions "the positive identifications some writers make, stating exactly who shot who, or whom."[34]

Contemporary newspapers and wanted circulars identify another gang member as Tod Carver, which has further compounded the confusion, especially because Will Carver's full name has been given as William Todd Carver.[35] But Tod Carver, as shown by subsequent events, was the go-by of an outlaw named T. C. Hilliard, who, the available evidence suggests, was present at the Triangle Springs fight.

The early wanted notices named one Bob Johnson, later changed to Mack Steen, alias Bob Johnson. This individual, whose name has also been given as Mac Stein and Max Stein, was included by Walters as one of the gang.[36] Perhaps this man was the Bob Johnson of the Erie Cattle Company whom Milton said Scarborough wanted to provoke into a fight in 1897 because of his association with known outlaws. No evidence has surfaced to confirm this, but at least one of the gang must have been very familiar with the Chiricahuas to elude so completely the posses searching for them, and this was the range with which Bob Johnson of the Erie was intimately acquainted.

There is circumstantial evidence that Bob Johnson was in fact Ben Kilpatrick, a sometime member of the Hole-in-the-Wall gang, who has been named by several Wild Bunch historians as riding with the band in Arizona during this period.[37] Johnson's physical description in the wanted notices match those of Kilpatrick, nicknamed the Tall Texan by his cohorts. Ben and his brother George, also a gang member, hailed from Concho County, Texas, and it may be significant that a prominent family of the area was named Steen, perhaps prompting one or both of the brothers to adopt the name as a pseudonym. But the best argument for including Ben Kilpatrick in the outlaw band is the certain conviction of Edgar Scarborough, who had the strongest motivation to sort out the mystery, that Kilpatrick was one of those responsible for his father's death, as will be shown.

George Kilpatrick is an even more shadowy figure than his brother. There is no reason to place him at the Triangle Springs fight other than that the Kilpatricks generally rode together and, if there were five members of the band and Ben was present, George was probably the fifth man.

Based on the scattered information available at this time, these, then, would appear to be the members of the gang who fought Scarborough and Birchfield at Triangle Springs: Tom Capehart, alias Tom Wilson, alias Smith; Will Carver, alias Jeff (or Jess) Black, alias George W. Franks; T. C. Hilliard, alias Tod Carver, alias John Hunter, alias Skeet Jones, alias Dick Smith, alias Frank Laughlin; Ben Kilpatrick, alias Bob Johnson, alias Mack Steen (or Mac or Max Stein); George Kilpatrick. Others named by various writers as participants in this battle include Dan ("Red") Pipkin, Harvey Logan, and Butch Cassidy.

The involvement of Pipkin, the outlaw who escaped at the time of Scarborough's capture of Broncho Bill, would have been impossible because he was jailed in Graham County, Arizona Territory, on April 2, 1900.[38] The confusion caused by Harvey Logan's use of the alias Tom Capehart appears to be the only basis for his consideration.

The alleged participation by Cassidy can be traced to a story that the death of Scarborough was not the tragic result of an unfortunate confrontation with a band of outlaws on the move, but a premeditated, cold-blooded murder planned and executed by Butch Cassidy and cohorts. The genesis of this tale seems to have been a magazine article written and published in 1928 by Michael Williams:

> My chief informant [was] a man I know very well, who was a great friend of the gang, [but] cannot be named for obvious reasons. . . . Billy Carver, Gus [sic] Cassidy, Tom Capehart and a man whose

name never got known, got together and started out with the express purpose of killing George Scarborough [who] had always been a bitter enemy of the Black Jack gang and these four men made up their minds to have it out with him for good and all. . . .

The four outlaws went up near the Triangle ranch in the San Simon Valley and . . . they killed a cow, and then ripped the carcass open and got out a tenderloin and rode leisurely on. This they had done deliberately and following a well-laid plan which worked out perfectly. The foreman of the Triangle cattle outfit came along and saw his cow by the road and at once telegraphed to George Scarborough to come to San Simon to take the trail.

After the gunfight at Triangle Springs, the gang pulled out, leaving the wounded Scarborough behind his rock fort. Williams's informant said he "rode one hundred miles to where he knew the outlaws would be hiding to tell them how the fight had ended. When he came into their camp he said: 'Well, you've got him, boys,' and they threw their hats into the air."[39]

In another article two years later, writer Carl B. Livingston repeated the story of the planned ambush, saying he got his information from "a reliable man" who had talked to Butch Cassidy in "a certain republic" of South America. This unidentified informant said Cassidy had told him he planned the assassination of Scarborough and had been one of the party who did him in, although he would not name his accomplices.[40]

Another element was added to this story by Henry Brock, onetime manager of the Diamond A, in interviews conducted by Lou Blachly in the early 1950s. Brock indicated that not only was Scarborough deliberately ambushed and assassinated, but Walt Birchfield was an accomplice in the conspiracy:

> George Scarborough, he's one they hated . . . and they just deliberately—Cassidy's gang—they just trapped him before they pulled out for South America. . . . I got all this from Walter [Birchfield] himself. Him and I was good friends, you know. We'd worked together for years. So I'm telling you this right from Walter. . . . [Scarborough] might have not had much faith in Walter because him and Walter had had several toughs around Deming about [Walter's] cutting up, you know. I know Walter didn't like him. Scarborough knew it too. . . . [Walter] didn't tell me that he got Scarborough up there in order to get him killed because he didn't have to.[41]

The tale of the gang's entrapment of Scarborough is accepted by
Jeff Burton in his *Dynamite and Sixshooter*, an otherwise well-
researched and reasoned account of outlaw activities in the southwestern territories at the turn of the century. "In order to eliminate
him the gang devised a lethal variant of hare and hounds, in which
the roles of hunter and quarry are reversed at the kill," writes Burton.
"Brutal and calculating as their strategy was, its style was not alto-
gether dissimilar to his own, and he ought not to have been deceived
by it." Scarborough's killers are named with great certitude: "Besides
Cassidy and Capehart [Logan], the ambush party contained Will
Carver and at least one of the Kilpatrick brothers." While subscribing
to the Cassidy-plotted assassination yarn, he does not accept Brock's
allegation of Birchfield's involvement, noting, with some logic, that
had Birchfield been a party to the plot, he would hardly have risked
rifle fire to build a fort around Scarborough or undertaken a dangerous
and arduous journey through storm-lashed mountains to get help for
the wounded man.[42] Perhaps because acknowledgment of the gang's
responsibility for the Apache County possemen murders would not
jibe with the assassination conspiracy theory, Burton states, again
with great certainty but no proof: "None of the outlaws who were
involved in the assassination of Scarborough could have had anything
to do with the murder of . . . Frank LeSueur and Gus Gibbons . . .
on March 27th, 1900."[43]

The entire Cassidy conspiracy story rests on the flimsiest of hear-
say evidence, the reported testimony of Williams's "great friend of
the gang," and Livingston's "reliable man," who are nameless for
all time. But there are many other good reasons to doubt this tale.
The idea of an assassination plotted and executed by Butch Cassidy
is completely out of character for this outlaw, who captured public
popularity in large part because, during a long and spectacular criminal career, he evidently never killed a man and took pride in that
fact.

Other contradictions are readily apparent. The weight of the evidence points toward the Apache County killers and the Triangle
Springs outlaws being the same, making the idea of an engineered
ambush of Scarborough ludicrous. If Birchfield was not a party to
the plan, what assurance did the gang have that he would send for

Scarborough? If he was a conspirator, why did he go to such lengths in an attempt to save Scarborough's life?

As an assassination attempt, this would have been one of extraordinary ineptitude. Scarborough came under rifle fire from a distance of several hundred yards and was struck in the leg by one round, suffering a wound that under normal circumstances would not have been fatal. The outlaws did not follow up their advantage, even after Birchfield left. Had the whole object been to kill Scarborough, certainly further action would have been taken to accomplish the mission.

Planned assassinations of officers during this period were not uncommon but were almost invariably carried out at short range and without the presence of a surviving witness. The murder of Edward Beeler, the Apache County sheriff, almost a year to the day after Scarborough's death, is a case in point. On April 11, 1901, Beeler, no longer sheriff, was ambushed on a backcountry lane some thirty miles from Saint Johns. Waiting killers hidden behind rocks some sixty to seventy feet from a pasture gate blasted him as he got down from a wagon to open the gate. Three heavily armed men had been seen in the vicinity shortly before the shooting, and although no one was ever brought to trial for the murder, it was believed by many in Apache County that Beeler's killers were outlaws he had harassed during his days as sheriff.[44]

Perhaps Beeler was murdered by those he was convinced had killed LeSueur, Gibbons, and Scarborough in Arizona Territory and Sheriff Tyler and Sam Jenkins in Utah; perhaps his death, which was a true assassination, somehow got twisted in the telling around the outlaw campfires to become that of George Scarborough, a much better-known officer.

If Beeler's killers were indeed part of the gang who had caused so much excitement the previous year, they did not include Will Carver, for only a few days before, on April 2, 1901, he and George Kilpatrick had been gunned down in Sonora, Texas, by Sheriff E. S. Briant. Kilpatrick survived, but Carver lived only a short time before expiring.[45]

Tom Capehart's movements are unknown after the fight at Triangle Springs. Henry Brock thought he went to South America with Butch

Cassidy, but there is no confirmation of this. Lorenzo Walters said that he went to Colorado and received a life sentence on a murder charge. If this report is true, he was using another name, for the Colorado State Penitentiary has no record of an incarceration of a prisoner named Tom Capehart.[46]

Bob Johnson, or Mack Steen, also disappears from the pages of western outlaw history after April 1900. Lorenzo Walters said he "left Cochise County and a short time afterward was killed in Utah while assisting in a train robbery."[47] Ben Kilpatrick, who may have been the mysterious Johnson or Steen, did in fact die of wounds he suffered in an abortive train robbery, but it was not a short time afterward and was not in Utah. In November 1901, Kilpatrick was arrested in Saint Louis for robbery and the following month was given a sentence of twelve to fifteen years in prison. Released in June 1911, he and a former cellmate, Ole Beck, attempted a holdup of the Southern Pacific near Sanderson, Texas, in which both were killed.[48]

T. C. Hilliard, alias Tod Carver, the last of the suspected killers of LeSeuer, Gibbons, and Scarborough, was the only one ever brought before the bar of justice in Arizona Territory for those crimes. His apprehension was the result of a determined effort by young Edgar Scarborough, who seemed to be following the tough frontier-lawman tradition established by his father.

George Scarborough's son Ed was no good.
—JUDGE JAMES C. HANCOCK, AUGUST 23, 1936

-15-

Ed

Edgar Scarborough's career as a peace officer after the death of his father began auspiciously. In July 1900 he captured a man named Jerome Adams, accused of the murder of Oliver Gruell in Old Mexico. After what a newspaper termed "an exciting chase" in which "Scarborough displayed great courage," Ed collared his quarry on Deer Creek and brought him to Silver City, where he was jailed to await extradition by Mexican authorities.[1]

The following month, Keechi Johnson was murdered, and in the ensuing investigation, Ed killed his first man. On August 16, Deputy Sheriffs Johnson and Miles Marshall had headed north out of Silver City into the Upper Gila country in search of cattle rustlers, who had become increasingly active in that area. They picked up a trail and followed it four days. When it split, Johnson took one fork and Marshall the other. Marshall lost his trail and returned to Silver City. Johnson, meanwhile, had apprehended a suspect named Ralph Jenks and started back.

On Monday morning, August 27, Jenks appeared at a ranch on Whitewater Creek and said that Johnson had been shot from ambush and killed at McKinnie Park, some forty miles from the town of Mogollon. When the news reached Silver City, Sheriff Blair, together with Don Johnson, son of the dead deputy, Miles Marshall, and Rangers McMahan, Scarborough, Doak, Collier, and J. Marvin Hunter headed for the scene. By the time they reached it, a coroner's jury had been impaneled from Mogollon, an inquest held at the death site with Ralph Jenks the only witness, and the body buried. After inspecting the area and conducting inquiries, Blair decided that

247

J. Marvin Hunter served briefly as a Scarborough Ranger. *Courtesy Western History Collections, University of Oklahoma Library.*

Jenks, his brother Roy, and a man named Henry Reinhart were
rustlers and guilty of Johnson's murder. He dispatched McMahan
and his rangers to Mogollon to apprehend Ralph Jenks and Reinhart,
while he, Marshall, and Don Johnson went into the hills in search
of Roy Jenks.[2]

At Mogollon, McMahan's party took custody of Jenks and Reinhart and headed for Silver City. They were riding along Duck Creek
about nine o'clock on the night of September 3 when Jenks suddenly
reached over and jerked Ed Scarborough's shotgun from its scabbard.
Hunter told what happened:

In trying to work the gun it must have jammed. Jenks jumped from his horse and kept trying to work the gun. Scarborough called on him several times to drop the gun, and then shot him three times with his six-shooter—twice in the breast and once in the head, and as Jenks fell he threw the shotgun at Scarborough. . . . We covered the corpse of Jenks with a tarp and went on to Silver City . . . arriving there the next day. McMahan had placed Scarborough under arrest and when we reached Silver City placed him in jail. District court was in session, and the grand jury no-billed Scarborough immediately and he was released. McMahan as well as the other men of our force, believed that Ralph Jenks and his brother, Roy Jenks, were the ones who killed officer Keechi Johnson.[3]

Not everyone in Grant County was convinced of Jenks's guilt or that his death had been necessary. The killing also focused attention on the unofficial rangers, especially Ed Scarborough, and actions considered by many to be high handed and imperious. George Scarborough had not been liked by everyone in Grant County, but he had commanded respect from all. Ed Scarborough had not earned that respect, and his tactics were resented.

By October the *Silver City Independent* felt the need to defend Sheriff Blair, who had come in for a share of criticism because he had issued deputy commissions to what was essentially a private police force:

Some complaint having been made about Sheriff James K. Blair giving deputy commissions to the range riders for the Southwestern New Mexico Cattle Protective Association, the *Independent* deems it just to him to state to the public the facts concerning these deputyships. . . . The commissions were applied for by the executive committee of the cattle association in order that its men might have proper authority to carry out the work which they were employed to do.

The paper pointed out that the range riders also held deputy papers from Sierra, Dona Ana, and Socorro counties in New Mexico Territory and Cochise County in Arizona Territory "in order to complete the circuit of the territory over which the men might have to work."[4]

In a later edition the paper added that Blair had nothing whatever to do with appointment of the rangers, who were selected and paid by the cattle association, which was entirely responsible for their acts. "If these men have oppressed or illegally arrested anyone," said the paper, "the courts are open to such person for redress, and is the proper forum in which to air his complaint against the cattle association and its men. Tax payers should consider the fact that these men are no expense whatever to the county, and judge accordingly."[5]

The controversy played a major part in the November election and contributed to the defeat of Blair in his bid for reelection. On taking office, Sheriff Goodell, his successor, promptly withdrew Ed Scarborough's deputy commission. Ed had also become a problem for the cattlemen's association, as evidenced by a meeting held in Silver City in January 1901 which nearly broke up in a fistfight and forced the resignation of President William Jack. Said a Lordsburg paper:

> The chief point of discussion seemed to have been the ranger system. Up to the time of the death of George Scarborough there was no trouble about the way the system was worked, but after he was killed and his son took the position there has been considerable trouble. Young Scarborough has arrested many men for stealing cattle but was unable to present enough evidence to warrant indictments, and the men arrested had to be turned loose. It looked to the citizens as though the rangers were trying to bulldoze men more than they were trying to secure convictions of cow thieves.[6]

Ed was not entirely without support, at least in Deming, where he managed to get himself elected constable during this period of controversy, and by June his deputy's commission had been restored.[7] That month he pulled off a coup that made many forget his past mistakes: he nabbed one of the suspects in his father's killing.

After lying low in Texas for almost a year, Tod Carver had drifted back into New Mexico. Following up reported sightings of the outlaw, Scarborough dogged his trial for several months. He and another officer named Ed Halverson finally closed in on Carver at a remote campsite.

"Up with your hands!" demanded Ed, throwing down on the pair with a six-shooter.

"Not for any officer!" Carver retorted as his companion reached for the sky.

"Up with your hands or you'll soon be in hell!" Ed snapped.

"Then," said the newspaper reporting this story, "the outlaw's hands went up."[8]

Another man with Carver was released by Scarborough because he had no reason to hold him other than consorting with bad company. Enlisting the help of a man named Pollard Pearson, Ed took his prisoner cross-country to Saint Johns, where warrants were still outstanding for Carver's arrest in the slaying of the Apache County possemen the previous year. "There is not much doubt that this criminal [was] one of the murderers of our beloved townsmen Frank LeSueur and Augustus Gibbons fifteen months ago today," said the *St. Johns Herald*. "That he is Tod Carver there is no doubt. There is a pretty clear case against him. Witnesses are being sent for and justice will be done."[9] Although this Arizona paper made no reference to Carver's involvement in the death of George Scarborough, it was not forgotten in Grant County. "Deputy Sheriff Ed Scarborough of Deming . . . seems very modest and reticent over his famous capture," said the *Silver City Enterprise*, "[but] it is believed Carver is the man who shot and killed the father of young Scarborough . . . several months ago."[10] The capture was publicized as far away as Sonora, Texas, where the *Devil's River News* noted that "the son of the late George Scarborough . . . has unremittingly followed the trail of Carver."[11]

On July 3, Carver, under his true name, T. C. Hilliard, was bound over for action of the Apache County grand jury. But authorities in Utah, claiming an iron-clad case against Carver in the slaying of Grand County Sheriff Jesse Tyler and posseman Sam Jenkins in May 1900, submitted a requisition for extradition and took custody of the prisoner on August 7. It was understood that if the Utah authorities were unsuccessful in obtaining a conviction against Carver, he would be returned to Arizona Territory to stand trial. However, in January 1902, charges against Carver were dropped because of insufficient evidence and he was released. He never answered charges in Arizona in either the Scarborough or Apache County possemen cases.[12]

Arizona Territory had lost one of its most wanted fugitives, but in that year of 1901 it finally moved to establish the force of rangers which George Scarborough had wanted so much to lead, either in Arizona or New Mexico. In March a bill had been signed into law providing for a force of fourteen men, consisting of one captain, to be paid $120 a month; one sergeant, $75 a month; and twelve privates at $55 a month. Those enrolled in the Arizona Rangers were to provide their own mounts and weapons "and all necessary accouterments and camp equipment." Ammunition, food, and forage would be furnished by the territory for each man and his mount, not to exceed one dollar a day for meals and fifty cents for horse feed. Rangers had the power of arrest throughout the territory but were to turn prisoners over to officials within the county in which the crime had been committed.[13]

Gov. N. O. Murphy chose as captain a fiery cattleman named Burt Mossman, who had bossed the Hash Knife, the Aztec Land and Cattle Company west of Holbrook. Mossman had impressed lawmen and ranchers throughout the territory with the way he ran the big spread, cleaning out dishonest cowboys and rustlers who had been preying on the Hash Knife herds. On August 30, 1901, Mossman took command as the first captain of the Arizona Rangers and began selection of likely recruits for the new organization. Ed Scarborough was one of those chosen, perhaps more out of a recognition of his father's stature as a law enforcement officer than Ed's own. On September 6, Ed was one of the first four men to sign enlistment papers in the new elite organization. Don Johnson, son of the late W. D. ("Keechi") Johnson, was another of the first recruits. He and Ed had much in common, each being the son of an officer killed in the line of duty and, at twenty-two, being the youngest in the ranger company, whose members average thirty-three years in age.[14]

Ed's appointment was noted in the *Tucson Citizen*, which said the "daring young Arizona Ranger" had recently been on the trail of members of the notorious Smith gang from Black River but had lost them near Alamogordo, New Mexico. "He is a determined fellow and much like his father," said the paper. "When he joined the Arizona Rangers this fall it was considered one of Captain Mossman's best acquisitions. Scarborough was brought up in the saddle and is an excellent marksman. He don't know what fear is and when he succeeds in coming up with the Smith outlaws, a lively scrap can safely be promised." According to this account, Ed was now blaming the Smith gang for the death of his father. "I will devote the rest of my life to the capture of the Smith outlaws, one of whom is the slayer of my father," he was quoted.[15]

But Ed Scarborough's career as an Arizona Ranger was short and undistinguished. His enlistment had been for a year, but he lasted less than nine months. Mossman found that the young man was "a bit on the harum-scarum side and traveled quite a little on his father's reputation." The captain had already "had a little trouble" with Ed when he rode into Tombstone one day in May 1902 and learned that the young ranger "had disobeyed orders and gone over to the courthouse and picked a fight." County officers grabbed him but hesitated to jail a ranger.

Mossman told his biographer that he placed Scarborough under arrest and knocked him down when Ed went for his gun. "He almost fell under the heels of one of the horses, and he was lucky he didn't get kicked to death." Mossman, who was preparing to leave on a scout into the mountains above Clifton, turned the obstreperous ranger over to the sheriff with instructions to hold him until his return. Ed was locked up in a cell for almost three weeks and, according to Mossman, "pulled every possible string to get himself out of jail. He even appealed to the Governor, but neither the Governor nor the sheriff would budge."[16] On his return, Mossman took Ed to ranger headquarters at Bisbee, where he was discharged on May 31. As reason for termination on the discharge document, Mossman wrote "services no longer required" and evaluated the former ranger's character as "good."

Ed quickly signed on as an inspector with the Wagon Rods, the Boquillas Land and Cattle Company on the San Pedro River. The day after his discharge, the *Tombstone Epitaph* noted: "Detective Ed Scarborough was to the city today. Ed is now permanently located on the San Pedro."[17]

After his discharge from the rangers, Ed's path led downward. He had about played out the strong hand he had been dealt as the son of George Scarborough, and never again would he command respect as an officer in his own right. "Ed was not the man his father was," says a cousin, Mrs. Evelyn Linebery.[18] Cochise County pioneer Judge James C. Hancock was less compassionate, saying bluntly: "George Scarborough's son Ed was no good,"[19] but salty old John Cox said it even more pithily: "They shoulda hung him when he was a pup."[20]

By December of 1902, Ed was back in Deming, where he was arrested for unlawfully carrying a deadly weapon. He retained the services of attorney James S. Fielder to represent him in this case.

Fielder managed to gain continuance for four years until the charges were finally dropped in November 1906.[21]

In August 1904, Ed was in more serious trouble. He was arrested in Deming and charged with robbery, assault with intent to rob, and two counts of assault with a deadly weapon.[22]

At two o'clock on the morning of Saturday, August 20, "a man disguised in a mother hubbard dress and a lady's silk stocking made into a cap with a handkerchief over the lower part of the face" appeared at the lunch counter of the Harvey House restaurant at the Deming depot and demanded cash "at the point of a sixshooter." The cashier produced twenty-four dollars, which the holdup man stuffed into another stocking. The "bold bad man" then marched the cashier and another man from the restaurant some two hundred yards up the track, where he released them with a warning that they would be killed if they sounded an alarm. Sheriff D. B. Stephens was called for and arrived to find "Ed Scarborough, known as 'Kid' in Arizona, . . . a well known character throughout the southwest," seated at the counter quietly eating. Ed was arrested when the robbery victims claimed they recognized him as the holdup man. According to one newspaper story, the arrest was made "with some difficulty."

A room in the rear of the Ranch Saloon that had been occupied by Scarborough was searched, and officers found the dress and stocking cap used in the holdup. A man named Lester Noal, who had recently accompanied Scarborough to Deming on the train from El Paso, was also arrested and charged as an accessory.[23] Further sensationalism was added to the case by a newspaper allegation that Scarborough was the leader of a "gang of seven men who had planned to hold up one of the Southern Pacific trains."[24]

At a preliminary hearing on August 22, Scarborough was bound over to the grand jury and released on five thousand dollars bail. He was indicted in December on four charges and his attorney, James Fielder, requested and was granted a change of venue to Grant County. The case was moved from Deming, seat of the new county of Luna, to Silver City, where Fielding employed his stalling tactics, requesting and receiving continuances until the charges were eventually dropped.

George Scarborough must have revolved in his casket. His son, a cheap holdup man—and gussied out in women's clothes to boot! The history did not get better.

In 1909, Ed was being sought by authorities in Socorro County for horse theft. Fred Fornoff, who now held the job George Scarborough had coveted, captain of the New Mexico Mounted Police, was being requested to apprehend George's son as a common horse thief. District Attorney John E. Griffith of Socorro wrote to Fornoff on June 18, 1909, advising him that two indictments for larceny of a horse had been returned against "your friend, Ed. Scarborough," and "if you can find him the service will be appreciated."[25] Wanted notices were issued for Scarborough and Jesse Ely for horse theft. Ed Scarborough was said to be known all over the Southwest and to have "been in trouble before."[26]

Ed appears to have escaped the law in New Mexico. He was living at Los Angeles, California, in March 1912 when he read in a newspaper that Ben Kilpatrick was dead. Arrested in Saint Louis in the fall of 1901, Kilpatrick had entered a guilty plea to a twelve-count indictment for passing unsigned currency traced to a Great Northern train robbery near Wagner, Montana on July 3, 1901. He was sentenced to fifteen years in the federal penitentiary. Released on June 11, 1911, he and a former cellmate named Ole Beck attempted a holdup of a Southern Pacific express near Sanderson, Texas. A tough messenger named D. A. Trousdale killed Kilpatrick with an ice mallet and Beck with Kilpatrick's rifle.[27]

On March 29, 1912, Ed Scarborough penned an ungrammatical but easily understood letter to the warden of the federal penitentiary in Atlanta, Georgia:

> I was surprised a few days ago to hear that one of the two men that was killed in attempted train robbery in western Texas was Ben Kilpatrick whom you had in your prison for handling some unsigned currency that was claimed to have got in a train robbery in Colorado in 1901 or 1902.
>
> As I was under the impression that he was to serve 20 yrs. in your prison.
>
> I dont recognize the dead train robber picture as Kilpatricks, but have not seen him since 1900 in New Mex.
>
> This man Kilpatrick and some others of his gang waylayed and killed my father who was an officer at the time.

If you would kindly send me one of Kilpatricks pictures taken at the time of his release I would consider it a great favor as it would enable me to identify him from the picture taken of the dead bandit that is claimed to be Kilpatrick.

P. S. There was never a warrant swore out for him for my fathers murder but I know he did and if I can get on his trail if he is alive I can be able to prove it. My father was sheriff in Jones Co Tex from 85 until 89 Deputy U. S. M. under Dick Ware from 92 until 94.

The warden responded on April 5 that one of the two men killed in the train holdup attempt in West Texas "was John Arnold, a man of many aliases, but whose true name was Ben Kilpatrick, a resident of Concho County, Texas."[28]

Perhaps with receipt of this letter, Ed finally gave up his twelve-year quest to hunt down his father's killers. Will Carver and George Kilpatrick had gone down before the guns of Sheriff Briant and his deputies eleven years earlier, and now Ben Kilpatrick had joined them in death. Tom Capehart and Tod Carver had disappeared, perhaps to the wilds of South America, and had not been heard of in years.

By February 1915, Ed was back in Cochise County, Arizona, punching cows on the Wagon Rods for Superintendent Henry K. Street of the Boquillas Land and Cattle Company. Street was a tough little cattleman of the old school who had herded for the Millett Ranch and had known George Scarborough back on the Clear Fork in the 1870s. He had later worked on the Spur Ranch near Luna and with Walter Birchfield on the Diamond A. When the Boquillas acquired Colonel William C. Greene's vast San Pedro range, a spread reaching from the international line almost to Benson, Street was selected to ramrod the outfit.[29]

Ed soon was having trouble with a rancher named John Clinton, who ran a herd of cattle near Hereford. It was reported that the difficulty arose when Clinton allowed his cattle to graze in a Boquillas pasture and that Ed had words with him over the matter and at one point "had drawn a gun upon Clinton, who laughed the cowboy out of the notion of shooting."[30]

About eight o'clock on the evening of June 18, 1915, Ed Scarborough and another cowboy named Cal Cox rode up to the Clinton ranch house. Scarborough dismounted, went up onto the porch, and asked Clinton to come outside. The rancher had just finished his supper and had pulled off his boots in preparation for bed. Slipping on a pair of moccasins, he walked out into the yard with Scarborough. What happened then is not clear. Clinton's wife and young daughter later testified that they heard the men arguing and swearing and then heard gunshots. When they ran into the yard, Clinton lay dying with four bullet wounds. Cox said he never dismounted and had no part in the shooting. Scarborough admitted that he had drawn his six-shooter and shot Clinton but claimed he was in fear of his life when the rancher called to his wife, "Mamma, get the rifle and kill him!"[31]

Ed and Cox rode for the Mexican border, which was only two miles away, and separated. Scarborough then reversed direction and went north to Benson on the main line of the Southern Pacific, apparently with the intention of catching a train out of the state. But he was apprehended in Benson by deputies of Cochise County Sheriff Harry C. Wheeler and taken to Tombstone and jailed. Cox was arrested later. Both were charged with the murder of Jack Clinton.[32]

An inquest was held at the death scene on June 19 by Judge George R. Smith, after which the *Bisbee Daily Review* concluded that Scarborough would have "a difficult time in clearing himself before the courts."[33]

Responding to rumors that Scarborough was acting in the interests of the Wagon Rods when he killed Clinton, Henry Street published a letter denying the charges. "None of the employees of this company," he said, "has ever had a dispute with Mr. Clinton over the rights of his property or over any other question until this affair came up between him and Scarborough." He advised all to "wait until the preliminary examination before rendering a decision" as the "erroneous reports are doing the B L & C Co. a great injustice."[34]

On June 28, Ed was taken to Lowell for a preliminary examination before Judge Smith. On advice of his counsel, Eugene Ives of Tucson, Ed caused "not a little of a surprise" by waiving examination. Cal Cox had been brought from Tombstone by automobile for the hearing. Riding in the rear seat was Clinton's sister, who was also called to testify. During the trip the woman suddenly reached forward and attempted to throttle Cox and the officers had "some trouble [releasing] Cox from the grasp of the enraged woman."[35]

The preliminary hearing for Cox was held July 6 in Tombstone before Judge Fowler. Several witnesses testified that Cox had made threats against Clinton. Cox said that Scarborough had come to his camp and suggested he accompany him to Clinton's place, where he waited at the gate while Scarborough approached the house. He heard voices but could not make out the words as he claimed to be partly deaf. He saw gun flashes and heard the reports. He said Scarborough then "ordered" him to ride for the international boundary. Both suspects were returned to the Tombstone jail and held without bail.[36]

Ed was arraigned on November 13 and trial was set for Superior Court in Tombstone on December 2 before Judge Alfred C. Lockwood. Acting for the defense were Eugene Ives and Frank W. Doan. The prosecution was conducted by County Attorney John F. Ross, assisted by Bruce Stevenson and special prosecutor William F. Cleary, called the "best known criminal lawyer in the southern part of the state."[37]

Star witness for the prosecution was Rose Clinton, the small daughter of the deceased, who said she had witnessed the entire affair and answered all questions "without falter" and undoubtedly gained much sympathy for the state's case with the jury.[38]

Among the witnesses called by the defense to testify to Ed's ability and courage as a peace officer were Jeff Milton and Harry Wheeler. Ed testified in his own defense, spent most of two days on the stand, and was subjected to severe cross-examination. He said he believed Clinton had stolen some of his calves and they had argued over this on several prior occasions. He stuck firmly to his story that he shot Clinton because he believed his life was in danger.

Judge Lockwood's charge to the jury focused on the legal difference between first- and second-degree murder and the specific definition of justifiable homicide. At the request of defense counsel the following was inserted into that instruction: "If you believe that Clinton seized the defendant and prior to any shot by the defendant or effort by the defendant to shoot, said in effect, referring to Mrs. Clinton, 'Mamma, get the rifle and kill him,' referring by killing him to the defendant, and that at such time the defendant, as a reasonable man, believed himself in danger of death or great bodily injury, and acting under such belief, shot and killed Clinton, the homicide was justified and your verdict should be not guilty." The jury retired at five o'clock on the evening of December 10 to deliberate and returned at eleven the next morning with a verdict of guilty of murder in the second degree. That afternoon Ed was sentenced by Judge Lockwood to a term in the state prison of not less than ten years nor more than his natural life.[39]

At least one editor saw the verdict and sentence as a sign that the day of judge and jury liberality toward mankillers in frontier towns like Tombstone had finally passed:

> The other day a man was convicted at Tombstone of murder in the second degree. The killing took place at the house of the victim when he was called out in the nighttime and shot down. The settings of the crime were those of the old Arizona days, of the days of Curly Bill. It looked like plain assassination and there was nothing to remove that appearance except the word of the murderer and another man who was jointly indicted with him for the crime. Nine of the jurors believed it was assassination and they voted for a verdict of murder in the first degree. One juryman thought that second degree murder had been committed and one favored manslaughter. The remaining juryman, who must have been a person of superior superhuman intelligence, voted for acquittal. A compromise verdict was then agreed upon. Considering the verdicts of Cochise County jurors in the recent past in murder cases, where cold-blooded slayers have been acquitted because they stated that they thought that their unarmed victims had "motioned toward their hip pockets," we think this verdict of second degree murder is something of an advance.[40]

Attorney Ives filed an appeal on technical grounds while Ed languished in the Tombstone jail. Cal Cox was tried the following week and acquitted.[41] In May 1916, Ed asked his attorney to withdraw his appeal and announced that he was ready to serve his sentence.[42] He entered the Arizona State Prison at Florence on May 19, 1916, as Inmate No. 4787.[43]

Within months after Ed went to prison, his wife, Ruby, divorced him, married O. A. Ash, a brakeman on the El Paso and Southwestern Railroad, and moved to Douglas. There were reports that when Scarborough heard this, he swore "vengeance on both his former wife and on Ash and vowed he would escape from the pen and kill them both."[44]

On the night of May 25, 1917, one year and six days after he had entered the prison, Ed Scarborough went over the wall. Escaping

Edgar Scarborough in the Arizona State Prison
at Florence. *Courtesy Kansas State Historical
Society.*

with him were convicts Bob Pitts and George Townsend, each
serving a five-year term for burglary. Pitts and Townsend were
recaptured the following month near Roswell, New Mexico, and
returned to Florence, but Ed was still on the loose.[45]

Because of his reported threats against the safety of Ruby and her
new husband, officers in southern Arizona kept a sharp lookout for
him. "Being a gunman of the worst known type, it is feared that
[Scarborough] will make his way to Douglas where Mr. and Mrs. Ash
now reside and attempt to carry out his threat," said the *Tombstone
Epitaph*. "Officers all along the line have been warned to be on the

lookout and Ash has been notified to be on his guard while efforts are being made to effect his capture."[46]

So far as is known, Ed Scarborough never attempted to harm Ruby or her husband. He simply disappeared. Eleven years later, Scott White, the former Cochise County sheriff who had ridden stirrup to stirrup with George Scarborough on many a manhunt, was superintendent of the Arizona State Prison at Florence and still was offering a reward of one hundred dollars for the apprehension of George's son.[47]

Ed went to Mexico and remained, crossing back into the United States only occasionally to visit his mother and sisters, who were living in Southern California. He was still alive and well as late as 1945.[48]

Afterword

George Scarborough's old compadres, Frank McMahan and Jeff Milton, survived him by many years. After disbandment of the cattlemen's range riders, McMahan lived in San Diego, California, and patrolled the Mexican border as an officer in the United States Immigration and Naturalization Service until his unexpected death, apparently from a heart attack, at age sixty-nine in Yuma, Arizona, on March 6, 1940.[1]

The indomitable Jeff Milton, refusing to be slowed down by a crippled left arm, the memento of the express-car battle with train robbers at Fairbanks in February 1900, prospected for mineral deposits and oil for a time and then, in 1904, also joined the Immigration Service. In 1917, four days before his fifty-sixth birthday, he stumbled onto a bank robbery in progress at Tombstone, chased the bandit in a stripped-down Ford, and stopped him with a bullet in the arm from a .38 automatic pistol. Jeff finally married in 1919 and at seventy-two retired from the Immigration Service in 1932. He died in 1947 after eighty-five adventurous years.[2]

Mary Frances ("Mollie") McMahan Scarborough outlived her husband by almost half a century and was a resident of Southern California for most of that time. She died at the age of eighty-nine on July 3, 1949, at Burbank, where she had been living with her daughter, Eva McDowell. She was buried in Hollywood Cemetery. Her death notice listed as survivors, in addition to Eva, daughters Georgie May Kerr and Ethel Abbott and son Ray. Daughters Martha and Mary Ada Elizabeth had preceded their mother in death. Edgar

262

was not mentioned and apparently also had died since being reported as alive and well in 1945.[3]

Mollie Scarborough blamed her husband's untimely death on notoriety that had attached to him after the El Paso experience and especially the Selman killing. Apparently feeling that George had been marked for death by gunmen of the outlaw element because of this notoriety and blaming the press for its part in publicizing his adventures, she refused to talk to writers during her lifetime and urged her children to follow the same policy. Much of the distorted nonsense that was written and published about Scarborough in later years did nothing to cause Mollie to change her decision.

J. Marvin Hunter ran into this obstacle in the 1920s when he was helping his friend Noah Rose assemble the famous Rose Collection of photographs of western frontier celebrities. Hunter wrote in 1927: "My sister [Mrs. Frank McMahan] . . . has a splendid photo of George, but she will not let me nor anyone else have it, because they do not want any publicity in regard to George's career."[4]

Mollie's edict was honored through two succeeding generations; not only did her children rebuff writers, but so did her grandchildren. When western historian Robert Mullin attempted to obtain Scarborough information from George's grandson, Dan Abbott, Sr., through Dallas Scarborough of Abilene, Abbott wrote, "During my grandfather's lifetime he abhorred any publicity concerning himself, and this policy has been followed by my grandmother during her lifetime, and the remainder of the family."[5]

George Scarborough is remembered today primarily for that brief moment outside the Wigwam Saloon when he killed the man who killed the West's deadliest gunman. He deserves better.

Notes

Chapter 1

1. Jewel Davis Scarborough, *Southern Kith and Kin,* 15.
2. Mrs. Evelyn Linebery interview, Midland, Texas, May 6, 1989.
3. Scarborough, *Southern Kith and Kin,* 18.
4. Ibid., 73.
5. Ibid., 151; *Historical and Biographical Record of the Cattle Industry and the Cattlemen of Texas and Adjacent Territory,* 371.
6. G. W. Scarborough Family Bible.
7. Elizabeth Shown Mills to Robert K. DeArment (cited hereafter as RKD), January 26, 1985.
8. G. W. Scarborough Family Bible.
9. U.S. Census, Natchitoches Parish, Louisiana, 1860.
10. National Archives.
11. G. W. Scarborough Family Bible.
12. Ibid.
13. Ibid.
14. W. E. Paxton, *A History of the Baptists of Louisiana,* 563–64; Scarborough, *Southern Kith and Kin,* 151. In the Lee R. Scarborough archives at Southwestern Baptist Theological Seminary in Fort Worth, Texas, is a letter dated October 10, 1863, and signed by Capt. R. G. Buckner of the Confederate Quartermaster Corps, certifying the employment of "W. R. Rutland and Geo. W. Scarborough to transport gov't stores, they furnishing wagons and teams." Buckner agreed to pay ten dollars per day for each wagon and three yoke of Oxen, and sixteen dollars a day for each wagon and four yoke of oxen. In addition, he would provide rations for the drivers and forage for the teams.
15. Manie White Johnson, "The Colfax Riot of April, 1873," 399.
16. Ibid., 402.
17. Ibid., 403, quoting the *Grant Parish Enterprise,* September 20, 1928, and an interview with Judge J. A. Williams, an early-day resident of Grant Parish.
18. Johnson, "The Colfax Riot," 403, quoting the subsequent inquiry into the events by the Forty-third United States Congress.

19. Ibid., 404.

20. Quoted in Joe Gray Taylor, *Louisiana Reconstructed, 1863–1877.* 269.

21. Johnson, "The Colfax Riot," 416, quoting the *Colfax Chronicle*, April 9, 1921.

22. Ibid., 416.

23. Taylor, *Louisiana Reconstructed*, 270–71. W. Lod Tanner, a participant, said Shaw was taken to Calhoun's sugar house, where he was placed on a suspended plank with a noose around his neck. Just before he was pushed off, he gave the Masonic distress sign and his life was spared. Johnson, "The Colfax Riot," 400.

24. Johnson, "The Colfax Riot," 417, quoting remarks of a Grant Parish resident in the *Colfax Chronicle*, April 9, 1921.

25. Johnson, "The Colfax Riot," 417.

26. Taylor, *Louisiana Reconstructed*, 270.

27. Johnson, "The Colfax Riot," 418.

28. Those charged were William Cruikshank, John Pearce Hadnot, William Edwin, Clement C. Penn, Prudhomme Lemoine, Donas Lemoine, A. P. Gibbons, A. C. Lewis, and Thomas Hickman. At trials held in Federal court in New Orleans in February and May 1874, five of the defendants were acquitted and four were convicted of conspiracy against a peaceful assemblage, not of murder. The appeals process led to the U.S. Supreme Court, which on March 27, 1876, handed down in the case of *United States* v. *Cruikshank* a unanimous decision that the federal government had no jurisdiction in the case and had the effect of strengthening the argument for the doctrine of states' rights. "Thus the riot of April, 1873, in the little town of Colfax, Louisiana—at the time seemingly only the extreme manifestation of that bitter feeling engendered by the woes of Reconstruction—served to carry the Southern question into the highest tribunal of the United States, to definitely limit the operation of the Fourteenth Amendment, and to place the South legally, as well as actually, well on the road to home rule." Johnson, "The Colfax Riot," 424–425.

29. "The massacre at Colfax County courthouse ranks as the worst single day of carnage in the history of Reconstruction, exceeding in violence the massacres at New Orleans (1866), Memphis (1866), and Meridian, Mississippi (1871)." Ted Tunnell, *Crucible of Reconstruction: War, Radicalism and Race in Louisiana, 1862–1877*, 192.

Chapter 2

1. H. E. Dana, *Lee Rutland Scarborough*, 16; *Historical and Biographical Record of the Cattle Industry*, 371; Lee R. Scarborough Archives, Southwestern Baptist Theological Seminary, Forth Worth, Texas.

2. Dana, *Lee Rutland Scarborough*, 36.

3. Capt. James B. Gillett, "Beef Gathering in '71 was Thrilling," 6–7.

4. D. H. Henderson, "McCulloch County of Fifty-two Years Ago," 34.

5. Wyatt Anderson, "A Pioneer in West Texas," 14.

6. Ibid.

7. Mollie was one of five children born to Francis Marion McMahan and Mary Ann Liggett McMahan in Saline County, Missouri. The McMahan family moved to McCulloch County, Texas, in the early 1870s. They later followed the Scarbor-

oughs to Jones County. Information from William Reese Walker of Hot Springs Village, Arkansas; McMahan Family Bible; McLennan County, Texas, Marriage Records, vol. 2 (January 1871–July 1892), 30; John Marvin Hunter and Noah H. Rose, *The Album of Gunfighters*, 126.

8. Surveyor's Records, Jones County, Texas, vol. A, 343. Five hundred twenty-two and nine-tenths acres were granted to G. W. and M.E. Scarborough on December 16, 1877. The purchaser of record was Martha. The land had been surveyed April 18, 1877, and was described as being "situated on the waters of Elm fork and Clear fork, a tributary of the Brazos river, about 15 miles, 18 degrees from Phantom Hill, and known as survey No. 18 in Block No. 15." Information provided by Billie D. Lipham of Abilene, Texas, whose grandfather purchased part of this acreage from George's sister Ada and her husband in 1905.

9. Dana, *Lee Rutland Scarborough*, 27.

10. Hooper Shelton and Homer Hutto, *The First 100 Years of Jones County, Texas*, 21–25.

11. Ibid., 26–28.

12. John R. Hutto, "Emmett Roberts, a Pioneer of Jones County," 84.

13. Shelton and Hutto, *First 100 Years*, 34.

14. Hutto, "Emmett Roberts," 87.

15. Joe T. McKinney, "Reminiscences of a Texan," 14.

16. J. Evetts Haley, *Jeff Milton*, 15–20.

17. Letter, Mrs. Ada Phillips to RKD, October 20, 1981.

18. Ibid.

19. Dana, *Lee Rutland Scarborough*, 25.

20. Ibid.

21. McMahan Family Bible.

Chapter 3

1. Shelton and Hutto, *First 100 Years*, 35–36; *Western Enterprise*, August 24, 1933.

2. Shelton and Hutto, *First 100 Years*, 243. According to family tradition, when it became known that the parson was going to preach, "some fresh young man said he was not going to allow any preaching in the county." Parson Scarborough carried a shotgun with him and "stood the gun beside the improvised pulpit and preached. He was not interrupted." Mrs. Ada Phillips to RKD, November 6, 1983.

3. Shelton and Hutto, *First 100 Years*, 243.

4. Dana, *Lee Rutland Scarborough*, 36, 40; Shelton and Hutto, *First 100 Years*, 238.

5. *Western Enterprise*, August 24, 1933.

6. Ibid.

7. Ibid.; R. E. Sherill, *Haskell County History*.

8. *Western Enterprise*, September 7, 1933; Midland County Historical Society, "The Frying Pan Ranch."

9. Jones County Commissioner's Books, minutes of November 10, 1884, meeting.

10. J. F. Cunningham, "Experiences of a Pioneer District Attorney," 126–35.

11. Ibid. J. William Standifer served three terms as sheriff of Crosby County, from 1888 to 1894 (Sammy Tise, *Texas County Sheriffs*, 137). He was killed in a gunfight with Pink Higgins, a tough Panhandle cattleman and gunfighter at Higgins's ranch in Kent County, Texas, on October 4, 1903 (Bill O'Neal, *Encyclopedia of Western Gunfighters*, 140–41).

12. Jones County Commissioner's Books; *Western Enterprise*, August 24, 1933.

13. Mrs. Ada Phillips to RKD October 1, 1981, and November 6, 1983.

14. Jones County Commissioner's Books, November 1886.

15. *San Antonio Daily Express*, February 6, 1886.

16. Ibid.

17. Ibid., May 30, 1886; July 14, 1886.

18. Ibid., July 22, 1886.

19. Jones County Jailbook.

20. Jones County Commissioner's Books, minutes of December 1884 meeting.

21. Copies of undated clippings from the *Western Enterprise*, Anson, Texas, provided by Mrs. Ada Phillips and Irvin Munn, who had researched the Glazner family history. The *Western Enterprise* of August 24, 1933, commemorating Anson's fiftieth anniversary, carried an account of Glazner's death written by Mrs. W. E. Glazner, the wife of one of Will's sons. The killing of Will Glazner was the only murder recorded within the Anson city limits in the first fifty years of its history.

22. Perhaps one of the reasons Cannon was not captured was the inconsistency of his description in the Fugitive List from year to year. In 1891, for instance, Sheriff Ed Tyson had described him as having medium complexion, gray eyes, and brown hair; in 1886, Sheriff Scarborough submitted to the adjutant general's office a list of three men he wanted: George Sloan for horse theft and brothers Allen and Henry Swain for murder. Fourteen years later, Jones County Sheriff W. S. Swan still had all three on his 1900 list (Fugitive Lists, State of Texas, 1878, 1886, 1891, 1900; Adjutant General's Files, Austin).

23. Jones County Jailbook.

24. Letter, Irvin Munn to RKD, August 23, 1983.

25. Jones County jailbook.

26. Request for extradition in holdings of Texas State Archives, Austin.

27. Undated letter, Archie Jefferes to Homer Hutto. Jefferes's father and John Scarborough, first cousin to George, shared bachelor's quarters in Jones County in 1887–88 and were lifelong friends. The stories concerning George Scarborough originated in their mutual recollections. According to a short account of this capture in the *Las Vegas Daily Optic* of May 18, 1885, Tom Babb was the fugitive who had to be run down, making "a running fight for fifteen miles, shooting as he ran, but was finally captured without anyone of the party being hurt."

20. Abilene dispatch to the *San Antonio Daily Express*, May 23, 1885. See also the *Arizona Daily Star*, May 28, 1885.

29. Abilene dispatch to the *San Antonio Daily Express*, May 31, 1885.

30. Ibid., July 10, 1885.

31. Ibid.

32. *Western Enterprise*, Aug 24, 1933.

33. Ibid.; Jones County Jailbook.

34. Sherill, *Haskell County History*.
35. Ibid. Undated letter, Jefferes to Hutto.
36. Sherill, *Haskell County History*.
37. Case No. 82, Haskell County Court Records.
38. *Haskell City Free Press*, March 17, 1888.
39. Ibid.
40. Another undated letter from Archie Jefferes to Homer Hutto.
41. *Haskell City Free Press*, April 28, 1888.
42. Quoted in Ed Bartholomew, *Kill or Be Killed*, 102–103, from an Albany, Texas, newspaper.
43. Interview with Moliere Scarborough by Stuart M. Scarborough, December 1, 1984.
44. Jones County Commissioner's Books, February 1888 term.
45. Ibid. November 1888 term.

Chapter 4

1. From interviews with A. P. Black in the Earl Vandale Collection, Nita Stewart Haley Memorial Library. The Double Mountains were the two forks of the Brazos River: Double Mountain Fork in Lynn, Garza, and Kent counties and North Double Mountain in Lubbock, Crosby, Garza, and Kent counties. Black says this was the general roundup of 1887, but it most likely was in 1889 that he worked with Scarborough. Jess Hittson's HIT Ranch was in Stonewall and Fisher counties, adjoining Haskell and Jones counties to the west.
2. A. P. ("Ott") Black, *The End of the Long Horn Trail*, 32.
3. Ibid, 63–64. Black mangled names. He calls the LIX gunman "Pokesburg Hill" and consistently spells George's name "Scharbar." Poke Berryhill cowboyed in this area at the time (Sherill, *Haskell County History*, 57), and it is clear, from other remarks within the book and his interviews in the Vandale Collection, that George Scarborough is the man Black worked with on the roundup. He is less credible when he comments on events with which he had no firsthand knowledge. He says, for instance, that "Scharbar" killed John Wesley "Harding," who had killed thirty-one men, "Scharbar had killed thirty when they met. Scharbar killed his thirty-second when he put Harding away." Apparently, Black's arithmetic was as bad as his history.
4. C. L. Douglas, *Cattle Kings of Texas*, 306.
5. Franklin Reynolds, "One of the Last of the Old Time Rangers," 169–75. Doan's Crossing at this time supported a population of about three hundred with the hotel, a blacksmith and wagon repair shop, several eating places, and a drink-and-dance dive called the Cowboy Saloon. Angie Irons, "Doan's Crossing," 47.
6. Max Coleman, "Law and Order," 140.
7. Bob Beverly, *Hobo of the Rangeland*, 8.
8. Moliere Scarborough interviews, December 1, 1984, and February 23, 1985.
9. Richard C. Ware assumed the office of United States marshal for the Western District of Texas on April 25, 1893, and served until January 10, 1898 (letter from Robert R. Ernst, research consultant, U.S. Marshals Service, to RKD October 26, 1988).
10. Moliere Scarborough interviews, August 1984, December 1, 1984. Inter-

viewed at the age of ninety-three by his grandson, Scarborough said he clearly recalled this incident: "I distinctly remember George coming into the store, and the counter there and he just pulled out his sixshooter and put it on the table. . . . He said he was going to El Paso because he would rather run men than cattle, and that was it." But Moliere was only two years old when his Uncle George pulled out for El Paso. Apparently he had heard the story so many times from his father that he was certain he had witnessed the incident. Moliere also believed he remembered George as sheriff, but he was born three years after George left the sheriff's office.

11. C. L. Sonnichsen, *Pass of the North*, 310; Haley, *Jeff Milton*, 209.

12. Sonnichsen, *Pass of the North*, 310–13. Fusselman's killer was a man named Geronimo Parra, who was finally arrested by Ranger Captain Hughes. Tried and convicted, he was hanged on January 6, 1900.

13. Walter Prescott Webb, *The Texas Rangers*, 441–44; Sonnichsen, *Pass of the North*, 314–15; *El Paso Times*, July 1, 1893.

14. *El Paso Times*, July 6, 1893.

15. McMahan served as a member of Company D, Frontier Battalion, from September 1, 1893, to May 31, 1894. Texas Ranger Muster Rolls and Monthly Returns, Texas State Library and Archives, Austin.

16. *San Antonio Daily Express*, December 7, 1893. Dateline El Paso, Texas, December 6 (Special).

17. *El Paso Herald*, January 25, 1894.

18. Ibid., February 13, 1894.

19. *San Antonio Daily Express*, March 18, 1894, Dateline El Paso, Texas, March 17 (Special).

20. *El Paso Times*, May 15, 1894.

21. Ibid., June 16, 1894.

22. Ibid., July 27, 1894.

23. *San Antonio Daily Express*, March 4, 1894, Dateline El Paso, Texas, March 3 (Special).

24. *El Paso Times*, June 23, 1894.

25. Ibid., July 13, 1894.

26. Ibid., July 24, 1894.

27. Ibid., February 5, 1895.

28. *El Paso Herald*, April 20, 1895.

29. *El Paso Times*, April 28, 1895.

30. Ibid., June 12, 1895.

31. Ibid., September 18, 1894.

32. Ibid., February 19, 1895.

33. Ibid., October 13, 1894.

34. *El Paso Herald*, April 30, 1894.

35. Ibid., January 30, 1894.

36. *El Paso Times*, May 9, 1894.

37. Ibid., March 22, 1895.

38. Ibid., January 29, 1896; February 1, 1896.

39. Ibid., March 29, March 31, 1896.

40. Ibid., June 10, 1894.

41. Ibid., June 26, 1894.

42. *El Paso Herald,* January 28, 1895.

43. Ibid., April 12, 1895.

44. Ibid., February 16, 1894.

45. *El Paso Times,* April 25, 1894.

46. Ibid., April 6, 1895.

47. Ibid., June 23, 1895.

48. Clayton W. Williams, *Texas' Last Frontier,* 368; *San Antonio Express,* December 1, 1893; December 2, 1893.

49. *El Paso Herald,* February 8, 1894.

50. Williams, *Texas' Last Frontier,* 369.

51. Ibid.; Company D Monthly Returns, August 1894.

52. Williams, *Texas' Last Frontier,* 370–71.

53. *San Antonio Express,* October 24, 1894.

54. Williams, *Texas' Last Frontier,* 371; *El Paso Times,* October 25, 1894.

55. Williams, *Texas' Last Frontier,* 371. The quotation is from an unpublished manuscript of the author's father, Judge O. W. Williams, dealing with Sheriff A. J. Royal.

56. *El Paso Times,* October 25, 1894.

57. Williams, *Texas Last Frontier,* 372; *El Paso Times,* October 25, 1894; *San Antonio Express,* October 26, 1894. Ochoa was subsequently tried, convicted, and sentenced to two and a half years in prison for violation of the federal neutrality acts. In August 1895, Marshal Ware, assisted by Deputy Marshal Frank McMahan, escorted Ochoa and a Chinese alien on the long train ride to the Kings County Penitentiary in Brooklyn, New York. *El Paso Times,* August 9, 1895.

58. Robert K. DeArment, "Barney Riggs—Man of Violence."

59. Williams, *Texas' Last Frontier,* 372–75; *El Paso Times,* November 7, 1894; Company D Monthly Returns, November 1894.

60. Williams, *Texas' Last Frontier,* 376.

61. Ibid., 380–88.

62. *El Paso Times,* March 11, 1896.

63. Ibid., March 13, 1896.

64. Ibid., March 11, 1896.

65. Ibid., March 12, 1896.

Chapter 5

1. Outlaw was christened Baz at his birth in Georgia and was so listed in the Kimble County Census of 1880, which gave his age as twenty-three, but all contemporary newspaper accounts, Texas Ranger records and later reminiscences refer to him as Bass. Bill O'Neal, "The Latest on 'Bass' Outlaw."

2. In his *Encyclopedia of Western Gunfighters,* O'Neal lists 255 famous, infamous, and obscure gunmen. Because of the abbreviated life expectancy of young men who pursued this career, only 136 were still alive during the middle years of the 1890s. Of these, 23, or fully 17 percent, can definitely be placed in El Paso during the period. Since these fellows tended to drift toward centers of excitement and their comings and goings often went unrecorded, the figure is probably much higher.

3. Letter, J. P. Meadows to E. P. Lamborn, Lamborn Collection, Kansas State Historical Society, Topeka.

4. Frank Collinson, *Life in the Saddle,* 93.

5. This stockade is not to be confused with the town and fort by the same name in Jeff Davis County in West Texas.

6. Frank Collinson, "Three Texas Trigger Men."

7. Don H. Biggers, *Shackelford County Sketches,* 42.

8. Leon Metz, *John Selman,* 63–64.

9. Ibid., 83–84.

10. Andrew Jackson Scarborough, brother of the parson, moved to Jones County in 1880. He had lost his wife in 1870 and remarried in 1877, taking as his second wife a widow named Serena Bledsoe Selman. John Selman's mother, known in the Fort Davis country as Widow Selman, reportedly died in 1867 and was buried near the Clear Fork not many miles from the Scarborough Jones County home. It is not known whether there was any relationship between the former Widow Selman who became George Scarborough's aunt and the Widow Selman who was John Selman's mother. Metz, *John Selman,* 40; Scarborough, *Southern Kith and Kin,* 148.

11. Charles A. Siringo, *Riata and Spurs,* 171–73.

12. Metz, *John Selman,* 96.

13. Frederick W. Nolan, *The Life and Death of John Henry Tunstall,* 413.

14. Ibid., 388–89; Metz, *John Selman,* 101–104; Grady E. McCright and James H. Powell, *Jessie Evans,* 148–50; Robert M. Utley, *High Noon in Lincoln,* 115; John P. Wilson, *Merchants, Guns and Money,* 105; Maurice G. Fulton, *Maurice Garland Fulton's History of the Lincoln County War,* 292.

15. Metz, *John Selman,* 106–107.

16. Fulton, *Lincoln County War,* 333.

17. Utley, *High Noon,* 221.

18. Metz, *John Selman,* 109–11; Robert K. DeArment, "The Great Outlaw Confederacy," 14–19.

19. W. R. Cruger to John B. Jones, July 2, 1880 (Adjutant General's Files, Texas State Library, Austin), quoted in Metz, *John Selman,* 121–22.

20. Metz, *John Selman,* 61–62, 127–28.

21. Ibid., 132; Collinson, *Life in the Saddle,* 97.

22. Metz, *John Selman,* 138.

23. *El Paso Herald,* November 29, 1895.

24. Boyce House, *Cowtown Columnist,* 181; Boyce House, *Oil Field Fury,* 38.

25. Capt. John R. Hughes to Gen. W. H. Mabry, April 6, 1894, Adjutant General's Files, Texas State Library, Austin.

26. Eugene Cunningham, *Triggernometry,* 236.

27. Jack Martin, *Border Boss,* 104; Ed Bartholomew, *The Biographical Album of Western Gunfighters.*

28. *El Paso Herald,* April 6, 1894.

29. Collinson, *Life in the Saddle,* 98.

30. *El Paso Times,* April 6, 1894.

31. H. Gordon Frost, *The Gentlemen's Club,* 72–74.

32. Alonzo Van Oden, *Texas Ranger Diary and Scrapbook,* 21.

33. *El Paso Times,* April 6, 1894.

34. Ibid.; Collinson, *Life in the Saddle,* 98; Metz, *John Selman,* 148.

35. *El Paso Times,* April 6, 1894.

36. Collinson, *Life in the Saddle,* 99; *El Paso Times,* April 6, 1894.

37. Haley, *Jeff Milton,* 214.

38. Ibid., 214, 217.

39. Metz, *John Selman,* 150; Collinson, *Life in the Saddle,* 99. Selman's two sons were called to White's office. "I saw my father stretched out and covered with blood," John, Jr., wrote. "I was badly scared and thought that he would die as the blood kept spurting out of his leg. It was very hot in the office and I turned sick and started to keel over. Doctor White, who was the kindest man I ever met, gave me a glass of water and said, 'Here, kid, buck up. Your dad is all right' " (John Selman, Jr., "John Selman of El Paso," chap. 10, p. 3).

40. Owen P. White, *The Autobiography of a Durable Sinner,* 50–51.

41. Metz, *John Selman,* 150; *El Paso Times,* April 12, 1894; Hughes to Mabry.

42. Metz, *John Selman,* 150; *El Paso Times,* October 31, 1894.

Chapter 6

1. Haley, *Jeff Milton,* 23–24.

2. Ibid., 39. Clements ran for sheriff of newly created Runnels County in 1887 and during an acrimonious campaign was shot to death in a Ballinger saloon. His son, Mannie Clements, Jr., carrying on the family tradition of violence, was one of the gunslicks at El Paso during the turbulent turn-of-the-century years, served on the police force, and, like his father, was gunned down there in a saloon. Glenn Shirley, *Shotgun For Hire,* 13; Sonnichsen, *Pass of the North,* 341–44.

3. Haley, *Jeff Milton,* 50, 92.

4. Ibid., 113–14. This adventure of Milton has eerie overtones. He must have related the story to his close friend George Scarborough, who would later have an almost identical experience, but one without the salutary denouement. Nothing in J. Evetts Haley's Milton files or his book gives a hint that either biographer or subject ever remarked on the extraordinary similarity of the two incidents.

5. Ibid., 213.

6. House, *Cowtown Columnist,* 183–84.

7. Selman, "John Selman of El Paso," chap. 12, pp. 5–6.

8. Haley, *Jeff Milton,* 214.

9. Ibid., 209. A picture of John Selman holding his small son, John, Jr., adorned the personal photograph album of longtime El Paso madam Alice Abbott, along with a collection of madams, prostitutes, and pimps. Frost, *The Gentlemen's Club,* 70.

10. Ibid., 217.

11. Ibid., 218.

12. Metz, *John Selman,* 152.

13. Ibid., 153–56; *El Paso Times,* April 19, 1895.

14. Metz, *John Selman,* 153.

15. Haley, *Jeff Milton,* 222.

16. Ibid., vii.

17. Ibid., 229; T. Lindsay Baker, *The First Polish Americans,* 136. Texans had difficulty with the spelling of the name. It has appeared in contemporary publications

and later writings as "Marose," "Merose," "Morose," "Monrose," "McRose," and "M'Rose." Mroz was probably illiterate and did not know how to spell it himself.

18. Dee Harkey, *Mean as Hell*, 87.

19. John Marvin Hunter, ed., *The Trail Drivers of Texas*, 817–18.

20. Eve Ball, *Ma'am Jones of the Pecos*, 189.

21. A. P. Black interviews, Earl Vandale Collection.

22. Ball, *Ma'am Jones*, 201.

23. Black, *Long Horn Trail*, 61–62.

24. Bob Ford operated a dive in Walsenburg about this time and later opened another establishment in Creede, where he was killed in 1892. He never ran a place in Cripple Creek.

25. Harkey, *Mean as Hell*, 88. "General McKenzie" was Gene McKenzie, who with two brothers established the Dumb Bell Ranch on Monument Draw in 1885. Hervey E. Chesley, *Adventuring With the Old-Timers*, 127.

26. Lee Myers, "Two Lives of Sin Had Impact on Southwest," 3.

27. Harkey, *Mean as Hell*, 87–88.

28. Black, *Long Horn Trail*, 63.

29. *Eddy Current*, July 5, 1895.

30. Ibid.

31. Harkey, *Mean as Hell*, 78–79.

32. Lee Myers, "How Hell-Raising Phenix Dug Its Own Grave"; Harkey, *Mean as Hell*, 88.

33. *Eddy Current*, July 5, 1895.

34. Haley, *Jeff Milton*, 232. The marriage may have been a mock wedding; no official record has appeared. Writers have enthused over Beulah's beauty. Owen P. White, who may have seen her, described her as a "lovely creature . . . a vivid blonde . . . one who would decorate the establishment of any man who could afford to maintain her" (Owen P. White, *Lead and Likker*, 7). She was definitely seen by John Selman, Jr., who called her "a flashing blond lady . . . a regular queen for looks." The men of El Paso, he said, "never had . . . gazed upon such a beauty" (Selman, "John Selman of El Paso," chap. 13, pp. 1–2). Other writers have echoed this theme: Eugene Cunningham (*Triggernometry*, 60), "a dashing blonde lady of statuesque beauty"; J. Evetts Haley (*Jeff Milton*, 232), "a voluptuous blonde with big, baby-blue eyes"; Robert J. Casey (*The Texas Border and Some Borderliners*, 325), "a luscious blonde"; and C. L. Sonnichsen (*Pass of the North*, 321), "a handsome blonde woman." The only known photograph of Beulah hardly substantiates these claims, revealing a rather plain young woman.

35. Harkey, *Mean as Hell*, 88; *Eddy Argus*, March 22, 1895.

36. Haley, *Jeff Milton*, 232–33.

37. *Eddy Current*, July 5, 1895.

38. *Eddy Argus*, March 22, 1895.

39. Apparently, Mroz reverted to type and helped himself to someone's horseflesh during his short stay at Midland. Martin County, just north of Midland, issued a warrant for his arrest at this time. Deposition of J. D. Milton before W. D. Howe, Justice of the Peace, El Paso County, June 30, 1895.

40. John Wesley Hardin, *The Life of John Wesley Hardin;* Cunningham, *Triggernometry*, 50–51.

41. Hardin, *Life*. The introduction to this edition by Robert C. McCubbin is especially informative regarding Hardin's life after his release from prison and the publishing history of his autobiography.
42. Selman, "John Selman of El Paso," chap. 13, p. 1.
43. *El Paso Times*, April 7, 1895.
44. Ibid., April 2, 1895.

Chapter 7

1. *Eddy Argus*, April 5, 1895.
2. *El Paso Times*, April 12, 1895; *El Paso Herald*, August 9, 1895.
3. Haley, *Jeff Milton*, 238.
4. Harkey, *Mean as Hell*, 88–89. Harkey says a man named Charley Cochran escaped to Juárez with Mroz, but it is clear from all contemporary sources that Vic Queen was Mroz's partner in this affair.
5. Ibid., 89. There is some substantiation of Harkey's charge in an item in the *Eddy Argus* of April 19, 1895: "Thomas Fennessy [*sic*], ex-county clerk, and J. M. McKenzie were in El Paso last Tuesday, having brought up a lot of cattle from Agua Caliente, 200 miles south of Juarez. . . . Vic Queen . . . was in Juarez that day mourning over the incarceration of Martin Mrose." Gene McKenzie and his two brothers moved from Midland, Texas, to establish the Dumb Bell Ranch on Monument Draw in New Mexico Territory (Chesley, *Adventuring*, 127). A. P. Black wrote that there were wanted notices out for " 'General' McKenzie, Henry Harding [*sic*] and the rest of the outlaws operating around there. . . . The 'General' and his bunch were 'wanted' for burning the 'Jingle-Bob' brand of U into a dumbbell, O-O. Harding and the others were just wanted on general principles, they'd do anything that was profitable" (Black, *Long Horn Trail*, 65). Henry Hardin, a nephew of John Wesley Hardin, later became a prominent cattleman in the Amarillo country (Chesley, *Adventuring*, 117, 127).
6. Harkey, *Mean as Hell*, 89.
7. *El Paso Herald*, April 13, 1895. The jury in the Frazer trial became deadlocked, four holding fast for acquittal and eight for conviction. In a retrial at Colorado City, Frazer was acquitted on May 20, 1896. Jim Miller, as cold-blooded a killer as the West ever knew, exacted his own revenge. On September 14, 1896, he virtually decapitated Frazer with a shotgun blast at short range. He beat this murder charge as he beat many others both before and after. On April 19, 1909, in Ada, Oklahoma, he finally reached the end of a bloody trail, dangling at the end of a vigilante rope. Shirley, *Shotgun for Hire*.
8. *Eddy Argus*, May 17, 1895; *Eddy Current*, July 5, 1895.
9. *El Paso Times*, April 24, 1895.
10. Ibid.
11. Ibid. The man who sided Hardin on this occasion has never been identified. The newspaper accounts did not name him, nor did Milton do so in relating the story to J. Evetts Haley. A good guess would be Mannie Clements, Jr., who had accompanied Wes Hardin from Pecos to El Paso. Hardin had put his gun on the line for his cousin, Mannie's father, many times in the old days, and Mannie was kin and therefore more trustworthy by Hardin's lights. Scarborough is not named

in the newspaper stories, either, but Milton was clear that George was with him at this confrontation.

12. *El Paso Times,* April 24, 1895.

13. Ibid.

14. Haley, *Jeff Milton,* 240. Haley includes Vic Queen with the New Mexico men at this altercation, but it is evident that Queen and Mroz were still jailed at the time. The first story in the *Times* on the twenty-third made that clear: "The toughs who rallied around the imprisoned M'rose and Queen in Juarez gave it out that they would bulldoze Attorney John Wesley Hardin if he tried professionally to defeat extradition. Last night Mr. Hardin met the gang in Juarez and slapped their faces one after another."

15. Ibid., 234–35.

16. Deposition of J. D. Milton before Justice of the Peace W. D. Howe, June 30, 1895; *El Paso Times,* June 8, 1895.

17. *Eddy Argus,* May 17, 1895.

18. *El Paso Herald,* June 3, 1895.

19. *El Paso Times,* June 12, 1895.

20. *El Paso Herald,* June 22, 1895.

21. *El Paso Times,* June 23, 1895.

22. Ibid., June 30, 1895.

23. Ibid.

24. The *Times* of Saturday, June 29, reported: "Deputy U. S. Marshal Scarborough went down to Sierra Blanca yesterday to bring up a Chinaman . . . captured yesterday. The Celestial will have a hearing before Judge Sexton today."

25. Deposition of George A. Scarborough before Justice of the Peace W. D. Howe, June 30, 1895.

26. Ibid.

27. Ibid.

28. *El Paso Times,* June 30, 1895.

29. Scarborough deposition.

30. *El Paso Times,* June 30, 1895.

31. *El Paso Herald,* July 2, 1895.

32. Scarborough deposition.

33. *El Paso Times,* June 30, 1895.

34. Ibid.

35. Scarborough deposition.

36. *El Paso Times,* June 30, 1895.

37. Scarborough deposition.

38. *El Paso Times,* June 30, 1895.

39. Deposition of J. C. Jones before Justice of the Peace W. D. Howe, June 30, 1895.

40. Affidavit of Dr. Alward White, Case No. 1902, Thirty-fourth District Court, El Paso, in Robert Mullin Collection, Nita Stewart Haley Memorial Library, Midland, Texas.

41. *El Paso Times,* June 30, 1895.

42. *Eddy Current,* July 5, 1895, quoting the *El Paso Herald.*

43. Haley, *Jeff Milton,* 241.

44. J. Evetts Haley interview with W. H. Burges, April 22, 1946, in J. D. Milton Files, Nita Stewart Haley Memorial Library, Midland, Texas.

45. J. D. Milton deposition before Justice of the Peace W. D. Howe, June 30, 1895.

46. F. M. McMahan deposition before Justice of the Peace W. D. Howe, June 30, 1895.

47. *Eddy Current,* July 5, 1895, quoting the *El Paso Herald.*

48. Martin Mroz inquest held by W. D. Howe, Justice of the Peace, Precinct No. 1, El Paso County, Texas, June 30, 1895.

49. *Eddy Current,* July 5, 1895, quoting the *El Paso Herald.*

50. Highly respected former Texas Ranger Capt. George W. Baylor, who had tried to extradite Mroz, was in El Paso again a month after the shooting and defended the officers: "I would have disliked very much to have had to kill M'rose, but if I had attempted to arrest him I guess it would have resulted just as it did with Scarborough, Milton and McMahan. The boys no doubt thought M'rose would surrender when he saw there was no hope of escape. But they were mistaken and they either had to kill him or be killed themselves." *El Paso Times,* August 8, 1895.

51. *El Paso Times,* July 2, 1895.

52. Ibid.

53. Ibid. It should be noted that the men coming with the light were river guards Bendy and Dwyer, whose sole responsibility was to be on the lookout for smugglers. It is highly unlikely that two smugglers with sacks of contraband could be hidden this close to the scene of the shooting without ever being detected by either the officers involved in the shooting or the river patrolmen.

Chapter 8

1. *El Paso Times,* May 2, 1895.

2. Ibid., May 3, 1895.

3. *El Paso Herald,* May 4, 1895.

4. The Wigwam was quite spacious. The *Herald* of May 4, 1895, announced "a finish fight" to be held that night in the Wigwam sporting rooms between Professor James Davis and Reddy Gallagher, the latter a nationally known pugilist from Cleveland who later became a partner with Bat Masterson in a Denver fight club (Robert K. DeArment, *Bat Masterson,* 353).

5. It seems that just about every officer in El Paso, with the notable exception of George Scarborough, claimed the distinction of having arrested Hardin. Jeff Milton said Sheriff Simmons asked Milton to make the arrest as a favor, which he did. (Haley, *Jeff Milton,* 236.) John Selman, Jr., said Deputy Sheriff Ed Ten Eyke made the arrest for Simmons (Selman, "John Selman of El Paso," chap. 13, p. 3). In 1911, John Warren Hunter, father-in-law of Frank McMahan, credited McMahan with the arrest. He said McMahan volunteered for the job and was assisted by John Selman, Jr. "Hardin acknowledged service and handed over his pistols to McMahan. Young Sellman [*sic*] used language that greatly irritated Hardin in whose behalf McMahan interceded and Sellman was made to cease his remarks" (John Warren Hunter, "Inside Story of Life of John Wesley Hardin," 9). If true, this episode could have been the basis for Hardin's enmity toward young John, which ultimately resulted in Hardin's death. Young Selman claimed to have assisted in the arrest of

Hardin on two occasions, once with Ed Fink and Frank Carr at Hardin's rooms and again with the same officers and Joe Chaudoin in the Acme Saloon. In both instances, he said, the officers expected resistance but Hardin came along easily. The first arrest at Hardin's hotel room resulted in a ludicrous scene. "To our surprise, Hardin offered no resistance," Selman wrote, "Instead, he begged the Chief not to take him to jail as he was suffering from a bad case of piles and he went so far as to expose himself to convince the Chief." Showing great compassion, Fink allowed Hardin to remain in his room on his promise to appear in police court the next day, which he did (Selman, "John Selman of El Paso," chap. 17, p. 2).

6. *El Paso Herald,* May 9, 1895.

7. Ibid., May 16, 1895. Charles F. Jones was one of those who testified to seeing Hardin pull his gun. "When asked if he was playing himself, [Jones] said, 'No. I was broke.' Attorney Storms: 'Did you get broke there?' Witness: 'No. I have been broke ever since Cleveland has been president of the U.S.' " The *El Paso Times* of May 17 reported that Hardin was surprised by the verdict and planned to file for a new trial.

8. Harkey, *Mean as Hell,* 66–67. Dee Harkey included Scarborough and Milton in this category. "There were some shooting sheriffs, good and bad. George Scarborough and Jeff Milton were . . . both good officers; they used to say: 'Kill the outlaws and get rid of them.' "

9. *El Paso Herald,* May 24, 1895.

10. Larry D. Ball, "Lawman in Disgrace," 131. This incident, like others in which not much happened but there was an acute contemporary awareness of great tension and potential for violence, has produced distorted recollections. Dee Harkey tells the tale, complete with Perry's placement of two pistols on the bar, but with Hardin the one who refused to fight instead of Gladden (Harkey, *Mean as Hell,* 67). George Curry, another New Mexico officer and later governor of the territory, said he witnessed a Perry-Hardin confrontation when he was in El Paso as a special deputy the week of the Great Fistic Carnival, and he says he saw attorney Albert Fall, later United States attorney general, defuse the situation and disarm Hardin and Perry. However, at the time of the Great Fistic Carnival in February 1896, John Wesley Hardin had been dead for six months (H. B. Hening, *George Curry,* 91). It is possible Curry witnessed an altercation between Perry and M. Q. Hardin, a cousin of Wes. Both men were in El Paso at the time to which Curry refers, acting as deputies under U.S. Marshal Edward Hall. Curry was certainly a bit hazy on the happenings in El Paso that entire week. He claims to have witnessed the prizefight between Bob Fitzsimmons and John L. Sullivan, but Fitzsimmons's opponent was Peter Maher, not Sullivan.

11. *El Paso Times,* November 18, 1896.

12. The reporter interjected here that Hardin "referred, no doubt, to County Jailor J. C. Jones, because he lived in Comanche when Joe Hardin was lynched." The next day the *Times* carried a stern denial by Jones, who wanted "it distinctly understood that he never was a member of a lynching or any other kind of a mob" (*El Paso Times,* August 24, 1895). Strangely, the day before the publication of the article on Mrs. Williams, this item appeared: "The *Times* learned from an officer last night that several weeks ago John Wesley Hardin told the landlady of the

Herndon that he had to kill *three* more men before completing the history of his life, that John Selman was one of the men to be killed and a man, now living in El Paso, who assisted in the lynching of Joe Hardin, was another" (*El Paso Times,* August 22, 1895).

13. *El Paso Times,* August 23, 1895.

14. Ibid., June 30, 1895.

15. *El Paso Herald,* July 2, 1895.

16. Ibid., July 3, 1895; *El Paso Times,* July 3, 1895.

17. Collection of Robert G. McCubbin, El Paso, Texas.

18. *El Paso Herald,* August 2, 1895; *El Paso Times,* August 2, 1895.

19. Selman, "John Selman of El Paso," chap. 17, p. 3. As young John suggests, the two .41-caliber Colt pistols he took from Beulah were very likely the guns Hardin was carrying when he was killed.

20. *El Paso Herald,* August 3, 1895.

21. *El Paso Times,* August 23, 1895.

22. Ibid., August 7, 1895.

23. Ibid., August 23, 1895.

24. Ibid., August 7, 1895.

25. Metz, *John Selman,* 173–74.

26. *El Paso Herald,* August 10, 1895.

27. J. F. Hulse, *Texas Lawyer,* 60. Will Burges and others told J. Evetts Haley how Jeff Milton cornered Hardin and made him crawl because of his remarks, but Milton shrugged off the stories, telling Haley, "Twa'n't nothing to it" (Haley, *Jeff Milton,* 244–46). Some El Paso old-timers told Eugene Cunningham that Milton even slapped Hardin's face without response, but, wrote Cunningham, "Milton denies it" (Cunningham, *Triggernometry,* 62). The newspaper articles of the time mention Scarborough only.

28. *El Paso Times,* August 11, 1895.

29. *El Paso Herald,* August 12, 1895.

30. Ibid.

31. Ibid., August 13, 1895.

32. Ibid., August 19, 1895.

33. *El Paso Times,* August 15, 1895; August 20, 1895.

34. *El Paso Times,* August 18, 1895. The city of Chihuahua, more than two hundred miles due south of El Paso, not the province, obviously is meant here. The officers were wrong about Queen's involvement. The Valentine bandits, hunted for more than two weeks, were finally captured early in September and identified as cowboy brothers S. H. and Tom Holland from Sonora, Sutton County. Later in the month they were indicted for murder and robbery by the Presidio County grand jury (*El Paso Herald,* September 3, 1895; September 21, 1895).

35. Martin, *Border Boss,* 155.

36. *El Paso Herald,* August 20, 1895.

37. Ibid., August 22, 1895.

38. *El Paso Times,* August 21, 1895.

39. *El Paso Herald,* August 21, 1895.

40. *El Paso Times,* August 21, 1895.

41. *El Paso Herald,* August 22, 1895.

42. Ibid., September 3, 1895.

43. *El Paso Herald,* August 22, 1895.

Chapter 9

1. Reprinted in the *El Paso Times,* August 25, 1895. The list of undelivered messages at the Western Union office in this issue included one for Hardin.

2. Ibid., August 27, 1895.

3. Ibid., August 28, 1895; *El Paso Herald,* August 30, 1895.

4. *El Paso Times,* August 24, 1895.

5. Reprinted in the *El Paso Times,* November 10, 1895.

6. Reprinted in the *El Paso Herald,* November 18, 1895.

7. *El Paso Times,* November 10, 1895.

8. Ibid., November 11, 1895.

9. Ibid., February 12, 1896.

10. Robert G. McCubbin's introduction to Hardin, *Life,* xi; Chuck Parsons, "John Wesley Hardin as Author."

11. *El Paso Herald,* December 5, 1895.

12. Ibid., January 16, 1896.

13. Ibid., February 5, 1896; see also the *Herald* for January 31, 1896, and the *Times* for February 1, 1896.

14. *Silver City Enterprise,* December 16, 1904. According to Dee Harkey, Queen was free on bond on a murder charge at the time he was killed, and, ironically, the Freeman involved in Queen's death was the son of Judge A. A. Freeman, who was Queen's attorney in the case (Harkey, *Mean as Hell* 91–92).

15. *El Paso Times,* September 3, 1895; *El Paso Herald,* September 3, 1895.

16. *El Paso Times,* September 7, 1895; *El Paso Herald,* September 7, 1895.

17. *El Paso Herald,* October 15, 1895.

18. Metz, *John Selman,* 189.

19. Ibid., 188–93. Unable to attend court with a pistol openly displayed, Selman cut down the barrel of a Colt .45 to fit his pocket and appeared in court "heeled."

20. *El Paso Times,* February 12, 1896; *El Paso Herald,* February 13, 1896. The *Times* said the jury was split ten to two for acquittal. The *Herald* gave more detail, reporting that on the first ballot the voting was eight to four for acquittal; on the second and third, nine to three; and on the fourth, seven to five.

21. This was the same Reverend Millican who united Frank McMahan and Alice Hunter in marriage in the Scarborough home in September 1895, just as the prizefight controversy was heating up. Owen P. White (who called him "Pastor Billican") said that he "ran a dairy on the side and could swear better when a cow kicked him than any man [he] ever heard" (White, *Autobiography,* 61).

22. *El Paso Herald,* October 17, 1895.

23. Larry D. Ball, "The Lawmen and the Pugilists." Leader of the effort to push this measure through was J. V. Cockrell, the judge from Anson, Texas, who was now representing western Texas in the halls of Congress.

24. Harold J. Weiss, Jr., " 'I Will See It Through.' "

25. Ball, "The Lawmen and the Pugilists." These deputies included some hard cases who only added to the city's already explosive atmosphere. Charles Perry of

Roswell, who had come to town the previous year gunning for Wes Hardin, was there, as was Wes's cousin, M. Q. Hardin, who was allied with the murderous Jim Miller crowd in Pecos. During this period, Perry, trying to settle an old score, almost shot Texas Ranger W. J. L. Sullivan. Perry also may have attempted to provoke a gunfight with fellow Deputy Marshal M. Q. Hardin (see n. 10, chap. 8).

26. White, *Autobiography*, 60. C. B. Scarborough also came to El Paso from Anson to share in the excitement (*El Paso Times*, January 27, 1896).

27. *El Paso Herald*, February 4, 1896.

28. *El Paso Times*, February 4, 1896; *El Paso Herald*, February 5, 1896.

29. *El Paso Herald*, February 18, 1896.

30. *El Paso Times*, February 19, 1896.

31. *El Paso Herald*, February 21, 1896.

32. *El Paso Times*, February 18, 1896.

33. Weiss, "I Will See It Through."

34. *El Paso Herald*, February 21, 1896.

35. Ball, "The Lawmen and the Pugilists."

36. Metz, *John Selman*, 195–97.

37. Ibid., 198.

38. G. A. Scarborough Expense Report, May 2, 1896.

39. *El Paso Times*, April 4, 1896.

40. The time of the shooting was never definitely established. Scarborough thought it was "between 12 and 1." Graham was even more indefinite, saying it was "some time before day break." Metz places the time at "nearly four o'clock." *El Paso Times*, April 7, 1896; Metz, *John Selman*, 198.

41. *El Paso Herald*, April 6, 1896; *El Paso Times*, April 7, 1896.

42. Inquest proceedings on death of John Selman, April 8 and 11, 1896, before W. D. Howe, J. P., acting as coroner. Testimony of Frank Carr, April 8, 1896.

43. *El Paso Times*, April 7, 1896.

44. Testimony of physician S. T. Turner at inquest proceeding on death of John Selman, April 8, 1896.

45. Dr. Turner's testimony was concurred in by Drs. J. J. Dooley, Howard Thompson, B. S. Roseberry, and C. F. Braden.

46. Bail bond signed by Scarborough April 6, 1896. Bob Stephens, Dallas, Texas, to RKD, July 14, 1980.

47. Inquest proceeding, April 8, 1896.

48. *El Paso Herald*, April 8, 1896; *El Paso Times*, April 9, April 10, 1896. Scarborough's sureties for the additional two thousand dollars were J. H. Nations, J. L. Whitmore, and Frank McMurray.

49. Testimony of Frank Carr at Selman inquest.

50. *El Paso Herald*, April 6, 1896.

51. Ibid., Tom Bendy told writer Boyce House in 1921 that on his rounds as a night patrolman he had been in the Wigwam shortly before the shooting and saw Scarborough playing faro upstairs. Leaving, he encountered Selman at the foot of the outside stairway and noticed he had been drinking heavily. Evidently aware of strained relations between the two gunfighters, Bundy told Selman: "I wouldn't go upstairs; Scarborough is there, and you are in no condition to look out for yourself." Selman, said Bendy, patted the handle of his six-gun and replied: "Old Betsy will

take care of me." Bendy had walked on only a block when the sound of shooting brought him back on the run (House, *Oil Field Fury,* 38–39).

52. *El Paso Times,* April 7, 1896.

53. Selman, "John Selman of El Paso," chap. 19, p. 9.

54. *El Paso Herald,* April 6, 1896.

55. *El Paso Times,* April 7, 1896.

56. Ibid., April 8, 1896.

57. Ibid.; also *El Paso Herald,* April 6, 1896.

58. *El Paso Times,* April 10, 1896.

59. Bob Stephens to RKD, July 14, 1980.

60. *El Paso Times,* May 2, 1896.

61. Hunter, "Inside Story," 9.

62. *El Paso Times,* May 2, 1896.

63. Ibid., April 8, 1896; Metz, *John Selman,* 203. On April 7, the day of Selman's funeral, the still-pending murder charges against him in the Hardin case were dismissed in the district court. Said the *Times:* "George Scarborough's bullet transferred [the case] to a higher court." *El Paso Herald,* April 7, 1896; *El Paso Times,* April 7, 1896.

64. *El Paso Times,* April 8, 1896.

65. Selman, "John Selman of El Paso," chap. 19, p. 9.

66. *El Paso Times,* April 8, 1896.

67. Ibid., April 10, 1896. Young Selman remained in the Juárez jail until May 7, when, with the aid of two friends, he broke out and made it back to the American side of the river. Señorita Ruiz had been sent away by her mother and he and his lover were never married. As he had indicated, he sought no confrontation with Scarborough and soon left El Paso (Leon C. Metz, "Why Old John Selman Died," 31, 64–65).

68. John Selman, Jr., as told to Franklin Reynolds, "John Selman."

69. *El Paso Herald,* April 11, April 20, 1896.

70. *El Paso Times,* April 8, 1896.

71. *El Paso Evening Telegram,* April 9, 1896.

72. Martin, *Border Boss,* 156.

73. Frontier Battalion of the Texas Rangers Miscellaneous Papers in the Mullin Collection, Haley Memorial Library.

74. *El Paso Times,* June 16, 1896. "I will go to his trial and am trying to get him to leave El Paso," Parson Scarborough wrote to son Lee on May 8, 1896. "He is clean broke" (Lee R. Scarborough Archives).

75. *El Paso Times,* June 16, 1896.

76. Ibid., June 20, 1896.

77. Frost, *The Gentlemen's Club,* 91.

78. *El Paso Times,* June 20, 1896.

79. Transcript of Case No. 1945, Thirty-fourth District Court, El Paso, in Mullin Collection, Haley Memorial Library.

80. *El Paso Times,* June 21, 1896.

81. Ibid., July, 1896. Belmont seemed to have a knack for being on hand at celebrated gunplays. When he completed his jail sentence, he went to Pecos and was in the Orient Saloon on October 3, 1896, when Barney Riggs shot and killed

Bill Earhart and John Denson, two of Jim Miller's gunmen. He testified at Riggs's May 1897 trial in El Paso and said he was born in 1871 and had lived in Indian Territory before coming to El Paso (*State of Texas* v. *Barney Riggs*, Case. No. 2068, Thirty-fourth District Court, El Paso; DeArment, "Barney Riggs"). John Selman, Jr., said that some time later, at the request of Sheriff Simmons, he arrested Belmont in Brownwood, Texas, on a charge of stealing a hack and team in El Paso. "Frank Simmons came a few days later and returned with him to El Paso, where I think he received a stiff sentence in Huntsville Prison." Selman was at the time acting as a deputy under Sheriff Ball of Brown County (Selman, "John Selman of El Paso," chap. 20, p. 9).

82. *El Paso Times,* June 27, 1896.

Chapter 10

1. Undated 1970 letter from Mrs. Pierson to Ed Bartholomew of Fort Davis in Ed Bartholomew Files.

2. Bartholomew Files.

3. Barry Scobee, *Old Fort Davis,* 89; Barry Scobee, *The Steer Branded Murder,* 20; Mrs. Evelyn Linebery interview, Midland, Texas, November 19, 1984.

4. Barry Scobee, *Fort Davis, Texas, 1583–1960,* 160.

5. Ibid., 160–61; Scobee, *The Steer Branded Murder,* 35; Hunter, *The Trail Drivers of Texas.*

6. *El Paso Herald,* April 20, 1897, quoting the *Presidio Guard.*

7. Haley, *Jeff Milton,* 250.

8. *El Paso Herald,* April 21, 1897.

9. Ibid., April 26, 1897.

10. Ibid.

11. Haley, *Jeff Milton,* 250.

12. *El Paso Herald,* April 27, 1897.

13. Ibid., April 28, 1897.

14. Copies of case records in Mullin Collection, Nita Stewart Haley Memorial Library, Midland, Texas.

15. *El Paso Herald,* April 28, 1897. Haley (*Jeff Milton,* 250) says Judge T. A. Falvey tried the cases, but the trial transcripts in the Mullin Collection show C. N. Buckler.

16. *El Paso Herald,* April 28, 1897.

17. Selman, "John Selman."

18. Collinson, "Three Texas Trigger Men."

19. Cunningham, *Triggernometry,* 63.

20. Metz, *John Selman,* 179.

21. Ibid., 179–80.

22. Collinson, "Three Texas Trigger Men."

23. Metz, *John Selman,* 178–79.

24. "No mention is made of [Martin's] money after his death. So where did it go?" Metz asks (*John Selman,* 178). One might well look across the river to Vic Queen. Perhaps Queen's letter to Beulah a month after Mroz's death saying he wanted to see her on "some business" for her "own benefit" alluded to Mroz's cash.

25. Jeff Milton interview, March 1938, in J. Evetts Haley Files.

26. Jeff Milton interview, December 2, 1942, J. Evetts Haley Files.

27. Collinson, "Three Texas Trigger Men."

28. Selman, "John Selman." In his previously written manuscript "John Selman of El Paso," John suggests that his certainty that Scarborough "would not have stood a chance in a gun battle" with his father was due to the manner of their pistol packing and not that old John had his gun lifted. "George carried his gun in a pocket holster, in his right hip pocket and wore a coat, making it difficult to draw quickly, while my father wore his gun in a holster with a belt and was in his shirt sleeves and in a position to make a quick draw" (Selman, "John Selman of El Paso," chap. 19, p. 10).

29. Sonnichsen, *Pass of the North,* 235.

30. White, *Lead and Likker,* 12.

31. William MacLeod Raine, *Guns of the Frontier,* 42.

32. Metz, *John Selman,* 202–203.

33. Jeff Milton interviews, March 1938 and December 2, 1942, J. Evetts Haley Files.

Chapter 11

1. Larry D. Ball, *The United States Marshals of New Mexico and Arizona Territories, 1846–1912,* 203.

2. Arie W. Poldervaart, *Black-Robed Justice,* 181.

3. Jeff Burton, *Black Jack Christian: Outlaw.*

4. Haley interviews with Milton, March 1938 and December 2, 1942.

5. Holmes Maddox, "George Scarborough, U.S. Deputy Marshal and Pioneer," 437.

6. Jeff Burton, *Dynamite and Sixshooter,* 36–38, 45–46.

7. Joseph ("Mack") Axford, *Around Western Campfires,* 22.

8. Henry Brock Interviews with Lou Blachly, Tape 106. Henry Brock was born in Ohio in 1867 and came to New Mexico in the early nineties. He worked on the Diamond A, first as a wrangler, later as wagon boss, and finally as ranch manager. From 1912 to 1916 he served as undersheriff of McKinley County, New Mexico. In the 1950s, when Brock was in his eighties, he was interviewed extensively by Lou Blachly.

9. *El Paso Herald,* November 23, 1897.

10. *Eddy Argus,* November 26, 1897.

11. Haley, *Jeff Milton,* 284.

12. Maddox, "George Scarborough," 438.

13. Jesse James Benton, *Cow by the Tail,* 194–95.

14. Leonard Alverson, "Reminiscences."

15. Walter C. Hovey, "Black Jack Ketchum Tried to Give Me a Break," 48.

16. Alverson, "Reminiscences."

17. Hovey, "Black Jack Ketchum."

18. Alverson, "Reminiscences."

19. Haley, *Jeff Milton,* 285. Alverson wrote that Tom Ketchum told him two years later that when the posse started down the canyon, it was watched by Ketchum and his cohorts. "They ranged themselves along the rim in such a position that they could have killed two or three of the posse with one shot if necessary and they

intended to shoot if they had us with them. . . . We came a few minutes behind in the wagon but the outlaws did not know this and had left" ("Reminiscences").

20. Haley, *Jeff Milton,* 285.

21. Ibid., 286.

22. Alverson, "Reminiscences."

23. *Silver City Enterprise,* March 11, 1898.

24. Ibid.

25. Ibid.

26. Burton, *Dynamite and Sixshooter,* 56–57; Hovey, "Black Jack Ketchum," 48.

27. Hovey, "Black Jack Ketchum," 49. Hovey exaggerates here. Never were rewards totaling that much offered for any of the Black Jack gang.

28. Ibid. Scarborough and Milton, while in Las Cruces to testify at the trial, were approached by Pat Garrett, who requested their assistance in hunting down Oliver Lee and Jim Gililland, suspects in the murder of Albert Fountain and his small son. They declined, saying they had all the problems they needed already (Haley, *Jeff Milton,* 291).

29. Alverson, "Reminiscences."

30. Ibid.

31. Before he died, Sam Ketchum is said to have made a statement to Robert Law and Antonio Borrego, cellhouse keeper and assistant, respectively, to the effect that Alverson, Hovey, and Warderman, then convicts at the prison, were innocent of the crime for which they were serving time and that he and his brother Tom and "their partners" had held up the train at Steins. Nothing, apparently, was done with this information until April 1903, when Borrego made a sworn statement affirming Ketchum's action (Alverson, "Reminiscences").

32. Jeff Burton, "Suddenly in a Secluded and Rugged Place," pt. 2, 15.

33. Ketchum suffered a particularly gruesome death. The drop distance for his two-hundred-plus pounds had not been calculated well; his head was snapped from his body. Ketchum also holds the distinction of being the only man in American history to be put to death for the holdup of a train.

34. Hovey, "Black Jack Ketchum," 51.

35. Alverson, "Reminiscences."

36. Burton, *Dynamite and Six Shooter,* 53–54.

37. Haley, *Jeff Milton,* 290.

Chapter 12

1. *Silver City Independent,* October 9, 1900.

2. Blachly-Brock Interviews, Tape 324; see also Blachly's interviews with Brock and John Cox, April 11, 1953.

3. Alverson, "Reminiscences."

4. Hovey, "Black Jack Ketchum," 10.

5. Ben W. Kemp, *Cow Dust and Saddle Leather,* 170. Kemp somehow got the idea Scarborough had served a term in the penitentiary and took the deputy's job when he was released.

6. James Emmitt McCauley, *A Stove-Up Cowboy's Story,* 34. McCauley says the hunted outlaws were Joe George and Grant Wheeler, who had held up a train

at Willcox. This crime took place in January 1895—before George Scarborough became active in Arizona Territory. Cochise County Sheriff C. S. Fly led the posse after George and Wheeler. It is likely that McCauley confused two incidents.

7. Maddox, "George Scarborough," 437.

8. Haley-Milton interviews, March 1938 and December 2, 1942.

9. Philip J. Rasch, "An Incomplete Account of 'Broncho Bill' Walters," 2. The Swingle aliases adopted by Walters were borrowed from a gunman and outlaw active in Arizona a decade earlier (see Philip J. Rasch, " 'Kid' Swingle, a Forgotten Highwayman," 6–7).

10. ("Salty John") Cox, "Salty John Cox and Bronco Bill," 25, 48. The *Silver City Enterprise* (October 24, 1890) said Walters and McGinnis were thwarted in their attempt to rob miners at Separ and shot up the place in frustration.

11. Rasch, "Broncho Bill Waters," 2; Cox, "Salty John," 48; *Silver City Enterprise*, February 20, 1891. A later story in the *Enterprise* said that Walters had "purloined a fresh horse from Henry Holgate at Deming" and, after reaching safety at Palomas, "returned the borrowed horse and sent a note to Holgate thanking him for the same" (March 13, 1891).

12. *Silver City Enterprise*, March 13, 1891; Rasch, "Broncho Bill Walters," 2.

13. Haley interview with Walt Birchfield, November 2, 1939, in J. D. Milton Files at Haley Library.

14. Cox, "Salty John," 48; Rasch, "Broncho Bill Walters," 3.

15. *Silver City Enterprise*, April 10, 1896.

16. *El Paso Times*, May 28, 1896.

17. Cox, "Salty John," 48.

18. Rasch, "Broncho Bill Walters," 3.

19. *Albuquerque Daily Citizen*, June 11, 1898, quoting the *Silver City Enterprise*.

20. Haley interview with Milton, December 2, 1942.

21. Ibid.

22. Rasch, "Broncho Bill Walters," 5.

23. Haley, *Jeff Milton*, 290.

24. Rasch, "Broncho Bill Walters," 5–6; Burton, *Dynamite and Sixshooter*, 176–77; Joseph Miller, ed., *The Arizona Story*, 217.

25. Burnett disappeared about this time; there were reports that the gang suspected him of betrayal and disposed of him. Rasch, "Broncho Bill Walters," 7; Haley, *Jeff Milton*, 291–92.

26. Michael Williams, "Iron Men of Arizona."

27. Langford Ryan Johnston, *Old Magdalena, Cow Town*, 50.

28. Quoted in *Albuquerque Daily Citizen*, June 11, 1898.

29. Haley interview with Milton, March 1938.

30. Ibid.

31. *Arizona Republic*, July 25, 1898; *Albuquerque Daily Citizen*, August 4, 1898; Haley, *Jeff Milton*, 294–95; Williams, "Iron Men of Arizona."

32. *Arizona Bulletin* (Solomonville), August 12, 1898.

33. Haley, *Jeff Milton*, 296.

34. *Arizona Bulletin*, August 12, 1898.

35. Climax Jim (Rufus Nephews) was arrested a year later by Apache County officers and taken to Springerville, charged with cattle theft. Left alone to change

clothes in a blacksmith shop, Climax went "out the same hole that the smoke does" and got away without his stolen stock, but also without his clothes. An undated 1899 article from the *Florence Tribune* telling the story is reprinted in Miller, *The Arizona Story*, 224–26.

36. J. E. Howard to Jeff Milton, July 24, 1945, J. D. Milton Files, Haley Library.

37. Ibid. Howard said the battle lasted about forty minutes. *Arizona Bulletin*, August 12, 1898.

38. *Arizona Bulletin*, August 12, 1898.

39. Haley, *Jeff Milton*, 298–99.

40. Ibid. The *Tombstone Epitaph*, August 3, 1898, reported that a telegram was sent "from Fort Apache to the sheriff of Solomonville, signed Scarborough and Milton: 'We have shot Broncho Bill and Johnson. We wait here till you come. Shooting occurred at Double Circle horse camp 75 miles from here.' "

41. *Arizona Bulletin*, August 12, 1898.

42. Williams, "Iron Men of Arizona."

43. Letter from J. E. Howard to Jeff Milton, J. D. Milton Files, Haley Library.

44. *Arizona Bulletin*, August 12, 1898.

45. Ibid.

46. Haley, *Jeff Milton*, 301.

47. *Arizona Bulletin*, August 12, 1898.

48. Lou Blachly interview with Henry Brock, April 11, 1953.

49. Rasch, "Broncho Bill Walters," 8.

50. Ibid., 10; Burton, *Dynamite and Sixshooter*, 177; undated clippings from the *Arizona Bulletin* reprinted in Otto M. Marshall, *Lest We Forget;* Blachly-Brock Interviews, June 13, 1952. Old cowboy Jack Thorpe said most of the loot from the Belen holdup was buried by the gang along the banks of the Rio Puerco and that "the youngest member of the gang," presumably Pipkin, returned after getting out of prison and searched unsuccessfully for the cache for months (Jack Thorpe, *Story of the Southwestern Cowboy, Partner of the Wind,* 148–49).

Chapter 13

1. *Silver City Independent,* December 12, 1898; 1900 census of Deming, New Mexico Territory.

2. J. Marvin Hunter conversation with Ed Bartholomew, May 1956. Bartholomew Files.

3. J. Evetts Haley interview with Walter Birchfield, November 2, 1939 (cited hereafter as Birchfield-Haley).

4. *Tombstone Epitaph,* January 2, 1889; *Deming Headlight,* April 16, 1889; Chesley, *Adventuring,* 134, 149.

5. Miller, *The Arizona Story,* 219.

6. Selman, "John Selman of El Paso," chap. 21, pp. 13–14.

7. *Santa Fe New Mexican,* January 19, 1899.

8. Selman, "John Selman of El Paso," chap. 21, p. 14.

9. *Arizona Republican,* January 22, 1899.

10. Quoted in the *Nogales Border Vidette,* October 27, 1898.

11. *Santa Fe New Mexican,* January 19, 1899.

12. A bill authorizing the formation of a company of Arizona Rangers was passed by the Twenty-first Legislative Assembly of Arizona on March 21, 1901, and immediately signed into law by Gov. Nathan O. Murphy. The first captain was Burton Mossman (Bill O'Neal, *The Arizona Rangers,* 3–4). The New Mexico Mounted Police Act was passed by the Thirty-sixth Legislative Assembly of New Mexico on February 15, 1905, and signed that day by Gov. Miguel A. Otero, who appointed John F. Fullerton captain (Chuck Hornung, "Fullerton's Rangers," 7).

13. No record of this arrangement seems to have been kept among the papers of Governor Otero or in the files of the cattlemen's organizations. However, there were frequent press references to Scarborough's "rangers," and J. Marvin Hunter, who served briefly as one of the group, confirms its existence: "I was with that 'Ranger' force barely five weeks—or 33 days to be exact—and was glad to get released from such dangerous work. . . . I am pleased to say that I still have my commission as issued by M. A. Otero, which is a treasured souvenir. It is dated September 10, 1900" (John Marvin Hunter, *The Story of Lottie Deno,* 171).

14. Letters, Mrs. Ada Phillips to RKD, September 9, 1981, and November 6, 1983. Mrs. Phillips, daughter of George's sister Ada and C. C. McCargo of Anson, was four years old when she went with her mother to her grandfather's bedside at Cameron. It was the only time she ever saw her celebrated Uncle George.

15. Dana, *Lee Rutland Scarborough,* 19–20. George's mother, Martha Scarborough, died in August 1908 and was buried in Anson.

16. Ibid., 61. In 1900, Lee Scarborough married Neppie Warren and fathered six children. He later rose to international eminence as an evangelist, theologian, writer, and teacher of the Baptist faith. He served as president of Southwestern Baptist Seminary at Fort Worth from 1914 to 1945 and wrote many books on evangelism, travels, and sermons. He died at Amarillo, Texas, on April 10, 1945.

17. William F. Scarborough's first ranch was a forty-section spread in Dawson County, Texas. He later acquired land in the Texas counties of Winkler, Loving, and Andrews and Lea and Eddy counties in New Mexico and established the Frying Pan Ranch near Kermit, Texas. Oil was discovered on some of his holdings, and the Scarborough Pool in Winkler County was named for him. On June 19, 1939, tragedy struck; at the age of 71, Will was fatally shot by his fifty-year-old son, Hollis, after a family argument. He died the following day and was buried at Midland. On June 24 an indictment for murder was brought against Hollis, but the following February, while confined at the United States Veterans Hospital at Waco, he hanged himself. Midland County Historical Society, "The Frying Pan Ranch"; *El Paso Herald-Post,* June 19, 20, 21, 1939, and February 20, 1940; *El Paso Times,* June 20, 21, 22, 25, 1939, and February 20, 1940.

18. *Tombstone Epitaph,* September 11, 1899. It was the day before payday at the Pearce mine and the bandits hoped to get seventy-five thousand dollars or more in payroll money. Their take was later estimated at between two thousand and three thousand dollars; the payroll had been taken from the train at Willcox and transported to Pearce by wagon (Vernon B. Schultz, *Southwestern Town: The Story of Willcox, Arizona, 41*).

19. *Arizona Bulletin,* November 3, 1899, quoting the *Lordsburg Liberal.* Louise Auer, "Arizona's Lady Bandit"; Burton, *Dynamite and Sixshooter,* 134–35; Wallace

E. Clayton, "Lady Bandit Demanded Equal Rights for Women," 18. In some accounts, Pearl's fugitive companion is identified as Ed Hogan.

20. *Tombstone Epitaph*, February 15, 1900; Haley, *Jeff Milton*, 305–307.

21. *Tombstone Prospector*, February 25, 1900; Bartholomew, *Kill or Be Killed*, 112.

22. Quoted through the courtesy of Mrs. Evelyn Linebery.

23. *Arizona Daily Citizen* (Tucson), April 4, 1900, quoting the *Lordsburg Liberal*.

24. Letter dated March 8, 1934, from A. F. Nolan, owner of the ranch where Triangle Springs was located, to Frank M. King, quoted in full in an undated copy of King's newspaper column "Longhorn," in the files of the Arizona Historical Society, Tucson. The name of the owner of the Triangle has been variously spelled "Rook," "Ruke," and "Ruck." The spelling used here is Birchfield's.

25. Birchfield-Haley.

26. *Arizona Bulletin* (Solomonville), August 12, 1898.

27. A. F. Nolan to Frank M. King, March 8, 1934.

28. Birchfield-Haley. Holmes Maddox, who was one of the first to talk to Birchfield that night and was at the scene of the fight the next day, confirms this: "After they got up in the canyon about a mile the trail turned out on the south side . . . and headed back down. . . . They then saw the outlaws below them on top of a boulder-strewn hill. . . . Birchfield told Scarborough they could go out over a high saddle at the head of Triangle Spring and over into Dun Springs Canyon and avoid the ambush but Scarborough said, 'No, we are going back down and see who those fellows are.' When they got down about opposite the outlaws, Scarborough opened the fight" (Maddox, "George Scarborough," 439).

29. Letter, Walter Birchfield to W. F. Scarborough, April 21, 1900, courtesy of Mrs. Evelyn Linebery (cited hereafter as Birchfield letter). Birchfield's spelling and punctuation have been corrected for purposes of clarity.

30. Birchfield-Haley. The *Silver City Independent* of April 10, 1900, reported that Scarborough insisted that they ride slowly, "for fear that a run might be taken for cowardice."

31. Birchfield letter.

32. Birchfield-Haley.

33. A F. Nolan to Frank M. King, March 8, 1934.

34. Birchfield letter.

35. Birchfield-Haley.

36. Birchfield letter.

37. Birchfield-Haley.

38. Ibid.

39. Birchfield letter.

40. Birchfield-Haley.

41. Birchfield letter.

42. Birchfield-Haley.

43. Birchfield letter.

44. Birchfield-Haley. Two inches of snow fell that night (Maddox, "George Scarborough," 439).

45. "The San Simon wagon had left the day before for the Triangle Ranch to begin the spring work" (Maddox, "George Scarborough," 439).

46. Joe Schaefer, who was working a mining claim at nearby White Tail, heard about the fight and went to Triangle Springs and viewed the scene the same day. "The outlaws just literally drilled that oak tree and half-a-dozen bullets hit the rock," he said. "They were shooting from four hundred yards and had those high-powered, .30–.40 rifles." Chesley, *Adventuring*, 133.

47. *Silver City Independent*, April 10, 1900.

48. *El Paso Herald*, April 5, 1900.

49. "The doctor told me he'd taken a sliver of bone right out—six inches long." Blachly-Brock Interviews.

50. *Silver City Enterprise*, April 6, 1900. Strangely, it was four years to the day after Scarborough had mortally wounded Selman in the alley beside the Wigwam Saloon and six years to the day since Selman had dispatched Baz Outlaw in Tillie Howard's parlor house.

51. Haley interview with Milton, December 2, 1942. George's nephew Moliere got a different story from the doctor: "I was talking to the doctor that operated on him . . . and he told me that he had lost so much blood . . . that is what killed him" (Moliere Scarborough interview, December 1, 1984).

52. *Silver City Enterprise*, April 13, 1900.

53. Hunter and Rose, *The Album of Gunfighters*, 126. Hunter attended the funeral. Scarborough's grave is in Lot 14, Row J, IOOF section of the Deming cemetery.

Chapter 14

1. *Tombstone Prospector*, April 5, 1900.

2. *Silver City Independent*, April 10, 1900.

3. Undated clipping from a Memphis, Texas, paper provided by Mrs. Evelyn Linebery of Midland, Texas.

4. *El Paso Herald*, April 5, 1900.

5. *El Paso Times*, April 5, 1900.

6. *Tombstone Epitaph*, April 15, 1900, quoting the *El Paso Herald*.

7. The *Argus* (Holbrook, Arizona), April 28, 1900.

8. John Marvin Hunter, *Peregrinations of a Pioneer Printer*, 126.

9. Letter from A. F. Nolan to Frank M. King.

10. Dana, *Lee Rutland Scarborough*, 47.

11. *Silver City Independent*, July 10, September 4, 1900.

12. Ibid., April 24, 1900.

13. Clipping from an unidentified Texas newspaper provided by Mrs. Evelyn Linebery of Midland, Texas.

14. The *Tombstone Prospector*, April 5, 1900, named Kid Carver; the *Los Angeles Times*, April 6, 1900, reporting a dispatch from Benson, Arizona, said Tod Carver.

15. *Silver City Independent*, April 17, 1900; *Silver City Enterprise*, April 20, 1900.

16. *Silver City Enterprise*, April 13, 1900.

17. *El Paso Herald*, April 28, 1900.

18. *Silver City Independent*, June 26, 1900. Stevenson was killed April 17, 1901,

by Superintendent H. O. Bursum of the territorial prison while attempting to escape. *Silver City Independent*, April 23, 1900; Miguel Antonio Otero, *My Nine Years as Governor*, 109–10.

19. *Arizona Weekly Journal Miner*, June 13, 1900.

20. Ibid., June 20, 1900.

21. Charles A. Siringo, *The Lone Star Cowboy*, 241. "Walter Birchfield was with Scarborough when he was killed," wrote Siringo. "The boys used to tell in my presence of how Birchfield's life was spared, as they liked him on account of his many acts of kindness toward Capehart when he was a cowboy near Deming."

22. Alverson, "Reminiscences."

23. Owen P. White, *Trigger Fingers*.

24. Brown Waller, *Last of the Great Western Train Robbers*, 143–44.

25. Burton, *Dynamite and Sixshooter*, 135–36.

26. *Silver City Independent*, April 17, 1900.

27. *Silver City Enterprise*, April 20, 1900.

28. *St. John's Herald*, March 31, 1900.

29. Cochise County Sheriff's Reports, handwritten on Sheriff Scott White's stationery, dated April 1899. Copy in files of Ed Bartholomew.

30. Blachly-Brock Interviews, Tape 324. Reported the *Silver City Independent* of April 10, 1900: "During the afternoon one of the outlaws gave a cowboy yell which was answered by Birchfield."

31. *Silver City Independent*, April 17, 1900. The first reward notices had included one Coley. On May 2, 1900, Sheriff Beeler, on receipt of a report this man was in Globe, Arizona, went there and arrested William Morris, alias Coley, who admitted acquaintanceship with the gang but claimed an alibi for the time of the Apache County killings. Apparently, charges against him were later dropped. (Philip J. Rasch, "Death Comes to Saint Johns," 6–7)

32. Williams, "Real Men of Arizona"; Lorenzo D. Walters, *Tombstone's Yesterday*, 170.

33. Lorenzo D. Walters, "Seven Links in a Chain," 437–38. Eugene Cunningham repeated this assertion in 1934 (*Triggernometry*, 347).

34. John Eaton, *Will Carver, Outlaw*, 57.

35. Dan L. Thrapp, *Encyclopedia of Frontier Biography in Three Volumes*, 238.

36. Walters, *Tombstone's Yesterday*, 172.

37. An early chronicler of the exploits of the Hole-in-the-Wall gang, Charles Kelly, identifies the killers of LeSueur and Gibbons as Harvey Logan, Bill Carver, and "probably George and Ben Kilpatrick," although he makes no connection with this crowd and the Scarborough shooting (Charles Kelly, *The Outlaw Trail*, 262–63). He is followed by Burton, *Dynamite and Sixshooter*, 136, and others.

38. Pipkin is named in Maurice Kildare, "Killers' Trail to Nowhere." The impossibility is shown in Rasch, "Death Comes to Saint Johns," 6.

39. Williams, "Iron Men of Arizona."

40. Burton, *Dynamite and Sixshooter*, 209, quoting Carl B. Livingston, "Hunting Down the Black Jack Gang," *Wide World* (August–September–October 1930).

41. Blachly-Brock Interviews, Tape 324.

42. Burton, *Dynamite and Sixshooter*, 135–36.

43. Ibid., 209–10.

44. *St. Johns Herald,* April 13, 1901; Rasch, "Death Comes to Saint Johns," 7–8.

45. Eaton, *Will Carver, Outlaw.* April 1901 was a bad month for New Mexico outlaws. Not only was Will Carver killed that month, but Bruce ("Red") Weaver, another cohort of the gang, was shot dead at Alma on April 8 by William ("Pad") Holliman, George Stevenson was killed in an escape attempt at the territorial prison by Superintendent H. O. Bursum on April 17, and Tom Ketchum was hanged on April 26.

46. Rasch, "Death Comes to Saint Johns," 8.

47. Walters, *Tombstone's Yesterday,* 172.

48. Thrapp, *Encyclopedia of Frontier Biography,* 780–81.

Chapter 15

1. *Silver City Independent,* July 24, 1900.

2. *Silver City Independent,* September 4, 1900. Keechi Johnson had been a very popular officer. Said Henry Brock: "You could just depend on [Keechi]. If there was anything you wanted . . . you were liable to see old Keechi" (Blachly-Brock Interviews, April 11, 1953).

3. Hunter, *Lottie Deno,* 170–71. The *Silver City Independent* reported on September 25, 1900, that Reinhart had been arraigned on sixteen cattle-theft indictments.

4. *Silver City Independent,* October 9, 1900.

5. Ibid., October 23, 1900.

6. *Lordsburg Western Liberal,* January 18, 1901.

7. *Silver City Independent,* April 12, 1901.

8. *St. Johns Herald,* June 29, 1901. There is confusion in the press reports of the location of this capture. The Saint Johns paper placed it "in the wild country known as Tularosa near Luna, New Mexico." Luna is in Valencia County, far north of the Tularosa country, which lies east of Silver City. But the *Silver City Enterprise,* August 16, 1901, which for some reason did not report the capture for almost two months, placed the site in "the Black and Blue country, as the New Mexico–Arizona boundary line west of here is called."

9. *St. Johns Herald,* June 29, 1901. Pollard Pearson later served in the Arizona Rangers.

10. *Silver City Enterprise,* August 16, 1901.

11. *Devil's River News,* July 20, 1901.

12. Rasch, "Death Comes to Saint Johns," 4–5.

13. O'Neal, *The Arizona Rangers,* 4.

14. Don Johnson was sheriff of Luna County, New Mexico Territory, in 1907–1908.

15. An undated *Tucson Citizen* story quoted in Miller, *The Arizona Rangers,* 31. The Smith gang gave the rangers one of their first and worst battles. On October 8, 1901, a posse fought the outlaws at a camp on Black River, and Ranger Carlos Tafolla and posseman Bill Maxwell were killed. The outlaws were not killed or captured, but the battle brought an end to the gang's activities in Arizona. Ed Scarborough was not involved in the fight (O'Neal, *The Arizona Rangers,* 13–17).

16. Frazier Hunt, *Cap Mossman,* 183.

17. *Tombstone Epitaph*, June 1, 1902.

18. Mrs. Evelyn Linebery interview, November 19, 1984.

19. Letter from J. C. Hancock to E. P. Lamborn, August 23, 1936, E. P. Lamborn Collection, Kansas State Historical Society, Topeka.

20. Blachly-Cox interview, April 11, 1953.

21. Cause No. 69, Luna County Court Records. Luna County was organized in 1901. Ironically, George Scarborough's son was represented in this and later cases by Fielder, the same lawyer who had unsuccessfully defended Alverson, Hovey, and Warderman, the suspects arrested by Scarborough in the Steins Pass train robbery cases in 1898.

22. Cause Nos. 239, 240, 241, 247, Luna County Court Records.

23. *Silver City Enterprise*, August 26, 1901.

24. *Silver City Independent*, August 23, 1904.

25. Territorial Archives of New Mexico, Micro. Roll 91, Letters Received.

26. Ibid., Micro. Roll 93, Notebook of Reward Posters, Strayed or Stolen Stock, Wanted Men and Related Correspondence, 1906–1912.

27. Thrapp, *Encyclopedia of Frontier Biography*, 780–81; James D. Horan and Paul Sann, *Pictorial History of the Wild West*, 222.

28. Copies of Edgar's letter of March 29, 1912, and April 5 response from Warden U.S. Federal Prison, Atlanta, Georgia, headed "IN RE JOHN ARNOLD, REGISTER NO. 1035," provided by Arthur Soule. Edgar was listed in the 1912 *Los Angeles City Directory* as a carpenter by trade, living at 326 East Fifty-fifth Street. His mother lived next door at 324 with seventeen-year-old Ray, an apprentice.

29. Haley, *Jeff Milton*, 375.

30. *Bisbee Daily Review*, June 20, 1915.

31. *State of Arizona* v. *George Edgar Scarborough*, Cause No. 634.

32. Arizona Territory became a state in 1912. Harry Wheeler headed the Arizona Rangers before becoming sheriff.

33. *Bisbee Daily Review*, June 20, 1915.

34. Ibid., June 27, 1915.

35. Ibid., June 29, 1915.

36. Ibid., July 7, 1915.

37. Ibid., June 29, 1915.

38. *Tombstone Epitaph*, December 6, 1915.

39. Ibid., December 12, 1915; *Arizona* v. *Scarborough* trial record. Lee Scarborough had suggested to his brother Will that they go to Arizona and try to help their wayward nephew in his trouble, but Will refused, saying that Ed had created his own problems and had to pay the penalty (Mrs. Evelyn Linebery interviews, November 19, 1984; May 6, 1989). "Lee went out to the trial and said he had never seen such an outrageous trial in his life. The thing was set before anything was said, that [Edgar] was going to be convicted. Lee was just terribly disgusted with it" (Moliere Scarborough interview, December 1, 1984).

40. *Tombstone Prospector*, December 15, 1915, quoting the *Arizona Republican*.

41. *Tombstone Epitaph*, December 19, 1915.

42. Ibid., May 7, 1916. The paper said there were fifty-one prisoners in the

county jail at the time, with four convicted of murder, including Scarborough. *Tombstone Prospector,* May 10, 1915; May 17, 1915.

43. Kay Dargitz, State of Arizona Department of Corrections, Phoenix, Arizona, to RKD, May 4, 1984.

44. *Tombstone Epitaph,* June 3, 1917.

45. Ibid.; *Florence Blade-Tribune,* June 2, 1917; June 16, 1917. There is a story within the family that Edgar withdrew the appeal applications after a promise that parole would follow soon after conviction, and when no parole was forthcoming, Ed escaped because he felt he had been double-crossed. Moliere Scarborough interview, December 1, 1984: "Uncle Lee got in touch with the fella . . . that was running for governor in New Mexico, and [Lee told] me that . . . he agreed that if he was elected he was going to pardon Edgar [but when] he *was* elected, he got scared of politics, he was afraid to do it and he didn't do it. . . . Lee saw him afterwards but couldn't get anything out of him. I have forgotten his name; he was a Mexican." Ezequiel Cabeza de Baca took office as governor of New Mexico in 1917. Of course the governor of New Mexico could not pardon a convict in Arizona. If a deal was promised, it was to exert influence for a pardon.

46. *Tombstone Epitaph,* June 3, 1917. The paper incorrectly reported on June 24 that Ed had been captured at Engle, New Mexico. Apparently it was another Florence escapee who was nabbed.

47. Letter from Scott White to E. P. Lamborn, February 24, 1928, in Lamborn Collection, Kansas State Historical Society, Topeka.

48. Moliere Scarborough interview, December 1, 1984: "We were out there once, in southern California where it joins Mexico, and that's where George's wife was. We visited in her home some. She was telling us about George's boy, living across and would sneak over every once in a while from his ranch—he had a Mexican ranch over there—and stay with her some and then scoot back because he still hadn't been pardoned." Mrs. Evelyn Linebery interviews, November 19, 1984 and May 6, 1989; letter from Hal S. Kerr to Jeff Milton, February 10, 1947, in J. D. Milton Files, J. Evetts Haley Collection, Nita Stewart Haley Memorial Library. Hal Kerr was raised on ranches in the Davis Mountains of Texas and southern New Mexico; was an officer at Douglas, Arizona; and knew the Scarboroughs well. George's daughter, Georgie May, married Thomas Fulton Kerr, taught school at San Simon, and ranched in New Mexico before moving to Southern California.

Afterword

1. *San Diego Union,* March 9, 1940.

2. Haley, *Jeff Milton.*

3. *Burbank Daily Review,* July 5, 1949. George's third daughter, Ethel, settled in El Paso and married a lawyer, William G. Abbott. Displaying the independence and dogged determination that had characterized her father, she tackled the law-books, passed the bar examination, and became a member of the legal profession in the early years of the century when a female lawyer was a rarity indeed. Her son, Dan Abbott, studied law while working as a Texas highway patrolman and obtained a law degree. His wife, Sarita, inspired by the example of her mother-in-law, also passed the bar and became a lawyer. Their son, Dan Scarborough Abbott, practices

law in Abilene, representing the third generation to follow the profession. Interviews, RKD with Dan Scarborough Abbott and Mrs. Sarita Abbott, May 5, 1989; *Abilene Reporter-News,* April 18, 1989.

4. Letter, J. Marvin Hunter to E. P. Lamborn, June 21, 1927, Lamborn Collection, Kansas State Historical Society, Topeka.

5. Letter, Dan Abbott to Dallas Scarborough, April 23, 1951, Mullin Collection, Nita Stewart Haley Memorial Library.

Bibliography

Books

Adams, Ramon. *Six-Guns and Saddle Leather,* Norman: University of Oklahoma Press, 1969.

Axford, Joseph ("Mack"). *Around Western Campfires.* Tucson: University of Arizona Press, 1969.

Baker, T. Lindsay. *The First Polish Americans: Silesian Settlements in Texas.* College Station and London: Texas A&M University Press, 1979.

Ball, Eve. *Ma'am of the Pecos.* Tucson: University of Arizona Press, 1968.

Ball, Larry D. *The United States Marshals of New Mexico and Arizona Territories, 1846–1912.* Albuquerque: University of New Mexico Press, 1978.

Bartholomew, Ed. *The Biographical Album of Western Gunfighters.* Houston: Frontier Press of Texas, 1958.

———. *Kill or Be Killed,* Houston: Frontier Press of Texas, 1953.

Beck, Warren A., and Ynez D. Haase. *Historical Atlas of New Mexico.* Norman: University of Oklahoma Press, 1969.

Benton, Jesse James. *Cow by the Tail.* Boston: Houghton Mifflin Co., 1943.

Beverly, Bob. *Hobo of the Rangeland.* Lovington, N.Mex.: N.p., n.d. (ca. 1941).

Biggers, Don H. *Shackelford County Sketches.* Albany and Fort Griffin, Tex.: Clear Ford Press, 1974 (first published in 1908).

Biographical and Historical Memoirs of Northwest Louisiana. Nashville and Chicago: Southern Publishing Co., 1890.

Black, A. P. ("Ott"). *The End of the Long Horn Trail.* Selfridge, N.Dak.: Selfridge Journal, n.d. (ca. 1936).

Burton, Jeff. *Black Jack Christian: Outlaw.* Santa Fe, N.Mex.: Press of the Territorian, 1967.

———. *Dynamite and Sixshooter,* Santa Fe, N.Mex.: Palomina Press, 1970.

Casey, Robert J. *The Texas Border and Some Borderliners.* Indianapolis and New York: Bobbs-Merrill Co., 1950.

Chesley, Harvey E. *Adventuring With the Old-Timers: Trails Travelled—Tales Told.* Midland, Tex.: Nita Stewart Haley Memorial Library, 1979.

Collinson, Frank. *Life in the Saddle.* Norman: University of Oklahoma Press, 1963.

Coolidge, Dane. *Fighting Men of the West*. New York: E. P. Dutton & Co., 1932.

Cunningham, Eugene. *Triggernometry: A Gallery of Gunfighters*. Caldwell, Idaho: Caxton Printers, 1962 (first published in 1934).

Dana, H. E. *Lee Rutland Scarborough: A Life of Service*. Nashville, Tenn.: Broadman Press, 1942.

DeArment, Robert K. *Bat Masterson: The Man and the Legend*. Norman: University of Oklahoma Press, 1979.

Douglas, C. L. *Cattle Kings of Texas*, Dallas, Tex.: Cecil Baugh, Publisher, 1939.

Eaton, John. *Will Carver, Outlaw*. San Angelo, Tex.: Anchor Publishing Co., 1972.

Frost, H. Gordon. *The Gentlemen's Club: The Story of Prostitution in El Paso*. El Paso, Tex.: Mangan Books, 1983.

Fulton, Maurice G. *Maurice Garland Fulton's History of the Lincoln County War*. Tucson: University of Arizona Press, 1968.

Haley, J. Evetts. *Jeff Milton, A Good Man With a Gun*. Norman: University of Oklahoma Press, 1948.

Hardin, John Wesley. *The Life of John Wesley Hardin*. Norman: University of Oklahoma Press, 1961 (first published in 1896).

Harkey, Dee. *Mean as Hell*. New York: Signet Books, 1951 (first published in 1948).

Harrison, Mabel Fletcher, and Lavinia McGuire McNeely. *Grant Parish, Louisiana: A History*. Baton Rouge: Claitor's Publishing Division, 1969.

Hening, H. B., ed. *George Curry, 1861–1947*. Albuquerque: University of New Mexico Press, 1958.

Historical and Biographical Record of the Cattle Industry and the Cattlemen of Texas and Adjacent Territory, Vol. 2. Saint Louis: Woodward & Tiernan Printing Co., 1895.

Horan, James D. *Desperate Women*. New York: G. P. Putnam's Sons, 1952.

———. and Paul Sann. *Pictorial History of the Wild West*. New York: Crown Publishers, 1954.

House, Boyce. *Cowtown Columnist*. San Antonio, Tex.: Naylor Co., 1946.

———. *Oil Field Fury*. San Antonio, Tex.: Naylor Co., 1954.

Hulse, J. F. *Texas Lawyer: The Life of William H. Burges*. El Paso, Tex.: Mangan Books, 1982.

Hunt, Frazier. *Cap Mossman, Last of the Great Cowmen*. New York: Hastings House, 1951.

Hunter, John Marvin. *Pereginations of a Pioneer Printer*. Grand Prairie, Tex.: Frontier Times Publishing Co., 1954.

———. *The Story of Lottie Deno*. Bandera, Tex.: Four Hunters, 1959.

———. ed. *The Trail Drivers of Texas*. New York: Argosy-Antiquarian Press, 1963 (first published in 1920–23).

———. and Noah H. Rose. *The Album of Gunfighters*. Bandera, Tex.: N.p., 1951.

James, Bill C., and Mary Kay Shannon. *Sheriff A. J. Royal. Fort Stockton, Texas*. Fort Stockton, Tex.: James and Shannon, 1984.

Johnston, Langford Ryan. *Old Magdalena. Cow Town*. Magdalena, N.Mex.: Bandar Log, 1983.

Kelly, Charles. *The Outlaw Trail*. New York: Devin-Adair Co., 1959 (first published in 1938).

Kemp, Ben W., and J. C. Dykes. *Cow Dust and Saddle Leather*. Norman: University of Oklahoma Press, 1968.

King, Frank M. *Wranglin' the Past*. Pasadena, Calif.: Trail's End Publishing Co., 1946 (first published in 1935).

McCauley, James Emmitt. A Stove-Up Cowboy's Story. Dallas, Tex.: Southern Methodist University Press, 1943.

McCright, Grady E., and James H. Powell. *Jessie Evans. Lincoln County Badman.* College Station, Tex.: Creative Publishing Co., 1983.

Marshall, Otto M. *Lest We Forget*. Pima, Ariz. · Chamber of Commerce, n.d.

Martin, Douglas D. *Tombstone's Epitaph*. Albuquerque: University of New Mexico Press, 1951.

Martin, Jack. *Border Boss*. San Antonio, Tex.: Naylor Co., 1942.

Metz, Leon. *John Selman, Texas Gunfighter*. New York: Hastings House, 1966.

Middagh, John. *Frontier Newspaper: The El Paso Times*. El Paso, Tex.: Texas Western Press, 1958.

Miller, Joseph, ed. *The Arizona Rangers*. New York: Hastings House, 1972.

———. *The Arizona Story*. New York: Hastings House, 1952.

Nolan, Frederick W. *The Life and Death of John Henry Tunstall*. Albuquerque: University of New Mexico Press, 1965.

Oden, Alonzo Van. *Texas Ranger Diary and Scrapbook*. Dallas, Tex.: Kaleidograph Press, 1936.

O'Neal, Bill. *The Arizona Rangers*. Austin, Tex.: Eakin Press, 1987.

———. *Encyclopedia of Western Gunfighters*. Norman: University of Oklahoma Press, 1979.

Otero, Miguel Antonio. *My Nine Years as Governor of the Territory of New Mexico, 1897–1906*. Albuquerque: University of New Mexico Press, 1940.

Paxton, W. E. *A History of the Baptists of Louisiana*. Saint Louis: C. R. Barns, 1888.

Poldervaart, Arie W. *Black-Robed Justice*. N.p.: Historical Society of New Mexico, 1948.

Raine, William MacLeod. *Famous Sheriffs and Western Outlaws*. New York: Doubleday, Doran & Co., 1929.

———. *Guns of the Frontier*. Boston: Houghton Mifflin Co., 1940.

Scarborough, Jewel Davis. *Southern Kith and Kin: A Record of My Children's Ancestors*. Vol. 3. Abilene, Tex.: Abilene Printing Co., 1957.

Schultz, Vernon B. *Southwestern Town: The Story of Willcox, Arizona*. Tucson: University of Arizona Press, 1964.

Scobee, Barry. *Fort Davis, Texas, 1583–1960*. El Paso, Tex.: Barry Scobee, 1960.

———. *Old Fort Davis*. San Antonio, Tex.: Naylor Co., 1947.

———. *The Steer Branded Murder*. Houston, Tex.: Frontier Press of Texas, 1952.

Shelton, Hooper, and Homer Hutto. *The First 100 Years of Jones County, Texas*. Stamford, Tex.: Shelton Press, 1978.

Sherill, R. E. *Haskell County History*, Haskell, Tex.: Haskell Free Press, 1965.

Shirley, Glenn. *Shotgun for Hire*. Norman: University of Oklahoma Press, 1970.

Simmons, Don. *Graves Co., Ky. Census of 1840.* N.p., n.d..

Siringo, Charles A. *A Lone Star Cowboy.* Santa Fe, N.Mex.: 1919.

———. *Riata and Spurs.* Rev. ed. Boston and New York: Houghton Mifflin Co., 1927.

Sonnichsen, C. L. *Pass of the North: Four Centuries on the Rio Grande,* El Paso: Texas Western Press, 1968.

Taylor, Joe Gray. *Louisiana Reconstructed, 1863–1877.* Baton Rouge; Louisiana State University Press, 1974.

Thorpe, Jack. *Story of the Southwestern Cowboy, Partner of the Wind.* Caldwell, Idaho: Caxton Printers, 1945.

Thrapp, Dan L. *Encyclopedia of Frontier Biography in Three Volumes.* Glendale, Calif.: Arthur H. Clark Co., 1988.

Tipton, Ennis Mayfield. *Index to U.S. Tract Books, Northwestern Land District (Old Natchitoches District) in the Louisiana State Land Office.* Bossier City, La.: Tipton Printing & Publishing Co., 1980.

Tise, Sammy. *Texas County Sheriffs.* Albuquerque, N.Mex.: Oakwood Printing, 1989.

Tunnell, Ted. *Crucible of Reconstruction: War, Radicalism and Race in Louisiana, 1862–1877.* Baton Rouge and London: Louisiana State University Press, 1984.

Utley, Robert M. *High Noon in Lincoln: Violence on the Western Frontier.* Albuquerque: University of New Mexico Press, 1987.

Walker, Henry P., and Don Bufkin. *Historical Atlas of Arizona.* Norman: University of Oklahoma Press, 1979.

Waller, Brown. *Last of the Great Western Train Robbers.* South Brunswick, N.Y.: A. S. Barnes and Co., 1968.

Walters, Lorenzo D. *Tombstone's Yesterday.* Glorieta, N.Mex.: Rio Grande Press, 1968 (first published in 1928).

Webb, Walter Prescott. *The Texas Rangers: A Century of Frontier Defense.* Boston and New York: Houghton Mifflin Co., 1935.

White, Owen P. *The Autobiography of a Durable Sinner.* New York: G. P. Putnam's Sons, 1942.

———. *Lead and Likker.* New York: Minton, Balch & Co., 1932.

———. *Trigger Fingers.* New York: G. P. Putnam's Sons, 1926.

Williams, Clayton W. *Texas' Last Frontier: Fort Stockton and the Trans-Pecos, 1861–1895.* College Station, Tex.: Texas A&M University Press, 1982.

Wilson, John P. *Merchants, Guns and Money: The Story of Lincoln County and Its Wars.* Santa Fe: Museum of New Mexico Press, 1987.

Articles

Anderson, Wyatt. "A Pioneer in West Texas," *Frontier Times* 3, no. 5 (February 1926).

Auer, Louise. "Arizona's Lady Bandit," *Golden West,* March 1966.

Ball, Larry D. "Lawman in Disgrace: Sheriff Charles C. Perry of Chaves County, New Mexico," *New Mexico Historical Review* 61, no. 2 (April 1986).

Burton, Jeff. "Bureaucracy, Blood Money and Black Jack's Gang," *Brand Book of the English Westerners' Society* 22, nos. 1 and 2 (Winter 1983 and Summer 1984).

————. "Suddenly in a Secluded and Rugged Place," *Brand Book of the English Westerners' Society* 14, Nos. 3 and 4 (April and July 1972).

Clayton, Wallace E. "Lady Bandit Demanded Equal Rights for Women," *Tombstone Epitaph National Edition,* March 1987.

Coleman, Max. "Law and Order," *Frontier Times* 9, no. 3 (December 1931).

Cox ("Salty John"), transcribed by Eve Ball. "Salty John Cox and Bronco Bill," *True West* 24, no. 5 (May–June 1977).

Cunningham, J. F. "Experiences of a Pioneer District Attorney," *West Texas Historical Association Year Book* 3 (June 1932).

DeArment, Robert K. "Barney Riggs—Man of Violence," *Old West* 20, no. 1 (Fall 1983).

————. "The Great Outlaw Confederacy," *True West* 37, no. 9 (September 1990).

————. "Manhunter George Scarborough," *True West* 29, no. 4 (April 1982).

Gillett, Capt. James B. "Beef Gathering in '71 Was Thrilling," *Frontier Times* 3, no. 7 (April 1926).

Henderson, D. H. "McCulloch County of Fifty-Two Years Ago," *Frontier Times* 4, no. 10 (July 1927).

Hovey, Walter C. (ed. by Doris Sturgis), "Black Jack Ketchum Tried to Give Me a Break," *True West* 19, no. 4 (March–April 1972).

Hunter, J. Marvin, Sr. "George Scarborough, Peace Officer," *Frontier Times* 24, no. 9 (June 1947).

Hunter, John Warren. "Inside Story of Life of John Wesley Hardin," *Frontier Times* 1, no. 7 (April 1924).

Hornung, Chuck. "Fullerton's Rangers," *Tombstone Epitaph National Edition,* January 1981.

Hutto, John R. "Emmett Roberts, a Pioneer of Jones County," *Frontier Times* 11, no. 2 (November 1933).

Irons, Angie. "Doan's Crossing," *True West* 36, no. 11 (November 1989).

Johnson, Manie White. "The Colfax Riot of April, 1983," *Louisiana Historical Quarterly* 13, no. 3 (July 1930).

Kildare, Maurice. "Killers' Trail to Nowhere," *Golden West* 6, no. 3 (March 1970).

McKinney, Joe T. "Reminiscences of a Texan," *Frontier Times* 3, no. 9 (June, 1926).

Maddox, Holmes. "George Scarborough, U.S. Deputy Marshal and Pioneer," *The Cattleman,* June 1947; reprinted in *Frontier Times,* June 1947.

Metz, Leon C. "Why Old John Selman Died," *Frontier Times* 39, no. 6 (October–November 1965).

Midland County Historical Society. "The Frying Pan Ranch," *The Staked Plain* 2, no. 3.

Myers, Lee. "How Hell-Raising Phenix Dug Its Own Grave," *The West* 1, no. 3 (July 1964).

————. "Two Lives of Sin Had Impact on Southwest," *Sundial,* November 10, 1963.

O'Neal, Bill. "The Latest on 'Bass' Outlaw," *Real West* 25, no. 186 (August 1982).

Parsons, Chuck. "John Wesley Hardin as Author," *Quarterly of the National Association and Center for Outlaw and Lawman History* 5, no. 2 (January 1980).
Rasch, Philip J. "An Incomplete Account of 'Broncho Bill' Walters," *The Brand Book of the English Westerners' Society,* 19, no. 2 (January 1977).
————. "Death Comes to Saint Johns," *Quarterly of the National Association and Center for Outlaw and Lawman History* 7, no. 3 (Autumn 1982).
————. " 'Kid' Swingle, a Forgotten Highwayman," *Quarterly of the National Association and Center for Outlaw and Lawman History* 9, no. 3 (Winter 1985).
Reynolds, Franklin. "One of the Last of the Old Time Rangers," *Frontier Times* 31, no. 2 (April–May–June 1954).
Selman, John, Jr., as told to Franklin Reynolds. "John Selman," *All Western Magazine,* no. 15 (November 1935).
Walters, Lorenzo D. "Seven Links in a Chain," *Frontier Times* 5, no. 11 (August 1928).
Williams, Michael. "Iron Men of Arizona," *Pearson's Magazine* (September 1912).

Manuscripts

Alverson, Leonard. "Reminiscences." Arizona Historical Society.
Ball, Larry. "The Lawmen and the Pugilists: The Great Fistic Carnival of 1896." Paper presented at the annual meeting of the Western History Association, Los Angeles, California, October 7–10, 1987.
Collinson, Frank. "Three Texas Trigger Men." Collinson Papers, Research Center, Panhandle-Plains Historical Museum, Canyon, Texas.
Selman, John, Jr. "John Selman of El Paso." Texas State Library, Austin.
Weiss, Harold J., Jr. "I Will See It Through: The Rangers and the World of Prizefighting in El Paso and Beyond." Paper presented at the annual meeting of the Western History Association, Los Angeles, California, October 7–10, 1987.

Government Documents

Adjutant General's Files, Texas State Library and Archives, Austin.
Fugitive Lists, State of Texas, 1878, 1886, 1891, 1900.
McLennan County, Texas, Marriage Records (January 1871–July 1892).
Scarborough, Deputy Marshal G. A., Expense Records, National Archives.
Territorial Archives of New Mexico, Micro. Roll 91, Letters Received; Roll 93, Notebook of Reward Posters, Strayed or Stolen Stock, Wanted Men, and Related Correspondence, 1906–1912.
Texas Ranger Muster Rolls and Monthly Returns, Texas State Library and Archives, Austin.

Collections

Henry Brock Interviews with Lou Blachly, Zimmerman Library, University of New Mexico, Albuquerque.
John Cox Interviews with Lou Blachly, Zimmerman Library, University of New Mexico, Albuquerque.
E. P. Lamborn Collection, Kansas State Historical Society, Topeka.
Robert G. McCubbin Collection, El Paso, Texas.

J. D. Milton Files, J. Evetts Haley Collection, Nita Stewart Haley Memorial Library, Midland, Texas.
Robert Mullin Collection, Nita Stewart Haley Memorial Library, Midland, Texas.
Lee R. Scarborough Archives, Southwestern Baptist Theological Seminary, Fort Worth, Texas.
Earl Vandale Collection, Nita Stewart Haley Memorial Library, Midland, Texas.

Letters

Dan Abbott to Dallas Scarborough, April 23, 1951.
Walter Birchfield to W. F. Scarborough, April 21, 1900.
W. R. Cruger to John D. Jones, July 2, 1900.
Kay Dargitz to Robert K. DeArment, May 4, 1984.
Edna Selman Haines to Ed Bartholomew, November 20, 1953.
J. C. Hancock to E. P. Lamborn, August 23, 1936.
J. E. Howard to J. D. Milton, July 24, 1945.
J. Marvin Hunter to E. P. Lamborn, June 21, 1927.
Archie Jefferes to Homer Hutto, undated.
Hal S. Kerr to J. D. Milton, February 10, 1947.
J. P. Meadows to E. P. Lamborn, January 30, 1927.
Elizabeth Shown Mills to Robert K. DeArment, January 26, 1985.
A. F. Nolan to Frank M. King, March 8, 1934.
Mrs. Ada Phillips to Robert K. DeArment, September 9, 1981; October 1, 1981; October 20, 1981; November 6, 1983.
Mrs. Mary Pierson to Ed Bartholomew, undated (ca. 1970).
Vic Queen to Beulah Mroz, July 30, 1895.
George F. Scarborough to Warden, Federal Penitentiary, Atlanta, Georgia, March 29, 1912.
Bob Stephens to Robert K. DeArment, July 14, 1980.
Warden, Federal Penitentiary, Atlanta, Georgia, to George E. Scarborough, April 5, 1912.
Scott White to E. P. Lamborn, February 24, 1928.

Interviews

Daniel Scarborough Abbott, May 5, 1989.
Sarita Abbott, May 5, 1989.
J. Marvin Hunter by Ed Bartholomew, May 1956.
Mrs Evelyn Linebery, November 19, 1984; May 6, 1989.
Moliere Scarborough by Stuart M. Scarborough, August, 1984; December 1, 1984; February 23, 1985.
Moliere Scarborough, Jr., November 21, 1984.

Newspapers

Abilene Reporter-News
Albuquerque Daily Citizen
Arizona Bulletin
Arizona Daily Citizen
Arizona Daily Star

Arizona Republican
Arizona Weekly Journal Miner
Bisbee Daily Review
Burbank Daily Review
Deming Headlight
Devil's River News (Sonora, Texas)
Eddy Argus
Eddy Current
El Paso Evening Telegram
El Paso Herald
El Paso Herald-Post
El Paso Times
Florence Blade-Tribune
Haskell City Free Press
Holbrook Argus
Las Vegas Daily Optic
Lordsburg Western Liberal
Los Angeles Times
Nogales Border Vidette
St. John's Herald
San Antonio Daily Express
Santa Fe New Mexican
Silver City Enterprise
Silver City Independent
Tombstone Epitaph
Tombstone Prospector
Western Enterprise (Anson, Texas)

Court Records

State of Arizona v. *George E. Scarborough,* Cause No. 634.
Haskell County, Texas, Court Records, Case No. 82.
Jones County, Texas, Commissioner's Books, 1884–88.
Jones County, Texas, Jailbook, 1884–88.
Jones County, Texas, Surveyor's Records, vol. A.
Luna County, New Mexico, Court Records, Cause Nos. 69, 239, 240, 241, 247.
State of Texas v. *George Scarborough,* Cause No. 1902, Thirty-fourth District Court, El Paso.
State of Texas v. *Jeff Milton,* Cause No. 1903, Thirty-fourth District Court, El Paso.
State of Texas v. *Frank McMahan,* Cause No. 1903, Thirty-fourth District Court, El Paso.
State of Texas v. *Barney Riggs,* Cause No. 2068, Thirty-fourth District Court, El Paso.

Miscellaneous

Depositions before Justice of the Peace J. C. Jones, El Paso, Texas, June 30, 1895.
Los Angeles (California) *City Directory,* 1912.

McMahan Family Bible.
G. W. Scarborough Family Bible.
U.S. Census Records:
    Graves County, Kentucky, 1840.
    Clairborn Parish, Louisiana, 1850.
    Natchitoches Parish, Louisiana, 1860.
    Grant Parish, Louisiana, 1870.
    Jones County, Texas, 1880.
    Kimble County, Texas, 1880.
    Grant County, New Mexico, 1900.

Index

307